The Origins of Elected Strongmen

The Origins of Elected Strongmen

How Personalist Parties Destroy Democracy from Within

ERICA FRANTZ
ANDREA KENDALL-TAYLOR
JOSEPH WRIGHT

OXFORD
UNIVERSITY PRESS

Great Clarendon Street, Oxford, OX2 6DP,
United Kingdom

Oxford University Press is a department of the University of Oxford.
It furthers the University's objective of excellence in research, scholarship,
and education by publishing worldwide. Oxford is a registered trade mark of
Oxford University Press in the UK and in certain other countries

© Erica Frantz, Andrea Kendall-Taylor, and Joseph Wright 2024

The moral rights of the authors have been asserted

All rights reserved. No part of this publication may be reproduced, stored in
a retrieval system, or transmitted, in any form or by any means, without the
prior permission in writing of Oxford University Press, or as expressly permitted
by law, by licence or under terms agreed with the appropriate reprographics
rights organization. Enquiries concerning reproduction outside the scope of the
above should be sent to the Rights Department, Oxford University Press, at the
address above

You must not circulate this work in any other form
and you must impose this same condition on any acquirer

Published in the United States of America by Oxford University Press
198 Madison Avenue, New York, NY 10016, United States of America

British Library Cataloguing in Publication Data

Data available

Library of Congress Control Number: 2023949187

ISBN 9780198888079

DOI: 10.1093/oso/9780198888079.001.0001

Pod

Links to third party websites are provided by Oxford in good faith and
for information only. Oxford disclaims any responsibility for the materials
contained in any third party website referenced in this work.

Acknowledgements

The origins of this book lie in 2016, when the three of us—all quite familiar with the world of personalism in dictatorships—noted similar dynamics operating in new territory: democracies. Just as personalists tend to bring great harm to author-itarian systems, our hunch was that the same was true for democracies too. Testing this hunch required data, however, the collection of which was far more time con-suming than any of us had anticipated. The actual writing of the book was no easier. But the domino of real-world events bearing out our expectations—and the importance of the book's findings—kept us motivated.

This book would not have been possible without the support—in resources, generosity, and time—of an array of individuals and institutions. We are grateful to a number of colleagues for their inciteful feedback on parts of the manuscript, particularly Miles Armaly, Jessica Maves Braithwaite, Abel Escriba-Folch, Steph Haggard, Gregory Love, Bill Mishler, Michael Nelson, Eric Plutzer, Paul Schuler, Julie Wronski, and Vineeta Yadav, as well as audiences at Arizona State, the Uni-versity of California Institute on Global Conflict and Cooperation at UCSD, the National University of Singapore, the University of Alabama, the University of Arizona, the University of Mississippi, and the University of Tübingen.

Generous support provided by the Luminate Foundation, Charles Koch Foun-dation, and The McCourtney Institute for Democracy at Penn State, gave us the resources to pursue the project in the first place and carry out the extensive data collection that is its backbone. We also are indebted to dozens of students in Polit-ical Science 414 at Penn State, Carisa Nietsche, Nick Lokker, and Nikolai Rice at the Center for a New American Security, Nikolas Frantzeskakis, and especially Jia Li for their research assistance. And, of course, we are grateful to the editors and staff at Oxford University Press for excellent assistance throughout all stages of the book's publication process. Lastly, we would like to thank our families for their steadfast support and encouragement.

Democracy brings with it many good things. We dedicate this book to the tireless actions of citizens and groups around the world engaged in the effort to preserve it.

Contents

List of Illustrations	x
List of Tables	xii

1.	Introduction	1
	1.1 Introduction	1
	1.2 The Rise of Personalist Politics	5
	1.3 Previewing the Argument	7
	1.4 What Do We Mean by Democracy?	10
	1.5 Contemporary Patterns of Democratic Collapse	11
	1.6 Existing Explanations of Democratic Backsliding	14
	1.7 Contributions of the Book	17
	1.8 Plan of the Book	19
2.	What Are Personalist Parties?	22
	2.1 Conceptualizing Personalist Political Parties	23
	2.2 Measuring Personalism in Ruling Political Parties	25
	2.2.1 Addressing Endogeneity	27
	2.2.2 Underlying Indicators	29
	2.2.3 What Our Measure Can and Cannot Capture	31
	2.3 Related Concepts and Measures	33
	2.3.1 Party Personalism and Populism	33
	2.3.2 Other Related Concepts and Measures	38
	2.4 Basic Facts and Features of Ruling Personalist Parties	40
	2.4.1 Trends in Ruling Party Personalism over Time	40
	2.4.2 Geographical Distribution of Personalist Parties	42
	2.4.3 Personalist Parties and Ideology	44
	2.4.4 Personalist Parties and Populism	47
	2.4.5 Institutional Arrangements and Personalist Parties	50
	2.5 Why Do Personalist Parties Win Elections?	52
	2.6 Conclusion	54
	2.7 Appendix A: Measurement Model of Ruling Party Personalism	56
	2.7.1 Internal Consistency and Reliability	57
	2.7.2 Face Validity	58
	2.7.3 External Validity	59
	2.8 Appendix B: Regression Results	60
	2.9 Appendix C: Selection into Ruling Party Personalism	60
3.	The Argument	63
	3.1 The Argument	64
	3.1.1 Underlying Assumptions	65

viii CONTENTS

3.2 Executive Restraint in Incumbent Support Parties — 67
   3.2.1 Incentive — 67
   3.2.2 Capacity — 71
3.3 Empirical Patterns — 74
   3.3.1 The Political Experience of Elites — 76
   3.3.2 Party Nominations — 84
   3.3.3 Local Party Strength and Party Funding — 86
   3.3.4 The Duration of Cabinet Appointee Tenures — 88
3.4 Conclusion — 93
3.5 Appendix A: Regression Results — 94

4. The Evidence — 97
4.1 Case Studies — 99
   4.1.1 El Salvador under Nayib Bukele — 101
   4.1.2 Hungary under Viktor Orban — 104
4.2 Ruling Party Personalism and Democratic Backsliding — 108
   4.2.1 Repression of Political Civil Liberties — 108
   4.2.2 Democratic Backsliding Broadly — 111
   4.2.3 How Do Democracies Collapse? — 120
   4.2.4 Personalism Matters Most When Ruling Parties
       Dominate — 125
4.3 Conclusion — 130
4.4 Appendix A: Regression Results — 131

5. Institutional Pathways — 132
5.1 Executive Constraints in Democracies — 134
   5.1.1 Legislatures — 136
   5.1.2 Judiciaries and Bureaucracies — 137
   5.1.3 How Do We Know When Institutional Actors
       Constrain? — 139
5.2 Empirical Tests — 140
   5.2.1 Legislative Constraints on the Executive — 141
   5.2.2 Judicial Constraints on the Executive — 144
   5.2.3 Bureaucratic Constraints on the Executive — 145
   5.2.4 Term Limit Extension Attempts — 147
5.3 Conclusion — 149
5.4 Appendix A: Regression Results — 150

6. Societal Pathways — 151
6.1 Are Citizens to Blame for Decreasing Vertical Constraints? — 154
6.2 Polarization — 155
6.3 Shifting Democratic Norms — 159
6.4 Case Studies — 161
   6.4.1 Turkey under Reccep Tayyip Erdoğan — 161
   6.4.2 Brazil under Jair Bolsonaro — 163

CONTENTS ix

6.5 Empirics	166
6.5.1 Does Ruling Party Personalism Boost Polarization?	166
6.5.2 Does Ruling Party Personalism Shift Norms?	177
6.6 Conclusion	189
6.7 Appendix A: Regression Results	190
7. Personalist Politics, Democracy, and the Path Ahead	193
7.1 Summary of the Book	195
7.2 Countering the Perils of Personalism	197
References	202
Index	220

List of Illustrations

1.1.	How personalist parties erode democracy	4
1.2.	Modes of democratic collapse, 1991–2020	12
2.1.	Populism in Turkey under AKP rule	37
2.2.	Party personalism time trend	41
2.3.	Personalist parties and ideology	46
2.4.	Empirical overlap between party populism and personalism	49
2.A-1.	Item characteristic curves from the IRT model	57
2.A-2.	External validity tests	60
2.B-1.	Personalist parties, presidentialism, and electoral systems	61
2.C-1.	Selection into ruling party personalism	62
3.1.	Elite political experience, Global Leadership Data	78
3.2.	Elite political experience, Comparative Candidate Survey	81
3.3.	Elite political experience by party type	83
3.4.	Leader control over parties	85
3.5.	Leaders who create their own parties appoint elites with shorter tenures	90
3.6.	Personalist parties keep cabinet members on a short leash	91
3.A-1.	Within-country comparisons of leaders' control over parties	95
3.A-2.	Leaders backed by personalist ruling parties have cabinet members with shorter tenures	96
4.1.	Democracy indicators, difference of means tests	114
4.2.	Democratic collapse, difference of means tests	116
4.3.	Personalist parties increase the risk of democratic collapse	119
4.4.	Ruling party personalism and modes of democratic collapse	124
4.5.	Ruling party personalism and legislative majorities	127
4.A-1.	Personalist parties increase government repression of civil liberties	131
5.1.	Personalist ruling parties decrease executive constraint	143
5.A-1.	Ruling party personalism boosts presidential attempts to extend term limits	150
6.1.	Polarization in Benin, United States, and Venezuela	167
6.2.	Macro- and micro-polarization trends	169
6.3.	Attacks on the state increase polarization in personalist ruling parties	173
6.4.	Party personalism boosts polarization via attacks on the state	177

6.5.	Ruling party personalism and support for political violence	183
6.6.	Trends in non-state election violence	186
6.7.	Election violence when personalist parties lose	187
6.A-1.	Judicial attacks increase polarization	190
6.A-2.	Ruling party personalism and polarization	191
6.A-3.	Election losers, personalist voters, and support for political violence	192

List of Tables

2.1.	Pre-selection indicators of party personalism	30
2.2.	Party personalism is a global phenomenon	44
2.A-1.	Split-sample reliability	58
3.1.	Party personalism, party populism, and elite experience	79
4.1.	Party personalism and democratic backsliding	118
4.2.	Declining democracy prior to democratic collapse	122
4.3.	Personalist parties, incumbent approval, and democratic backsliding	129
5.1.	Party creation and legislative constraint	142

1

Introduction

1.1 Introduction

In 1998, Hugo Chavez was elected president of Venezuela in free and fair elections. At the time of Chavez's election, Venezuela was unique with its long history of democratic rule in a region known for bouts of authoritarianism. Despite this democratic tradition, Chavez implemented a number of policies after assuming the presidency in 1999 that reduced constraints on his rule. He curtailed the power of the opposition-led legislature, fiddled with presidential terms to extend his rule, and initiated a purge of the judiciary. Such actions polarized the Venezuelan electorate and intensified criticism of Chavez, culminating in a failed coup attempt in 2002. By 2004, the political opposition had galvanized a recall referendum, but Chavez won this vote, which was generally deemed free and fair, and he continued to consolidate power.

By the end of that year, the quality of Venezuelan democracy began to deteriorate, as Chavez leveraged his position of strength to attack his opponents. Those individuals who had supported the recall petition were dismissed from public jobs and lost their access to welfare benefits after the government made their names public. The Venezuelan government passed laws to intimidate the media, forced television outlets to broadcast Chavez's speeches, all while the government spearheaded a campaign to target and instill fear in those who opposed Chavez, who were now deemed to be 'anti-revolutionaries'.

By the time of the 2005 legislative elections, five opposition parties vowed to boycott them, citing fears of government intimidation and suspicions the race would be biased. To no one's surprise, Chavez's Fifth Republic Movement (MVR) won a majority of seats in the contest, with smaller parties that were allied with it winning the rest. This all signalled the end of Venezuelan democracy in the eyes of most experts.

The story of Venezuela's democratic decay and ultimate collapse has become a common one. The watchdog organization, Freedom House, for example, documented seventeen consecutive years of decline in political rights and civil liberties in its 2023 global report (Gorokhovskaia et al., 2023). While some of these declines have occurred in countries that were already autocratic (as in Belarus), the rest took place in democracies, reflecting either a weakening of democracy (as in El Salvador) or a movement from democracy to autocracy (as in Serbia).

The Origins of Elected Strongmen. Erica Frantz, Andrea Kendall-Taylor, and Joseph Wright, Oxford University Press.
© Erica Frantz, Andrea Kendall-Taylor, and Joseph Wright (2024). DOI: 10.1093/oso/9780198888079.003.0001

2 THE ORIGINS OF ELECTED STRONGMEN

Importantly, many of today's democracies are decaying from within, as occurred in Venezuela under Chavez, with freely and fairly elected leaders leading the charge to dismantle their countries' democratic institutions. Whereas in the past, democracies typically collapsed via force (through coups or other coerced seizures of power), today incumbent leaders are typically spearheading the drift to authoritarianism by pursuing grabs for power that ultimately deteriorate democracy and give way to dictatorship (Bermeo, 2016; Kendall-Taylor and Frantz, 2016; Waldner and Lust, 2018; Lührmann and Lindberg, 2019). News media and policy-makers have picked up this trend; by 2018, *Time Magazine* had declared that the 'Strongman era is here'. Recent examples include countries as diverse as Nicaragua under Daniel Ortega, Turkey under Recep Tayyip Erdoğan, and Benin under Patrice Talon. Thus, a key feature of the contemporary wave of democratic backsliding is that it is driven by the actions of democratically elected leaders, as opposed to their rivals, opposition forces, or armed groups.

This book shows that the origins of the new strongman era lie with the rise of personalist political parties throughout the world. Scholars have documented the personalization of politics in a variety of domains—ranging from political campaigns to media reporting.[1] We focus on its manifestation in political parties. All over the globe, leaders are increasingly coming to power backed by *personalist parties*—or those parties that exist primarily to promote and further the leader's personal political career rather than advance policy.

Take Venezuela. Chavez ran for the presidency in 1998 with the backing of the MVR. The MVR had its roots in the Revolutionary Bolivarian Movement (or MBR-2000), another group that Chavez had formed many years earlier in 1982, but it did not become an official political party until July 1997, just after Chavez had declared his intention to run in the election. For all purposes, the MVR was a vehicle for Chavez to secure power. In this book, we show that unique features of personalist parties, such as the MVR, make it easier for incumbent leaders to dismantle democracy from within, as occurred in Venezuela. In this way, the upsurge in personalism in the support parties of leaders worldwide helps explain the contemporary wave of democratic erosion.

To illustrate this, we gather original data on levels of personalism in the political parties of democratically elected leaders around the globe in the thirty years since the end of the Cold War. This period covers both the rapid spread of democracy in the 1990s as well as the period of democratic backsliding since the 2008 Great Recession. As importantly, our data capture leader-party relations that predate the leader's election to office.[2] This enables us to evaluate the consequences of ruling

---

[1] See Cross et al. (2018) and Garzia and Ferreira da Silva (2019) for reviews of the personalization of politics literature. See, also, Rahat and Sheafer (2007) and Balmas et al. (2014) for typologies of different types of personalization.

[2] Our sample extends from 1991 to 2020 and includes nearly 600 leaders in 106 countries with democratic governments. Existing studies of party personalism (e.g., Rahat and Kenig, 2018; Rhodes-Purdy

party personalism for outcomes that may be endogenous to leader strategies once in office, such as incumbent power grabs.[3]

Indeed, once democratically elected leaders start to undermine democracy, pundits and policy-makers are quick to label them 'strongmen' and blame them for democracy's demise. Asserting they are 'strongmen' after they have successfully consolidated power and eroded democracy, however, tells us little about how or why they were able to do so. Our book investigates the origins of elected strongmen, focusing on the political parties that enable their behaviours. Using global data on all democratic leaders—those who eventually undermine democracy and those who do not—we show not only that ruling party personalism is on the rise worldwide—a trend consistent with the broader pattern of personalization of politics—but also that it is harmful for democracy.

Our theoretical starting point lies with the organization that helps democratic leaders win elections in the first place: political parties. Leaders' support parties vary in their levels of personalism. Some leaders assume power backed by parties organized to advance the leader's personal political career and frequently established for this purpose, where party personalism is high. Other leaders, by contrast, come to power backed by parties organized to advance policy goals; and the leaders of these parties have typically had to rise through the ranks of the party to be selected leader. In these parties, personalism is low. We argue that personalist parties differ from non-personalist parties in important ways, particularly in terms of the incentive and capacity of party actors to restrain the leadership. This sets in motion a number of consequential political dynamics for democracy, which we document in this book.

Figure 1.1 sketches the causal pathways linking personalist parties to democratic backsliding. First, party personalism enables leaders to attack horizontal checks on their power, weakening institutional constraints on the executive in a variety of domains. This impact is strongest when the ruling party has control of the legislature. These attacks on state institutions both directly contribute to democratic backsliding and have ripple effects throughout society, in ways that diminish vertical accountability mechanisms from ordinary citizens that prevent leaders from dismantling democracy. Specifically, the behaviour of leaders backed by personalist parties while in office deepens polarization and weakens supporters' commitment to democratic norms.[4] Personalist parties thus

---

and Madrid, 2020; and Marino et al., 2021) have region foci and/or include many fewer countries. Further, these studies measure personalist dynamics that occur after the leader takes power.

[3] Throughout this study, we are interested in levels of personalism in the parties of incumbent democratic leaders. We do not focus on levels of personalism in other parties in the country's party system. For this reason, we use the terms 'party personalism', 'ruling party personalism', and 'incumbent party personalism' interchangeably, unless otherwise noted.

[4] In this book, we use the term polarization to reference *affective* polarization specifically, or the tendency of partisans to like members of their own party and dislike members of the opposition.

4 THE ORIGINS OF ELECTED STRONGMEN

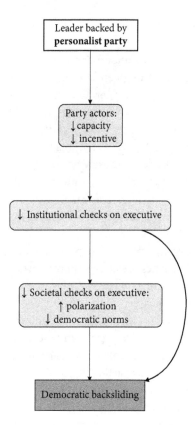

Figure 1.1 How personalist parties erode democracy

facilitate the erosion of both horizontal and vertical constraints on the executive, ultimately degrading democracy and making it vulnerable to collapse from within.

This book therefore offers critical insight into the political impact of the new personalist era and the harm it poses for democracy. In this introductory chapter, we begin with a detailed discussion of the rise of personalist politics and the factors underlying it. We then offer a preview of our argument, which sees personalization of politics—specifically of political parties—as a key contributor to the contemporary wave of democratic erosion. Next, we explain what we mean by democracy and movements away from it, before offering data on patterns of democratic collapse over time that illustrate how today's democracies fall apart. We then review existing explanations for contemporary democratic erosion and the ways in which our argument builds on and integrates them. Lastly, we highlight the central contributions of this study and close with a summary of the chapters to follow.

1.2 The Rise of Personalist Politics

Political personalization is a multi-faceted and broad concept, but at its core it encompasses the rising importance of individual political actors 'at the expense of parties and collective identities' (Karvonen, 2010, 4). All political systems feature some level of personalism, and personalist politics is by no means a new phenomenon (Frantz, et al. 2021). That said, scholars have observed a rise in personalism in democracies over the past few decades in a number of domains, particularly with respect to electoral systems (Rahat and Sheafer, 2007; Renwick and Pilet, 2016), voting behaviour (Garzia, 2014; Ferreira da Silva et al., 2021), media reporting (Adam and Maier, 2010; Stanyer, 2012; Balmas et al., 2014), and political parties (Blondel and Thiébault, 2010; Webb et al., 2012; Musella, 2015; Schumacher and Giger, 2017). Though empirical support for political personalization is weak and/or mixed in some areas (Adam and Maier, 2010; Karvonen, 2010; Kriesi, 2012), together the body of evidence suggests that 'political personalization occurs in democracies and influences numerous arenas' (Rahat, 2022, 2).[5]

Experiences with political personalization vary substantially across countries, of course. In long-standing democracies, for example, there is evidence that voters increasingly base their perceptions and actions on individual political actors rather than collective groups, but this varies quite a bit among the countries studied (Rahat and Kenig, 2018; Pedersen and Rahat, 2021). Likewise, looking solely at Western Europe, while there are country-level trends in personalization of political parties over time, no clear patterns appear at the regional level (Marino et al., 2021).

Regardless, the general message to emerge in the literature is that personalization of politics is a development that should not be ignored. Scholars point to it as a defining theme of the contemporary democratic era (Rahat and Kenig, 2018; Garzia and Ferreira da Silva, 2019), the 'central feature of democratic politics in the twenty-first century' (McAllister, 2007, 585), and a reflection of a major political shift in today's democracies (Renwick and Pilet, 2016).[6]

This begs the question, why now? While the rise of personalist politics is likely the consequence of many complex and interrelated processes, scholars have a good sense of the key factors that have contributed to it.[7] Two factors have

---

[5] Scholars have suggested that divergent findings in the literature are largely due to variation in the sample and time period under analysis, the particular type of personalization evaluated, and the way in which personalization is conceptualized and measured (Adam and Maier, 2010; Van Aelst et al., 2012; Holtz-Bacha et al., 2014).

[6] This shift is not confined to democracies; scholars have also documented a rise in personalism in autocracies in the past few decades (Kendall-Taylor et al., 2017).

[7] See Rahat and Sheafer (2007) for a discussion of how these processes might interrelate to influence personalization in multiple domains. For example, they point to declining party membership as a trigger for changes in party candidate selection methods, where parties gave members more influence

6 THE ORIGINS OF ELECTED STRONGMEN

been highlighted as particularly important: (1) *the changing media landscape*; and (2) *partisan dealignment* (McAllister, 2007; Garzia, 2011; Kostadinova and Levitt, 2014; Ferreira da Silva et al., 2021; Garzia et al., 2021; Quinlan and McAllister, 2022).

Changes in the structure of mass communication have been linked to the personalization of politics for some time, beginning with the spread of television (Sartori, 1989; Druckman, 2003; Postman, 2006; Lenz and Lawson, 2011; Garzia, 2017, 2011). As voters grew more attentive to visual images and cues about the personalities of political actors, issue-related concerns declined in importance. The spread of mass media weakened incentives for party building, as well (Levitsky and Cameron, 2003; Mainwaring and Zoco, 2007; Levitsky et al., 2016). As Mainwaring and Zoco (2007, 156–7) explain, 'it is easier and—in the short term—more effective to use the modern mass media than to build a party'. The advent of the Internet and social media has only supercharged these dynamics, further shifting voters' attentions away from issues and towards the leader's personal qualities, while also lessening the importance of parties by making it easier for political actors to directly connect with voters (McAllister, 2007; Hermans and Vergeer, 2009; Kruikemeier et al., 2013; Capati, 2019; Metz et al., 2020). As such, the changing nature of mass communication 'has been central in emphasizing the role of political leaders at the expense of parties' (Garzia, 2011, 698).

Partisan dealignment has also contributed to the personalization of politics (Garzia, 2013; Ferreira da Silva et al., 2021; Garzia et al., 2021). Looking primarily at evidence from advanced industrialized democracies, a large body of literature has documented the erosion of partisan identities, with voters feeling less attachment to political parties today than in decades past (Mair, 1984; Dalton and Wattenberg, 2002; Berglund et al., 2005; Renwick and Pilet, 2016). As voters' links to parties have weakened, the personality of the political leadership has grown more important (Blondel and Thiébault, 2010). The declining value of partisanship has created space for leaders to play a central role in structuring vote choice, such that political leaders—rather than partisanship attachments based on social or ideological identities—are the major short-term drivers of voting behaviour (Garzia, 2013, 2014; Garzia et al., 2022). As a consequence, we are seeing politics in democracies increasingly centred around political leaders as opposed to party brands (Lupu, 2016), resulting in 'deep transformations' of political parties (Garzia, 2011, 699).

While scholars have a good understanding of the factors contributing to the personalization of politics, we know far less about its consequences and implications, particularly with respect to its influence on democracy (Adam and Maier,

---

over candidate selection as a means of retaining them. This, in turn, changed how the media covered politics, leading to coverage more focused on candidates than parties, which likewise changed how politicians campaigned.

2010; Cross et al., 2018). Though many in the literature have suggested political personalization may be detrimental to the quality of democracy (see, for example, Mainwaring and Torcal, 2006, Balmas et al., 2014, Cross et al., 2018, and Rahat and Kenig, 2018), empirical work evaluating this relationship is limited (Adam and Maier, 2010, 239).

This study seeks to fill this void by showing how personalism in political parties harms democracy. In the section that follows, we explain our argument.

1.3 Previewing the Argument

One of the basic features of politics is that leaders seek to maximize power and, for this reason, standard theories of political science anticipate that leaders of all stripes look for opportunities to expand their influence (Bueno de Mesquita and Siverson, 1995). In democracies, this may stem from motivations to dismantle democracy and establish authoritarianism, but it may not. Rather, leaders may look to remove constraints on their power because they limit their ability to execute campaign promises or implement the reforms they see as necessary or that their voters support.

Regardless of motive, experience has shown that some leaders will operate within the confines of existing democratic norms and institutions in their endeavours, but others will ignore them (Levitsky and Ziblatt, 2018). As observers, it is impossible to know *a priori* the personality 'type' of a leader we are dealing with: one whose ambitions will be restrained by the rules of the democratic game or one whose aspirations know no bounds.[8] Importantly, the absence of a leadership power grab tells us little about the leader's 'type' because even leaders who aspire to be strongmen will be unlikely to pursue power grabs if they deem such moves likely to fail. Leaders who appear to be abiding by established democratic norms and processes, in other words, may only be doing so because they know it is unlikely they would get away with breaching them. While some scholars attempt to infer the preferences or beliefs of leaders from their age, military training, or prior education (see, e.g., Horowitz et al., 2015; Nelson, 2020), we propose that whether democratically elected leaders will succeed in undermining democracy can be explained, in part, by their history with and the nature of the party that supports them. We discuss these dynamics in greater detail in Chapter 3.

For these reasons, this study does *not* seek to understand the personality of individual political leaders, but rather examines the conditions under which their grabs for power are likely to be successful. In it, we emphasize the importance of

---

[8] Expert assessments of leaders' *personality* types are uniformly conducted *after* the expert observes the leader's behaviour in office (see, e.g., Rhodes-Purdy and Madrid 2020; Araya 2023). Thus an expert might infer personality from observed behaviour once a leader holds power. Such expert assessments of personality are likely endogenous to the outcome the researcher seeks to explain.

8   THE ORIGINS OF ELECTED STRONGMEN

personalist support parties. Building on theories of parties in democracies and personalism in autocracies (e.g., Laver (1981); Strom (1990); Aldrich (1995); Geddes et al. (2018)), we argue that personalist parties are fundamentally different than non-personalist parties in ways that have important consequences for whether leaders will encounter horizontal and vertical pushback to their efforts to consolidate control. With personalist parties backing them, it is easier for leaders to erode constraints to their rule, ultimately opening the door for actions that subvert democracy.

Our argument centres on key differences in personalist parties that reduce the incentives of party members to challenge the leader, as well as the party's capacity to do so. These differences are reflected in a variety of domains. For one, personalist parties are often created by leaders themselves, as was the case with Chavez and the MVR in Venezuela. In such instances, leaders usually control key appointments in the party and select the party's candidates. Leaders backed by personalist parties tend to eschew individuals from the political establishment, opting instead to fill high-level party positions with individuals from their personal network, such as friends and family members, who usually lack government experience. As such, elites in personalist parties often see their future as tied to that of the leader. In contrast to elites affiliated with other parties, those who are part of personalist parties are less likely to maintain their political careers without the leader. This means that they have a stronger incentive to maintain the incumbent leader in power—even if it means accepting executive aggrandizement—than do elites from non-personalist parties, who have greater potential to maintain their political careers in the leader's absence. As a result, elites in personalist parties are less likely to constrain incumbent attempts to consolidate power, instead aligning with and acquiescing to the leader's agenda. Elites in non-personalist parties, by contrast, are less tied to the leader's fortunes. They have to consider their long-term reputations, increasing the chance that they will push back against a leader's efforts to reduce constraints to their rule.

Moreover, personalist parties have less capacity to prevent executive power grabs. Indeed, an ideal-type stylization of political parties views their *raison d'être* as a vehicle to solve elite collective action problems (Aldrich, 1995, 45–7).[9] The organizational resources of non-personalist parties, including financial resources, human capital, and organizing knowledge, are less likely to be directly controlled by the chief executive and his or her personal network of family and friends. Leaders of personalist parties, by contrast, tend to have substantial control over the party, not only in terms of appointments but also in terms

---

[9] A stylized entrepreneurial leader unconstrained by a party would not seek votes or policy but rather maximize the chances of obtaining and remaining in office (Strom, 1990, 574). We discuss measurement elsewhere but reiterate here that our measurement strategy utilizes information on leader-party relations prior to the leader first gaining national executive power. The information used to code personalist parties does not, therefore, reflect the strategic behaviour of the leader once in power as the national executive.

of party resources (Kefford and McDonnell, 2018). This weakens the collective bargaining power of elites and increases the costs of collective action. The lack of political experience of the elite in personalist parties diminishes their ability to effectively act in concert, as well. They tend to have less skill in organizing and mobilizing activities needed to push back against a leader's efforts to expand power, in contrast to elites in non-personalist parties who tend to have a history of interactions with one another that makes it easier to cooperate when needed. This makes it more difficult for elites in personalist parties to act collectively—apart from the leader—to counter incumbent attempts to concentrate control. Personalist parties also feature more centralized internal structures and weaker local party branches, further diminishing the potential for party members outside of the leadership circle to contest and constrain the behaviours of the leader.

Less incentive and capacity to restrain the leadership means that once elected to power, it is easier for leaders backed by personalist parties to dismantle institutional checks to their rule. Ruling party personalism increases the chances that leaders will take actions such as reducing judicial powers, limiting bureaucratic oversight, and diminishing any other institutional obstacles to their ability to pursue their agendas. The nature of parties—whether they are highly personalist or not—matters most, we posit, when they are the strongest, specifically when they have majority control of the legislature. As such, when democratic leaders rule with strong partisan legislative support, the incentives and capacity of ruling party elites to constrain the executive become crucial determinants of whether the leader grabs power. Thus leaders should be most successful in curbing institutional checks when they are backed by a personalist party and have legislative majorities. While the leader's actions to consolidate power do not in and of themselves take down democracy, these behaviours hollow out institutional checks designed to prevent it.

Such actions, however, are not without consequence. They are often deeply divisive and set in motion increased polarization among voters, as well as a weakening of personalist party supporters' adherence to democratic norms of behaviour. The agenda of the leader becomes a rallying cry for supporters, diminishing the chances that the leader will face pushback from below in their consolidation of power. In this way, the actions of leaders supported by personalist parties send shockwaves throughout society, diminishing checks on their rule from the citizenry.

To summarize, we argue that leaders are more likely to get away with efforts to consolidate power when they are supported by personalist parties. Such parties feature elites with less incentive to take action to counter the leader, as well as less capacity to do so. The leader's push to deteriorate horizontal constraints to their rule sets in motion dynamics that diminish vertical checks as well, which party personalism makes worse. The end result is an environment friendly to subverting democracy from within.

1.4 What Do We Mean by Democracy?

We now turn to a discussion of how we conceptualize democracy in this book, so that it is clear what we mean when we reference its weakening and collapse in what follows. To do so, we draw from Dahl (1971, 3), who emphasizes the importance of free and fair elections to democracy, in addition to freedoms of association and expression. We see the integrity of the electoral process as a necessary condition for democracy, specifically whether executives achieve power through reasonably fair competitive elections (or via constitutional succession of a democratically elected executive) (Geddes et al., 2014). With this condition in mind, freedoms of association and expression are valuable for improving the quality of democracy. That said, the three concepts are often intertwined. Importantly, restrictions on freedoms of association and expression are frequently an indicator that an election is not likely to be reasonably competitive, such as when the media landscape is biased towards the incumbent or opposition groups are subject to government intimidation. In this study, we are interested in democratic backsliding broadly speaking, as well as its more brute manifestation, democratic collapse. Democratic backsliding—and its synonyms, democratic erosion, decay, and deterioration—encompasses a decline in the quality of this vision of democracy.[10] It is a movement away from democracy, whether due to regressions in the freeness and fairness of elections, freedom of association, or freedom of expression. Importantly, democratic backsliding can entail a weakening of democracy (e.g., the United States (US) under President Donald Trump) or its full collapse (e.g., Venezuela under Hugo Chavez). Democratic collapse represents transition from a democracy—as defined above—to a dictatorship or failed state. Which situation a country will fall under will depend on the quality of its democracy before the backsliding episode and the severity of the decline.

We measure whether countries are democracies using updated data from Geddes et al. (2014). To capture democratic backsliding, we look at small and large declines in these democracies using the Varieties of Democracy's *polyarchy* score (Coppedge, 2021). This measure aggregates indicators of the existence of elections and whether they are free and fair, freedom of association (such as the ability of political parties and civil society organizations to operate freely), and freedom of expression (such as freedom of the press and the ability of citizens to speak freely about politics). We measure democratic collapse by looking at transitions from democracy to dictatorship or a failed state, as provided by the Autocratic Regimes Data Set (Geddes et al., 2014). This measure captures the moment at which free and fair elections no longer determine the selection of the leadership,

---

[10] Though some in the literature conceptualize decay and erosion as distinct types of democratic backsliding (see, for example, Gerschewski 2021a, b), in this book we use these terms interchangeably, unless otherwise noted.

usually because the new leadership assumed power through force (e.g., coups or rebellions) or electoral contests grew so uncompetitive that the opposition no longer had the ability to effectively contest them.

Our conceptualization of democracy is therefore a minimalist or 'thin' version. It emphasizes the ability of ordinary people to influence politics and select their leadership. Importantly, mechanisms of horizontal accountability—while perhaps featured in 'thicker' definitions of democracy—are not included here. From this perspective, the deterioration of executive constraints does not necessarily mean democratic backsliding. There are certainly 'thicker' definitions of democracy that take into account horizontal accountability; we do not seek to arbitrate in this study which versions of democracy are 'right' or 'wrong'. Rather, we opt for a 'thinner' version of democracy because it offers theoretical and empirical clarity and is consistent with much of the literature (Kendall-Taylor et al., 2019).

As such, our definition of democracy—like many others—does not rest on checks and balances or constraints on the executive. Consolidation of power is therefore not indicative of deterioration of the quality of democracy. That said, specific actions on the part of the leadership to diminish horizontal accountability—via policy choices or institutional changes—often pave the way for subsequent behaviours that are harmful to democracy (Perez-Linan et al., 2019). As Chiopris et al. (2021a, 4) point out, 'in most instances, governments intent on pursuing an authoritarian agenda engage in institutional reforms that will, subsequently, make it easier to act in an authoritarian manner'. Efforts to expand executive power and influence do not always presage democratic erosion, in other words, but they do facilitate it. When executive power is largely unchecked, actions that undermine democracy are easier. In such environments, the pathway is open for behaviours that restrict freedoms of association and expression and ultimately threaten the integrity of electoral contests. The dismantling of constraints on the executive makes incumbent-led democratic erosion far easier, a subject to which we now turn.

1.5 Contemporary Patterns of Democratic Collapse

This study examines processes of democratic backsliding, broadly speaking, but draws insight from important changes in patterns of democratic collapse, specifically. During the post-World-War-II era, democracies typically fell apart on account of forces outside the executive office, at the hands of elite rivals, opposition groups, or foreign actors. Coups were the most common method of choice, often with members of the military storming a presidential palace to assert control or with troops seizing television and radio stations while the leader travelled abroad. Incumbent takeovers did occur on occasion, but they were often abrupt *autogolpes*, such as when Ferdinand Marcos declared martial law in the Philippines

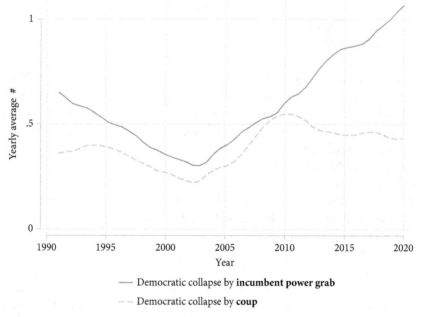

Figure 1.2 Modes of democratic collapse, 1991–2020

in 1972 or when Alberto Fujimori of Peru closed the legislature in 1992.[11] Today, however, incumbent takeovers have eclipsed coups as the most common mode of democratic collapse, usually the culmination of a broader process of democratic decline, as in the earlier example from Venezuela.

Figure 1.2 shows the global increase in democratic collapses, which are events that mark the change from democracy to dictatorship, even if in most cases these collapses are preceded by gradual declines in democracy.[12] We emphasize two patterns in the data. First, while the incidence of democratic collapse declined in the first decade after the fall of the Berlin Wall, it has been steadily increasing since the early 2000s. Second, throughout the entire thirty years after 1990, examples of democratic collapse at the hands of elected democrats (i.e., an incumbent power grab) outnumber those of coups that upend democracy. Together, these trends reveal that democratic collapse is increasing and incumbent power grabs are largely responsible.

Put simply, we are not only witnessing a significant increase in the number of democracies that collapse but also a change in the way they are doing so. From 2000 to 2010, nearly as many democracies were toppled by incumbent takeovers

---

[11] For recent discussion of different processes of democratic regression, see Diamond (2021), Ding and Slater (2021), and Gerschewski (2021b) to name a few.
[12] The trend line reflects the three-year moving average.

as were cut short by coups. Fast-forward to the 2010s and the numbers start to differ, with 64 per cent of democratic collapses being at the hands of incumbents and only 36 per cent via coups.

Rather than transpiring over the course of a day or two, contemporary democratic breakdowns often mark the end of many years of democratic decay, following a series of incumbent efforts to erode judicial independence, muzzle independent media, and restrict civil society. As this occurs, incumbent leaders undermine the liberal foundations of democratic rule. In the end, they succeed in dismantling democracy through a wide array of actions, including: jailing or banning prominent electoral opponents or parties; stacking the electoral deck in their own favour to such an extent that opposition groups stand little chance of organizing a serious electoral challenge; changing the electoral rules for how votes are counted such that a small numerical minority can rule; and imposing martial law or a state of emergency that suspends rule of law and normal legislative and judicial checks on executive power. In other words, there is a multi-faceted chipping away at the pillars of democracy that ultimately gives way to its breakdown.

And today, even in those instances where the *mode* of democratic breakdown is a military coup, incumbent-initiated backsliding is often the trigger. As one report states, '[democratic] regression has set the conditions for soldiers to seize power or at least use it as a pretext for military action' (Devermont, 2021).[13] For example, in Bolivia in 2019, President Evo Morales' push for a fourth term and the disputed electoral victory that followed led to protests across the country, ultimately prompting the coup that interrupted Bolivian democracy. Likewise, the 2021 coup that ousted President Alpha Condé in Guinea and ended democracy there resulted from his controversial decision to amend the constitution and run for a third term in 2020. Regardless of the *mode* of democratic collapse, actions on the part of democratically elected leaders to undermine democracy are the common cause.

To be clear, in some instances, incumbents' actions that weaken democracy do not succeed in toppling it. A good example of democratic decline that fell short of collapse is the experience of Ecuador under Rafael Correa (Freedom House, 2017a). After coming to power in 2007 in free and fair elections, Correa gradually undermined the country's democratic institutions by implementing policies that stifled the media and civil society, cracking down on social media and Internet activity, and placing limits on academic freedom. Even so, international observers assessed that elections under Correa had remained free and fair, suggesting that though the quality of democracy had deteriorated under Correa's rule, it had not yet slid to authoritarianism. In this instance, a change in the leadership post put a

---

[13] Even the 'royal coup' in Nepal in 2002, when the king dissolved parliament, was as a result of the elected prime minister asking the king to shut down the legislative body that had refused to extend the prime minister's emergency powers (Kräämer, 2003, 210).

14   THE ORIGINS OF ELECTED STRONGMEN

halt to the country's democratic erosion. Correa's chosen successor, Lenín Moreno, won the presidency, in 2017, in a contest that international observers deemed democratic. Upon his assumption of power, Moreno reversed many of Correa's actions, notably reopening up the space for the media and civil society (Freedom House, 2021b). Though Correa's efforts to consolidate control had weakened Ecuadorian democracy, in the end it survived his tenure. In many other instances, however, incumbent power grabs ultimately result in the demise of democracy.[14] We review existing explanations for democratic backsliding in the section that follows.

1.6 Existing Explanations of Democratic Backsliding

Despite the well-documented global tide of democratic backsliding in recent years, we know surprisingly little about the systematic factors that increase its likelihood. Some studies have examined the conditions that facilitate it, highlighting factors such as party system institutionalization (Diamond, 1994; Mainwaring and Scully, 1995); presidentialism (Linz, 1990); authoritarian legacy (Cheibub, 2007); electoral rules that cultivate candidate-centred politics (Carey and Shugart, 1995); public support for democracy (Claassen, 2020); and economic inequality (Acemoglu and Robinson, 2006)—yet the literature remains unsettled in terms of key causal pathways (Waldner and Lust, 2018). That said, two factors stand out in the predominant explanations for contemporary democratic backsliding: populism and polarization.

The academic literature on populism and its detrimental impact on democracy is enormous.[15] A common theme in this literature is that—by positioning ordinary people against a corrupt and inept elite—populists instil distrust in the institutions central to a well-functioning democracy, enabling them to be hollowed out.[16] The logic underlying this argument is compelling, yet this literature largely focuses on European and Latin American cases, with substantially less comparative analysis of other regions of the world, such as Africa and Asia, that are home to most new democracies. And, importantly, most approaches to measuring the concept of populism rely on observing the behaviour of elected leaders once in office, which makes the measurement of populism—as an explanation—perilously close to the outcome we care about, namely democratic backsliding. Even so, the populism literature offers rich insight into the processes at play in contemporary

---

[14] For a comparative case study analysis of when backsliding leads to breakdown, see Cleary and Ozturk (2022).

[15] See, for example, Mudde (2007); Mudde and Kaltwasser (2012); Muller (2016); Mudde and Kaltwasser (2017); Mounk (2018b); Weyland and Madrid (2019); and Grzymala-Busse et al. (2020).

[16] Note, however, that some scholars in the field argue that these very features of populism mean that it has the potential to strengthen democracy too (e.g., Bugaric, 2019; Mansbridge and Macedo, 2019).

democratic backsliding that we draw from in this study, in particular the way in which democratic institutions can be undermined from within. We discuss the commonalities and differences between populism and party personalism in detail in Chapter 2.

Other accounts of democratic backsliding look instead to polarization as the culprit.[17] A key argument in this literature is that polarization elevates the risk of democratic deterioration because it incentivizes voters to accept incumbents' undermining democratic principles in favour of advancing their partisan interests (Svolik, 2020). From this perspective, polarization is an exogenous feature of society that politicians exploit but which they do not strategically manipulate to their benefit; it is a societal condition that incumbent leaders leverage to subvert democracy. Our theory adopts a different perspective.[18] We suggest that polarization is endogenous to the erosion of democracy itself. Our theory starts with the political party of the leader and shows how ruling party personalism facilitates the weakening of executive constraints, which in turn triggers polarization. Polarization, in our account, is something leaders themselves endogenously produce by attacking state institutions. We draw from key insights in the polarization literature, however, to shed light on how these actions on the part of leaders influence citizens and weaken vertical accountability.

Other research indirectly related to democratic backsliding informs our understanding of it as well. Presidential term limit extensions, in particular, are often a clear indicator of a power grab even if they do not necessarily signal the end of democracy. This literature reveals that term limit extensions are more likely to be successful when leaders enjoy high approval ratings (Corrales, 2016), when they enjoy the benefits of rent seeking (Baturo, 2014), when presidential parties are less institutionalized (Kouba, 2016), and when incumbent party margins of victory are larger (McKie, 2017). These insights provide guidance in terms of the factors potentially at play in democratic demise from within, even if they are not directly devoted to this phenomenon.

Drawing from this body of work, we emphasize the key role of personalist political parties in facilitating democratic backsliding. We argue that the risks to democracy are greater where political leaders are backed by political parties that exist primarily to promote and further their personal political career. Our study expands on research by Rhodes-Purdy and Madrid (2020), who show using evidence from Latin America that when presidents rule their parties in a personalistic fashion, levels of democracy are likely to decrease. We

---

[17] See, for example, McCoy et al. (2018); Svolik (2019); Graham and Svolik (2020); Svolik (2020); Haggard and Kaufman (2021); Chiopris et al. (2021a); and McCoy and Somer (2021).

[18] In Svolik's (2020) model, policy-oriented candidates can endogenously shift their policy platforms to maximize electoral success, but voter polarization along the policy dimension is exogenous.

build on this work by advancing an original theory of how personalist parties erode democracy, using data that capture ruling party personalism prior to the leader's assumption of power, and testing this theory on a global sample of democracies.

Other research, though not directly related, implies potential links between personalist parties and democratic backsliding. Carreras (2014), for example, sees the election of political outsiders as a threat to democracy. Likewise, Mainwaring and Torcal (2006) point out that the election of anti-party politicians, such as Alberto Fujimori of Peru, is harmful to democracy. Such politicians typically govern weak parties which are less likely to hold them accountable. This is confirmed by a large literature citing political parties, broadly speaking, as important for a healthy democracy.[19] Our argument linking personalist parties with democratic deterioration fits within this broader perspective.

We note that a number of scholars have identified a decline of traditional parties starting as early as the mid-1990s, which brought with it a rise in non-ideological parties seeking to further the ambitions of their leaders (Ignazi, 1996; Kostadinova and Levitt, 2014). In a number of countries, this occurred in tandem with a shift towards more illiberal forms of democracy, implying that personalist political parties may be harmful in the quality of democracy (Rahat and Kenig, 2018). All of these connections are consistent with our expectations, though none underscore the theoretical mechanisms we emphasize which point to personalist parties lacking both the incentive and capacity to counter authoritarian threats from the party leader.

As a final point, while it has only been a few years since Waldner and Lust (2018, 95) insightfully assessed that 'efforts to explain backsliding remain inchoate', the literature has expanded remarkably in this time (and perhaps as a response). Noteworthy research has emerged in a variety of domains, including studies carefully documenting individual cases of democratic backsliding (e.g., Sadurski, 2019; Mettler and Lieberman, 2020), adopting a historical approach to understanding it (e.g., Berman and Snegovaya, 2019; Stasavage, 2020), documenting it in a handful of cases where it has transpired (e.g., Levitsky and Ziblatt, 2018; Applebaum, 2020), and offering formal models of the conditions under which we are likely to see it (e.g., Grillo and Prato, 2023; Horz, 2021; Miller, 2021). These studies are welcome additions to the literature and have enriched our understanding of the process through which democratic erosion occurs. This study—while informed by the insights derived from this wave of research—complements these approaches by developing and testing a theory of democratic backsliding using contemporary global data. In this way, this study sheds light on the vulnerabilities of the world's democracies today.

---

[19] See Levitsky and Cameron (2003) for a review.

1.7 Contributions of the Book

To our knowledge, this is the first study to empirically examine how personalist parties shape democratic decline in a global sample of democracies.[20] In it, we posit that to better understand the most common path of democratic breakdown in recent years—incumbent takeovers—we need to first understand why the political parties that back these democratically elected incumbents fail to stop their efforts to consolidate power and ultimately subvert democracy. As we discuss in Chapter 3, it is nearly impossible to identify elected strongmen *before* they are elected, but we can examine the political parties that help leaders win power and shape how they exercise it once elected. We can thus explain the origins of elected strongmen to demonstrate how personalism in the leader's support party contributes to the undermining of democracy.

To evaluate our argument, we gather systematic data on levels of personalism in the parties of incumbent leaders in democracies new and old across the globe. We document a variety of pathways through which personalist politics—as manifested by the election of leaders backed by personalist parties—sets in motion institutional and societal changes that weaken horizontal and vertical constraints on the leadership and ultimately contribute to the deterioration of democracy.

This book complements recent contributions to the literature on the hollowing of traditional parties and rise of new parties in Europe (Giglioli, 2020; Vries and Hobolt, 2020; Haughton and Deegan-Krause, 2021), as well as research on party system institutionalization and backsliding (Bernhard et al., 2020), legitimation strategies (Barker, 2001), and party brands (Lupu, 2016). In this way, this book unifies insights from a diverse body of research to provide a cohesive understanding of the nature and consequences of personalist ruling parties.

Our approach for measuring party personalism uses case-specific, historical information about the ties between leaders and the parties that support them in an election. It does not incorporate information about the leader's behaviours once in office and therefore does not reflect strategic actions that take place following the leader's election. This means that researchers can use these data to examine how personalism in the leader's party influences such activities. This contrasts with common measures of polarization and support for democracy, for example, which leaders may endogenously shape once in power. As such, the original data that underlie this study can be used in applied research to explore the causes of democratic backsliding.

Our measure of party personalism enables us to capture critical informal political practices and arrangements that can occur under democratic rule. Party

---

[20] Rhodes-Purdy and Madrid (2020) link personalism to democratic decline in Latin America but measure personalism with country experts' opinions about the president's behaviour in office, which may conflate explanation with outcome.

personalism, we posit, is conceptually distinct from and largely orthogonal to the formal institutional rules governing elections or extant cross-regional measures of party institutionalization based on electoral volatility. As such, we measure an existing concept in a new way, yielding a measure of as yet unexplained variations in the practice of democratic politics throughout the world. Using these data, we are able to gain an informed, systematic understanding of how personalist ruling parties influence democratic stability in different regions around the globe.

This approach marks an improvement on recent research on democratic backsliding which has tended to focus on experiences in handful of prominent cases (e.g., Levitsky and Ziblatt, 2018). Though such studies can inform our understanding of the processes at play, as Weyland (2020, 2) points out, 'they cannot assess the actual likelihood of this tragic outcome and identify the conditions under which it occurs and when not'. Our study leverages the full sample of the world's democracies from 1991 to 2020 to gain insight into these and other dynamics, offering a global comparative perspective. Further, we employ a mix of macro-evidence and survey data in democracies throughout the world to both document broad empirical patterns consistent with our theory and provide some intuitions about the micro-level, behavioural implications of the argument.

Personalism's harmful consequences for the quality of governance and the prospects of democratization has been explored in depth in the authoritarianism literature (see, for example, Geddes et al., 2018). Personalist dictatorships are among the most repressive and corrupt of all authoritarian systems and the least likely to democratize; when these regimes do fall from power, their departures are often bloody and violent.[21] In this book, we extend the intuitions from this line of research to democratic environments, focusing on personalism in the ruling political party. Though a number of democracy scholars have suggested that personalism could be detrimental to democratic rule, no study to date has empirically evaluated this relationship in a global sample of democracies (Adam and Maier, 2010; Rahat and Kenig, 2018). In this way our study speaks to and bridges distinct literatures on political personalism in autocratic and democratic settings.

The findings we present have clear policy implications. Where democratic leaders come to power with the backing of a personalist party, we are likely to see an elevated risk of democratic decay. In this way, the election of such leaders provides an early warning that trouble is on the horizon for a country's democracy. It is a clear and observable indicator that a country is at a higher risk of democratic decline, which in turn can inform democracy practitioners on how to prioritize their allocation of resources. This finding is particularly valuable given that most warning signs of democratic deterioration—such as leaders' sidelining or harassment of traditional media—are strategic behaviours only observed once a leader is

---

[21] See Frantz (2018) for a review of this literature.

in office. On the other hand, our measure of party personalism, which incorporates information that predates the leader's assumption of power, is not.

Our study also implies that ruling parties lie at the heart of democratic breakdown from within. Though observers are often tempted to look to voters and their disaffection with democratic politics, or the weakness and fragmentation of opposition parties and groups as key factors underlying the current democratic crisis, our findings suggest that the process is driven by features of the ruling party that favour consolidation of control in the executive—specifically, party personalism. While programmatic party building does not guarantee democratic resilience in the face of power-hungry incumbents—as the experience from Nazi Germany makes clear—the threat to democracy is far greater when personalist parties govern. Efforts to institutionalize political parties and de-link them from the leader who founded them may therefore be particularly effective in protecting democracy, a subject we address in our concluding chapter.

1.8 Plan of the Book

This book proceeds as follows. In the next chapter (Chapter 2), we lay out what personalist parties are, as we conceptualize them. We posit that personalism in political parties can be captured by the extent to which the party organization is a vehicle to advance the leader's personal political career such that the leader has more control over the party than do other senior party elites. Next, we detail our approach to measuring ruling party personalism and the original data collection effort underlying it. We highlight how our measure of ruling party personalism incorporates information that predates the leader's assumption of power, such that it is not endogenous to incumbent leaders' behaviours once in office. Thus, unlike other measures, ours does not conflate the explanation—personalist parties—with the outcome, namely anti-democratic behaviour and democratic backsliding. We then review related concepts and measures, paying particular attention to how party personalism differs from populism.

The rest of this chapter details the basic facts and features of personalist parties, demonstrating that party personalism is a truly global phenomenon, not simply a feature of one or two regions of the world. Nor are personalist parties ideologically different from non-personalist parties. Importantly, we show that ruling party personalism is on the rise globally but find little evidence that increasing political polarization or declining public support for democracy explain its rise. These insights offer a foundation for understanding personalist political parties in the chapters to come.

Chapter 3 articulates our theory linking personalist parties to the undermining of democracy. We posit that personalist parties are structured in ways that reduce the party's incentive and capacity to constrain the leader. Consistent with

20 THE ORIGINS OF ELECTED STRONGMEN

our theoretical assumptions, we demonstrate—using candidate and elite survey data—that personalist parties tend to feature elites with less party and governing experience, resulting in a loyal cadre of actors whose careers depend more on the leader and less on the party. Leaders of personalist parties, as we show, are also more likely to control party resources and nominations, resulting in parties with weaker local organizations. As a result, we demonstrate that cabinet appointee tenures are shorter when leaders' support parties are personalist, suggesting that partisan cabinet elites are unlikely to challenge a personalist leader's agenda. These patterns are consistent with our expectation that personalist parties have less incentive and capacity to push back against a leader who attempts to expand executive control. This chapter thus creates the backdrop for understanding the ways in which ruling party personalism is harmful for democracy that we detail in the remaining chapters.

Chapter 4 tackles these themes directly. We begin by providing two detailed case studies from El Salvador and Hungary to illustrate the full arc of our argument. Next, we present empirical tests linking ruling party personalism with an elevated risk of the deterioration of democracy. We first show that the election of leaders supported by personalist parties leads to a ratcheting up of repression of freedoms of expression and association. We then look at its consequences for democratic backsliding more broadly. We demonstrate that ruling party personalism increases the chance of democratic backsliding, whether it is measured incrementally, sharply, or by total democratic collapse. Lastly, we show that party personalism matters most when ruling parties have legislative majorities; under these conditions opposition parties are too weak to stop leaders, making the ruling party the most consequential constraint on executive-led power grabs. The overall message to emerge is clear: ruling party personalism is detrimental to the health of democracy.

Chapters 5 and 6 offer empirical evidence illustrating the pathways through which this occurs. Chapter 5 documents the harmful impact of personalist parties on institutional checks on the executive. We first discuss the factors that explain the maintenance of executive constraints in democracies and how these factors diminish with ruling party personalism. We then show that because personalist parties lack the incentive and capacity to restrain leaders' attempts to grab power, we see constraints on the executive weaken when these parties win office. Specifically, we find that ruling party personalism decreases the chance that leaders will face constraints in the state's legislative, judicial, and bureaucratic institutions. Importantly, we find that the whittling away of executive constraints brought on by ruling party personalism is even more severe when the leader's party has a large legislative majority. This suggests that personalist parties do little to stand in the way of a power-seeking leader's agenda. In addition, we find that ruling party personalism increases the likelihood that we will observe direct actions on the part of the leader to expand their power, as reflected in attempts to change term limits.

By weakening executive constraints, ruling party personalism opens the door for subsequent actions that culminate in the deterioration of democracy.

Chapter 6 illustrates this. It shows that the behaviour of personalist leaders while in office has far-reaching consequences, ultimately lessening the chance that such leaders will face checks on their actions from below. We begin by asking whether declining citizen views of democracy might be responsible for weakened vertical constraints on personalist leaders. Drawing from our own findings in Chapter 2 and recent research, we dispel that connection, suggesting instead that citizens can value and support democracy, but go along with an agenda that undermines it anyway. We argue that leadership groups shape citizens' beliefs about political opponents and norms of acceptable behaviour, focusing on two mutually re-enforcing explanations for why citizens condone anti-democratic power grabs. The first is polarization, which incentivizes voters to accept democratic subversion to prevent their opponents from securing control. Though some scholars argue that polarization enables the success of anti-democratic leaders, the evidence we offer shows the opposite: with a mix of micro- and macro-empirical analysis, we demonstrate that leaders themselves endogenously drive polarization by attacking state institutions. The second is a shift in their supporters' view of what acceptable behaviours in democracy look like, which weakens their own commitment to adhere to them. Focusing on a particularly egregious breach of norms—support for political violence—and a moment during which we would be particularly likely to observe it—an election loss—we find that ruling party personalism increases the chance that supporters will justify the use of violence in elections in which they lose.

Together, our analyses show that ruling party personalism is harmful for democracy. Because key actors in personalist political parties lack the incentive and capacity to restrain their power-hungry leaders, we see executive constraints weaken. This in turn intensifies polarization and compels supporters of these leaders to loosen their commitment to democratic norms of behaviour. With both horizontal and vertical pathways for accountability diminished, the stage is set for personalist leaders to push the countries they rule towards dictatorship.

In our last chapter (Chapter 7), we summarize these key messages, before closing by discussing the path ahead. We identify the major policy implications to emerge from our findings, suggesting that efforts to strengthen programmatic party building and disincentivize party personalization will be critical to protecting democracy from this new threat that it faces from within.

2

What Are Personalist Parties?

Alberto Fujimori won the presidency of Peru in 1990 with the backing of Cambio 90, a party he had founded the year prior for the purpose of his presidential campaign. Rather than drawing from the traditional political establishment, Fujimori filled Cambio 90's ranks with a group of 'politically independent and small businessmen' (Werlich, 1991, 63). The party did not have a well-articulated policy agenda, such that Fujimori campaigned on a programme that was 'largely undefined' (Robinson, 1990). In these ways, Cambio 90 differed meaningfully from the party of his predecessor, Alan Garcia, who governed with the support of the Peruvian Aprista Party (APRA). APRA was founded decades earlier in the 1920s, its elite ranks were staffed with experienced politicians, and it had a clear policy platform, advocating policies supportive of workers and the middle class. Though Garcia's performance in office was disastrous, Peruvian democracy still withstood it; it collapsed, in contrast, under the tenure of Fujimori, who staged an *auto-golpe* and closed Congress in 1992.

As the example from Peru illustrates, levels of party personalism differ substantially from one party to the next. We argue that these differences are consequential for political outcomes once leaders gain office. It was not long after Fujimori closed the legislature in 1992 and began to rule by decree that the *New York Times* pointed to him as a leading example of a 'new breed of strongmen in the South', documenting the rise in South America of rule by elected 'political leaders and their parties [that] exercise vast powers centralized in the executive branch'.[1] Yet, when Fujimori was first elected in the summer of 1990, few observers labelled him a strongman. Instead, the *New York Times* described Fujimori by his occupation (an engineer) and noted that he won with 'strong left-wing support', only briefly referencing him as a political 'novice'.[2]

Once elected strongmen have taken anti-democratic actions—such as closing the legislature and ruling by decree—it is often too late to turn back the democratic tide. Indeed, with every power grab it becomes incrementally more difficult for citizens and opposition groups to uphold democracy. Protecting democracy, therefore, requires early warning signs that trouble may arise. In this book, we

---

[1] Nash (1994, sect. 4, p. 4).
[2] Brookes (1990, sect. A, p. 1).

The Origins of Elected Strongmen. Erica Frantz, Andrea Kendall-Taylor, and Joseph Wright, Oxford University Press.
© Erica Frantz, Andrea Kendall-Taylor, and Joseph Wright (2024). DOI: 10.1093/oso/9780198888079.003.0002

identify such a factor: personalist political parties. We argue that personalist political parties give rise to the elected strongmen we see today. In this way the upsurge of these parties is facilitating the erosion of democracy we are witnessing across the globe.

This chapter explains what these personalist parties are. The first section conceptualizes them. The second section explains how we measure and operationalize personalist parties in the empirical work we feature in the chapters to come. The third section discusses how our conceptualization relates to similar concepts and measures. We are careful to explain how party personalism—the concept we emphasize—contrasts with populism, another oft-cited term in the democracy literature and mainstream media.

We then dedicate the bulk of this chapter to offering some basic facts and features about personalist parties using our original measure of ruling party personalism. We show that personalist parties do not conform to one particular ideology, and that the empirical overlap between party personalism and populism may stem from the fact that party populism captures whether the leader undermines democracy once in power rather than pre-existing features of the party itself. Using the case of Turkish President Recep Tayyip Erdoğan as well global data on ruling party populism, we show that declining democracy leads observers to describe a leader as more 'populist' over time. This suggests that common measures of populism may be capturing democratic decline rather than being a feature of ruling parties.

We then document trends over time in ruling party personalism, which reveal an uptick in recent years, and show that rising personalism is a global phenomenon, not restricted to one or two regions of the world. Though ruling party personalism is slightly more common in presidential than in parliamentary systems, the impact of political system essentially disappears when accounting for relevant factors. Finally, we find that there is little difference in ruling party personalism across electoral institutions. We close the chapter by demonstrating that shifts in public attitudes—such as declining public support for democracy and increasing polarization—are not associated with the elections of leaders backed by personalist parties. We then summarize how these insights inform analyses in subsequent chapters.

2.1 Conceptualizing Personalist Political Parties

Political parties are a classic feature of democratic politics. A vast literature on political parties addresses their organizational structure, ideological content, and institutionalization (see Katz and Crotty, 2006). In this book, we are interested in the ability of parties to structure politics; we therefore focus on their role as institutions. Individuals and groups comprise parties, but the institution of parties is a combination of the formal rules that govern partisans' behaviour and informal power arrangements among party members. Here we highlight the importance of personalism as a distinguishing dimension of political parties.

Before doing so, it is important to clarify that when we reference the leader of a party, we mean the *de facto* head, unless otherwise noted. For example, when Emmanuel Macron was elected to the French presidency in 2017, his La République En Marche! Party (LREM) was technically led by Stanislas Guerini, who had the post of executive officer. Yet, for all practical purposes Macron is the party's leader, having established it in 2016 as a launching pad for his run for the presidency. As this case illustrates, the *de jure* and *de facto* leader of a political party often do not overlap. We emphasize the latter.

We define party personalism as:

The extent to which parties are vehicles to advance leaders' personal political careers such that the leader has more control and power over the party than do other senior party elites in advancing policy and making personnel choices.

Our conceptualization of personalist political parties builds on early work, such as Janda (1980), who describes them as those parties that leaders establish so that they can consolidate and legitimize their power. Like Janda (1980) and consistent with others in the literature (Kostadinova and Levitt, 2014; Calise, 2015; Kefford and McDonnell, 2018), we see the leader's creation of the party as a key indicator of party personalism.

That said, whereas Janda (1980, 39) ultimately operationalizes personalist parties by the 'extent to which new party militants seem motivated by "personalism" or the charismatic qualities of the party leader', our conceptualization excludes reference to leaders' personal characteristics. Instead, we build on work by Kostadinova and Levitt (2014, 492), who describe personalist parties as weakly structured organizations dominated by the leader, and Gunther and Diamond (2003), who view them as a vehicle for helping leaders win elections and gain power, functioning to promote the leader's career ambitions rather than advocate a particular policy platform.

Not surprisingly, the centrality of the leader to the party means that leadership transitions are more destabilizing to personalist parties than non-personalist parties, with the latter better able 'to survive a first generation of leaders' (Randall and Svåsand, 2002, 11). Power within personalist parties lies with their leader, making them more likely to disband after the leader's departure (Kefford and McDonnell, 2018). In this way, personalist parties are distinct from dynastic parties, which can survive leadership transitions by passing power to family members (Dal Bó et al., 2009; Smith, 2012; Chhibber, 2013; Querubin, 2016; Smith and Martin, 2017).

2.2 Measuring Personalism in Ruling Political Parties

Defining a personalist party is straightforward for the most part. Personalist parties, in our view, are parties where the leader has greater control over the party compared to other party elites. Measuring personalist parties, however, is complicated. There are two key issues that emerge. The first is that observed signs of ruling party personalism (such as greater leadership control over policy or personnel choices relative to other party elites) are frequently endogenous to larger leader strategies following the leader's assumption to power (and the party becoming the 'ruling' party). The second is that such observed signs are often the result of underlying bargaining processes that are unobservable. A weak leader, for example, is unlikely to put forward policies that go against the preferences of a strong party elite; likewise, a weak party elite is unlikely to mount a public challenge against the actions of a strong leader. This means that the absence of observable challenges to the leader from the ruling party elite could represent leader-elite agreement, leader strength, or party elite strength. In the measurement approach that we discuss in this section, we take great care to select indicators of ruling party personalism that avoid these issues.

Our theory, discussed in detail in the next chapter, details why support *parties* potentially constrain elected leaders. We therefore want to measure information about ruling parties, such as whether their leaders created them. However, our theory also focuses on how parties interact with *leaders* to produce the outcome we explain, democratic backsliding. We therefore want to include information about how leaders relate to parties, as well. Further, we must ensure that the information in our explanatory variable is not contaminated by information about how the leader behaves—towards either the party or the larger democratic environment—after the leader is selected chief executive. Our approach therefore infers information about the party and its elites from the political experience of the leader in the party.[3]

We therefore collect information on each democratically elected leader and the party that supports them. This chapter details how we measure ruling party personalism using objective information on leader-party relationships. The next chapter demonstrates that our measure identifies key ruling party features that correspond to the causal mechanisms in our theory: personalist ruling parties have elites with less political experience, weaker local party structures, and greater leadership control over nominations and party funding. In simple terms, we aim to classify every democratically elected leader into two categories, denoting whether the 'party picks the leader' or 'the leader picks her/his party'. This basic distinction,

---

[3] See Krcmaric et al. (2020) for a review of using personal biographies to examine behavioural outcomes.

26 THE ORIGINS OF ELECTED STRONGMEN

we posit, is an observable indicator of who has greater relative power within the party—the party elite or the leader—and something that can be objectively coded. Party personalism is, of course, continuous in practice—with some parties featuring greater personalism than others. Our data therefore include both a binary indicator of whether the chief executive created the support party and a continuous measure of personalism based on this and seven additional indicators, which capture information about how the leader participated in the support party prior to becoming chief executive. In our approach, we use a clear set of coding rules to measure objective facts about leaders and their parties, organized into case narratives and data points. Our sample includes all chief executives in democracies in office in January of a calendar year from 1991 to 2020. The sample of democracies is based on updated data on regime type from Geddes et al. (2014).[4]

We first identify *de facto* democratic leaders and the party (if one exists) supporting their candidacy in their initial election to the chief executive position. The leader—in our definition—is the *de facto* chief executive (i.e., president or prime minister) of a national-level democratic government. Chief executives who were technocratic appointments following resignations (e.g., Ertha Pascal-Trouillot in Haiti; and Shahabuddin Ahmed in Bangladesh) are excluded because they were not elected. Appointed prime ministers backed by leading parties in a parliamentary government are included, however, as are vice presidents elected to their vice presidential positions but constitutionally appointed to be chief executive following incumbent resignations (e.g., Alejandro Maldonado in Guatemala). In both cases, an elected government-leading party selected the chief executive or the chief executive was elected to a position that is part of the constitutional succession (i.e., vice president). Our sample includes 542 democratic leaders in 106 countries.

In our approach, a support party is a political organization, mass movement, or civic association that openly mobilizes voters to help elect candidates to office using its name or label. We identify support parties based on whether they backed a candidate in the first or second round of a national election from which the chief executive is selected. Political support from a party, in our definition, includes openly identified speech, financial backing, and/or organizational resources.

For nominally independent candidates, we identify the main party that backs their election bids, in contrast to data such as the Database of Political Institutions (DPI).[5] For example, DPI codes Colombian President Alvaro Uribe as a nominal

---

[4] Their original data spanned the years 1946 to 2010; our updates include a dichotomous coding of dictatorship and democracy through January 2020.

[5] Sufficient but not necessary signs of a support party include: an identifiable group of individuals and/or an identifiable wealthy individual who finances and provides organizational resources to both a party and the eventual winning candidate's campaign, even where a candidate labels her/himself as an *independent*; an eventual winning candidate who has the backing of a party for which this candidate is the sole candidate in the final round of an election even though the candidate labels her/himself as an *independent*; and a party that openly supports the eventual winner in the first round, even though the party did not stand its own candidate, the winner did not belong to the party, and the candidate labels

'independent', though the Conservative Party was the largest political party backing his candidacy in the first round of the 2002 presidential election. Though Uribe was not a formal member of this party at the time of the election, we treat the Conservative Party as his support party.[6] We then match these data with PartyFacts ID codes (Döring and Regel, 2019) and parties coded in the Varieties of Party data set (Lührmann, 2020).

Identifying all democratically elected leaders in the world and the *de facto* party that is the largest source of electoral support in their *first* election in which they are selected chief executive allows us to move—both theoretically and empirically—beyond country-wide measures of party systems, which predominate in the comparative literature on parties. Ultimately, party systems are comprised of parties and studying how individual parties influence politics brings us closer to identifying the human and organizational agents of political change.

Further, recording the main support party during that *first* election allows us to collect information on the relationship between the elected leader and the support party *prior* to the leader being in office. Thus, our measure of party personalism only uses objective information from the *pre-electoral* history of each leader and their party, rather than information about how the leader behaves once in power (a point we return to shortly in our discussion of endogeneity). Finally, the data cover the entire globe for a thirty-year period. These factors set it apart from the handful of existing data sets that measure party personalism (Rahat and Kenig, 2018; Lührmann, 2020; Marino et al., 2021).

2.2.1 Addressing Endogeneity

One challenge in measuring party personalism is that its telltale signs—such as the leader's dominance over policy or personnel choices vis-à-vis other party elites—are frequently endogenous to the leader's broader strategies to consolidate

---

her/himself as an *independent*. There are therefore only a handful of true independent candidates in our codings who did not receive support from an identifiable party during an election campaign.

[6] Dugas (2003) writes that '[i[n Alvaro Uribe's case he established the Movimiento Primero Colombia (Colombia First Movement) and, while never eschewing his own Liberal identity, eagerly welcomed support from Conservatives and Independents'. And (Crisp, 2009) writes that '[i]n his campaign for president, Uribe had split from the traditionally dominant Liberal Party and run as an independent. He established the Colombia First electoral movement'. Another observer notes that '[i]n the first round of the presidential elections held on May 26, 2002, Alvaro Uribe Velez, running as candidate of the right-wing Colombia First (Primero Colombia) coalition, secured 53.04% of the votes to secure an unprecedented outright win' (Szajkowski, 2005, 130). Finally, writing in 2001, Forero (2001) notes that '[a]s governor and, before that, a senator, Mr. Uribe was a member of the Liberal Party, one of Colombia's two main parties. With the Liberal Party supporting another candidate for the presidency, however, he formed his own movement, Colombia First'. Colombia First, however, was a coalition of supporting political parties. Because the Conservative Party was the largest party in this coalition that backed Uribe's 2002 campaign and because the Conservative Party did not run a candidate against Uribe in the first round of the election, we treat the Conservative Party as the electing support party in 2002.

control once in office, as we mentioned earlier. After leaders assume power, greater personalization of the party may occur seemingly in tandem with actions that undermine democracy. Examples we reference throughout this study—ranging from experience in Turkey with Erdoğan and the Justice and Development Party (or Adalet ve Kalkınma Partisi; AKP) or in the US with Donald Trump and the Republican Party—attest to this. Elected leaders may gain greater control over their party precisely as we see them chipping away at institutional constraints to their rule. We argue that the former is what enables the latter. That said, empirically demonstrating the direction of causality requires a measurement approach that addresses the potential endogeneity of this relationship.

Disentangling how leadership power concentration and institutional weakness interact is a well-known challenge for research on personalism in authoritarian environments (Pepinsky, 2014). In that research, it is difficult to assess whether personalism is observed because the leader weakened institutions or because weak institutions strengthened the leader. The empirical strategy we use to address endogeneity in this study draws from approaches used in that literature, where personalism is measured prior to the leader's assumption to power (Geddes et al., 2018).

The items in our measure record information about the leader and the party they were elected with by looking at the history of their relationship, particularly whether the leader created or helped establish the party and whether the leader served in political positions with that party prior to assuming leadership. The items therefore capture objective information on the pre-electoral history of leader-party relations, recording information that chronologically precedes the leader obtaining executive office. They do not include information about the leader's behaviour once in power, such that they cannot be endogenously produced by it. In the cases of Erdoğan and Trump, therefore, though personalism in each of their support parties likely increased in the years after they took office, we measure it at the time they assumed power based on pre-electoral historical information. This enables us to isolate their party's personalism from their strategic behaviours while in office.

In contrast, measures of polarization or populism based on the leader's rhetoric or citizens' opinions of the party or leader may capture information about what the leader does *after* they are elected to office and therefore may be consequences of behavioural attempts to undermine democracy once in power. Observing a leader deploy derogatory rhetoric to demonize political opponents or criticize incumbent elites, for example, might constitute information used to document populism or produce a more polarized citizenry but such strategies may also be recorded by researchers as an attempt to undermine democracy. (We explore this possibility in greater detail later on in this chapter.) Thus information on a leader's rhetoric might be observed as both an *explanatory* factor (polarization or populism) and a change in the *outcome* a researcher would like to explain (democratic erosion or decay). If we want to test theories of democratic erosion, we need to measure the explanatory concepts using information that is chronologically prior to and conceptually independent from the outcome under study, namely democratic erosion.

For this reason, our data collection approach uses historical information on leader-party relations that precedes the leader obtaining executive office. In this way, we are able to ensure that our measure of party personalism is not contaminated by information about the leader's behaviour in office—such as stacking the judiciary, arresting opposition leaders, or purging the state bureaucracy—that leads observers to label the leader a 'strongman' or that researchers might employ to document the decline of democracy. Our measure is thus not endogenous to leaders' strategic behaviour once the leader becomes the chief executive.

2.2.2 Underlying Indicators

After identifying leaders and their support parties, we lay out a clear set of coding rules to organize objective facts about the history of the relationship between the two, which we describe in case narratives (Frantz, Kendall-Taylor, Li, and Wright, 2022). The narratives are qualitative data that capture the complexity of real-world politics in a variety of formal institutional settings and party systems. They include all the information we need to code the data we are interested in, as well as reference material from the qualitative sources we used to gather it. As such, the narratives allow other researchers to see the information we collected to code the data points and check the coding themselves. They both facilitate research transparency and provide additional information that can be used in future research.

Using the narratives, we recorded quantitative data on eight objective, systematic indicators of personalist parties:

We use the eight items, listed in Table 2.1, to construct a latent index of ruling party personalism, with higher values suggesting greater personalism in the party and lower values, less. The concept we measure is:

The extent to which parties are vehicles to advance leaders' personal political careers such that the leader has more control and power over the party than do other senior party elites in advancing policy and making personnel choices.

The definition contains two subcomponents that are conceptually related: 'parties that advance leaders' careers' and leaders' 'control and power' relative to other senior party elites.

The first indicator measures whether a party is created by a politician. This indicator captures both subcomponents of the definition because creating the party

30 THE ORIGINS OF ELECTED STRONGMEN

Table 2.1 Pre-selection indicators of party personalism

Create party	Did the leader create the political party that backed them in the election for chief executive?
National appointment with electing party	Did the leader hold a national appointed position in government with the electing party prior to being selected chief executive?
National elected with electing party	Did the leader hold a national elected position with the electing party prior to being selected chief executive?
Party leadership position with electing party	Did the leader hold an appointed position with the political party (e.g., party leader or treasurer) prior to being selected chief executive?
Local appointed with electing party	Did the leader hold an appointed local position with the electing party prior to being selected chief executive?
Local elected with electing party	Did the leader hold an elected local position with the electing party prior to being selected chief executive?
Prior independent	Did the leader hold a political office or run as a losing candidate for the chief executive position as a political independent (i.e., without backing from an established political party) prior to being selected chief executive?
Party experience	How long has the leader been in an established electing political party prior to assuming office?

(prior to an election) enables the politician to get elected (career advancement) and party creation means having initial control of and power within the party.

Five additional indicators provide information about the leader's prior positions in the party that backed the leader in the election. Two of these items relate to prior experience with the party at a local level and two at the national level. Local service to the party (*local appointed* and *local elected*) indicates that the leader has experience serving the party *without* a national electoral following and adhering to party norms for power-sharing. We expect local elected and appointed positions to capture *less* party personalism.

National appointments and national elected positions with the party indicate that other senior elites in the party value the leader's contributions to party service and that the leader had previously served under other party elites. Both national appointments and elected positions should capture *less* personalism. That said, national elected positions might translate into a national electoral following that provides the would-be leader with a source of power external to the party. We would thus expect national elected positions to indicate more personalism than national appointed positions. Finally, having a national party position provides the leader a resource within the party and should indicate *more* party personalism.

A seventh indicator captures whether the leader had previously held an elected or appointed position as an independent or whether the leader had run for the national chief executive position as an independent but lost that race. A prior independent political career indicates that a leader may have electoral strength independent of the party, especially a party the leader did not create. We thus expect *prior independent* to capture *higher* levels of party personalism.

The final indicator combines information about how long the party has existed with information about how long the leader has been a member of the party. Older parties are comprised of elites who have a history of repeated interaction together, which should enable them to more successfully counter moves by the leader to take party power from them. And leaders who have served in prior positions in the party for a long time will be more likely to have internalized the norms of party, including sharing power with other elites. We thus expect party experience to capture *lower* levels of party personalism.

The Appendix to this chapter provides details about the measurement model that aggregates information from these individual indicators to create a continuous measure of party personalism. The Appendix also provides tests that demonstrate the internal reliability (Table 2.A-1) of our measure of party personalism and document its external validity (Figure 2.A-2).

2.2.3 What Our Measure Can and Cannot Capture

Coding the relationship between incumbent leaders and their support parties is difficult, given the complexities of the real world of politics. Many democratic leaders go up the ranks of an established party prior to becoming chief executive, but there are a variety of departures from this route. In some cases, leaders come from an established party but then leave it to create a new one that launches them into power (such as Emmanuel Macron in France). In other cases, leaders ally themselves with an established party before an election following a career serving in local elected positions (such as Rodrigo Duterte in the Philippines) or as political outsiders (such as Donald Trump in the United States). And, in yet other cases, leaders create a party to back them in their campaigns (such as Hugo Chavez in Venezuela), help win legislative seats prior to boosting them to national executive office (such as Evo Morales in Bolivia), or team up with established parties in a pre-electoral coalition. In some instances, leaders have even created a party, won office with that party, and then left it soon after assuming the leadership (such as Jair Bolsonaro in Brazil or Bingu wa Mutharika in Malawi). Our measurement approach captures information on these (and other) party routes to democratic leadership.

In the real world, party personalism often varies over the course of a leader's tenure. Because we measure party personalism *at the time that a leader assumes*

32   THE ORIGINS OF ELECTED STRONGMEN

power, however, our measure cannot capture such changes while a leader is in office. While our measure does vary within parties over time (with different levels possible across different leaders), it remains static while an individual leader is in office. An example from the Republican Party in the US illustrates this. Using our measure, ruling party personalism is .34 for the years 2001 through 2008, while Republican George W. Bush was in the presidency; it more than doubles (to .69) for the years 2017 through 2020 (the last year of our data) while Republican Donald Trump was in office. Because these values are derived using objective information from the *pre-electoral* history of each leader and the Republican Party, they do not change over the course of these leaders' tenures.

In those instances where leaders come to power more than once with the same party (as in Hungary, for example, when Viktor Orban won power with the backing of the Fidesz coalition in 1998 and again in 2010), party personalism is measured the year the leader first assumed office. In the case of Hungary, this means that party personalism has the same value from 1999 to 2002 (the years of Orban's first tenure) as it does from 2011 on (the years of his second). Our measure therefore does not capture changes in levels of party personalism that might occur if a leader comes to office with the same party but on two separate occasions.

Our measurement approach thus enables us to disentangle the main treatment concept (party personalism) from the outcome (democratic backsliding), but at the expense of limiting our ability to capture instances where party personalism changes under a leader's rule. We acknowledge that this limitation reduces the accuracy of our party personalism measure. That said, we see it as providing a harder test of our argument, given that the level of party personalism we use in our analyses is likely lower than what is observed later on over the course of a leader's rule. If we find evidence that party personalism at the time of the leader's assumption to power influences the outcomes we are interested in in the years to come, it is suggestive that these relationships may in fact be even stronger than what we report.

To illustrate how our measure of ruling party personalism works in practice, we briefly discuss how the measure translates the political history of three US presidents who were selected as leader from the same party. President Donald Trump has a substantially higher personalism score (0.70) than President George W. Bush (0.34) because the latter held a local elected position (governor of Texas) with the Republican Party prior to being selected president in 2000 by the US Supreme Court. Trump, in contrast, never held an elected position with the Republican Party, nor was he appointed to a political position with the party. In fact, he was briefly a registered Democrat in the state of New York in 2001, well before he hinted at running for president. And while neither G.W. Bush nor Trump created the party that backed their selection to the presidency, Bush had served in the party for more than two decades, first running for a US congressional seat as a Republican in 1978. His father, President George H.W. Bush, however, has the lowest personalism score

(0.21) among the post-1990 Republican leaders. He held both national elected positions (US representative and vice president) and national appointed positions (ambassador to the United Nations and head of the US intelligence agency) as a Republican. Further, G.H.W. Bush held a top party position, chair of the Republican National Committee, in 1973–4. His deeper experience in the Republican Party than his son pushes his personalism score lower.

2.3 Related Concepts and Measures

In this section, we discuss concepts and measures that are similar to party personalism. We begin with a lengthy discussion of how party personalism relates to populism in particular, given the latter's prominence in the literature and mainstream media and overlap with party personalism in practice.

2.3.1 Party Personalism and Populism

Many observers have tied the contemporary democratic decline we are witnessing to the rise of populist movements around the globe. In its 2018 report, for example, the watchdog organization Human Rights Watch urged the world to push back 'against the populist challenge', as did Freedom House, which titled its 2017 report, 'Populists and Autocrats: The Dual Threat to Global Democracy' (Puddington and Roylance, 2017; Roth, 2018). Indeed, there are many noteworthy examples in recent years of populist leaders who oversaw the deterioration of their country's democracies, including Erdoğan and the AKP in Turkey, Chavez and his Fifth Republic Movement (MVR) in Venezuela, and Orban and the Fidesz coalition in Hungary. In each of these cases, elected leaders backed by populist political organizations eroded democratic institutions and established authoritarian rule. Importantly, for the purposes of this study, these are support parties we would consider to be personalist in nature too. Given the overlap between populist parties and personalist parties in these (and other) instances, it is valuable to discuss populism as a concept briefly, what it shares in common with party personalism and how it differs, and why this study focuses on party personalism.

The concept of populism is widely debated in the literature, such that there is no consensus definition of what populism refers to and substantial uncertainty over its 'conceptual core' (Wuttke et al., 2020, 357). Though this is more problematic in popular discourse than in the body of scholarship devoted to populism, it remains a contested concept even in the latter (Mudde and Kaltwasser, 2018; Landau, 2020; Rhodes-Purdy and Madrid, 2020). As Kaltwasser et al. (2017) note, academic consensus on the meaning of populism has improved in recent years; nonetheless, divisions in this regard remain (Singer, 2018). Some see populism as a set of ideas,

34 THE ORIGINS OF ELECTED STRONGMEN

at its core pitting 'the pure people' against 'the corrupt elite' and emphasizing popular sovereignty as a key principle of governance (Mudde and Kaltwasser, 2018). Others, however, see populism as a political strategy, where leaders make direct appeals to the masses and govern with the support of weakly organized political vehicles (Weyland, 2001). Additional visions of populism exist too, highlighting the contrasting and diverse ways in which scholars conceive populism.[7]

Regardless of how scholars define populism, it has a clear overlap with the concept of personalism in practice. As Landau (2020, 296) notes, '[t]here seems to be something generally "personalist" about populist leadership'. Part of this is because the bond between the leader and the people is particularly important for populists, thus favouring the ascension of leaders with charisma and centralized power. The two concepts are further entangled by the fact that both share a tendency to gravitate towards anti-pluralism (Posner, 2017, 5). Populists' emphasis on the divide between the people and the elite, for example, naturally lends itself to political exclusion, making it the 'enemy of pluralism' in the eyes of some (Galston, 2018, 12). Likewise, concentration of power—which is the essence of personalist politics—is essentially the opposite of pluralism; one runs counter to the other. For these reasons and more, populists and personalists often overlap in practice. This is consistent with research on European political parties, which shows that those that are populist are more likely to have centralized internal structures (with power concentrated in the leadership) than those that are not populist (Bohmelt et al., forthcoming).[8]

That said, the two terms are not synonymous. Conceptually, personalism—as we use it here—refers to a structural feature of a political party, specifically the extent to which parties are leader-centric. Organizationally, personalist parties are top heavy, with the leader exerting disproportionate control over policy and personnel choices relative to other senior party elites. Populism, by contrast, does not have to do with a party's structure in any of the major ways in which it is conceptualized. For those who adopt the ideational approach of populism, for example, populist parties are differentiated by the set of ideas that underlie them. For those who instead see populism as a strategy, populist parties are distinguished by the choices their leaders pursue to maintain control. Because of these conceptual differences, it is therefore possible for a party to be populist but not personalist, and vice versa.

Take Macky Sall of Senegal and his support party, the Alliance for the Republic (APR), which he created in 2008. The APR ranks as one of the more 'personalist' parties using our measure of ruling party personalism (discussed in the section to follow), yet observers do not view Sall as a populist. For example, the Varieties of

---

[7] See Mudde and Kaltwasser (2018) for a review.

[8] As Bohmelt et al. (forthcoming) point out, the concentration of power seen in populist European parties reflects an inconsistency between the rhetoric they put forward, which emphasizes the 'people', and how they are organized in practice.

Party data set (also described later in this chapter) gives the APR a lower populism score than both the Democratic Party under Barak Obama and the Republican Party under George W. Bush in the United States. If anything, Sall has persecuted populist challengers to his power, as in 2021 when he jailed opposition leader Ousmane Sonko because of the latter's 'popularity [that] has galvanized the street movements against the perceived corruption and inequities of the Macky Sall administration' (Lu, 2021). Observers describe Sonko—not Sall—as 'a populist who has railed against corruption and poverty' (Dione and Larson, 2021). Though neither a populist nor even a political outsider, Sall's party is highly personalist because he created the organization to back his first presidential campaign.[9] As this example illustrates, though we often see a blurring between personalist and populist political movements in practice, personalism and populism are not one and the same; one does not guarantee the other.

In this study, we view personalism as a characteristic of a political party. We see many analytical advantages to our emphasis on personalism. For one, personalism offers us conceptual clarity. As Rhodes-Purdy and Madrid (2020) point out, using the term personalism enables us to avoid the fuzziness and contestation that accompany terms such as populism. Personalism is easy to define; there is scholarly consensus with respect to what it refers to. Personalism is also easy to measure, a trait that is important for comparative research. With populism, by contrast, there is often a misalignment between concept and measurement, regardless of whether populism is captured in terms of attitudes, party strategies, or communication styles, such that 'populism constructs often do not reflect what they are intended to measure' (Wuttke et al., 2020, 370).[10] Meijers and Zaslove (2020) build on these themes. They write that most existing data capturing populism in political parties lack construct validity and/or precision; those measures that better address these issues have only limited coverage.[11] Whereas debates persist over how to accurately measure populism, developing criteria to capture personalism is fairly straightforward.

Finally, too often 'populist' leaders are labelled such once we observe their antidemocratic behaviour in office. Turkish President Erdoğan, for example, was once extolled by the media as the leader of a liberal Islamist party, indeed a party that some thought could pave the way for the first Muslim-majority country to join the European Union (Goodman, 2018). In 2004, for example, *The Economist* hailed Erdoğan and his AKP as 'proving in office to be of the liberal variety that believes in

---

[9] Prior to creating his own party, Sall had been a legislator, minister, and even the legislative leader for the Senegalese Democratic Party, an established party created in the 1970s.

[10] The problem lies in the challenges inherent in trying to capture a multi-dimensional concept. Personalism does not suffer from these issues, given that it is essentially uni-dimensional, capturing the distribution of power.

[11] Meijers and Zaslove (2020) offer data capturing populism in political parties that addresses these issues, but it is limited to European cases.

36 THE ORIGINS OF ELECTED STRONGMEN

free markets and secular democracy'.[12] Once Erdoğan started to attack horizontal checks on his power, however, observers quickly switched their tune and started to describe Erdoğan as 'populist'.[13] Indeed, one observer even described Erdoğan, in 2019, as the 'inventor of 21st century populism' (McKernan, 2019).

To illustrate this point more systematically, we examine data on populism in Turkey from two sources. First, we collected data from articles in major English-language newspapers about President Erdoğan to calculate the proportion of these articles that use the terms 'populist' or 'populism' to describe Erdoğan or his ruling party.[14] This measure captures the extent to which informed observers characterize Erdoğan or his party as a 'populist'. Second, we use data, compiled by the Varieties of Party project, from country-expert coders who specialize in party politics. This measure (described in greater detail later in this chapter) captures experts' assessment of parties' use of populist rhetoric, defined as conveying either people-centric or anti-elite sentiment.

Erdoğan has ruled Turkey for over two decades with the support of the AKP, which was created in 2001 by Erdoğan along with Abdullah Gül and elites from older, then-defunct parties. The AKP won the 2002 general election, selecting Gül as the prime minister to lead a new Turkish government. But Erdoğan, the leader of AKP at the time of the 2002 election, replaced Gül as prime minister in 2003. In 2014, while still prime minister, Erdoğan was elected president and subsequently transformed the government structure into a presidential system, giving him more power.

Figure 2.1 shows three trend lines for the period of AKP rule. The dashed line marks the level of democracy in Turkey during the past three decades. In the first years of AKP rule, the level of democracy rises, peaking in 2004. After that, however, democracy declines steadily, particularly once the AKP wins general elections in 2007 and 2011. This trend in democracy shows that while Erdoğan presided over a steep decline in democracy prior to democratic collapse in 2016, the first few years of his rule actually produced small *increases* in democracy.

The other two trend lines show that assessments of 'populist' rule have increased in response to the trajectory of democracy. The dark solid trend line shows the share of news stories about the AKP that describe the party (or Erdoğan) as populist. During AKP's initial election in 2002, less than 2 per cent of news stories contained descriptions of the AKP or Erdoğan as populist. That figure climbs to well over 2 per cent in 2007 and remains relatively steady through the 2011 election. However, after that election, the AKP presided over a steep

---

[12] *The Economist* (2004).

[13] Erdoğan and Öney (2014).

[14] We examined all news articles published in the *New York Times*, the *Financial Times* (UK), and *The Guardian* (UK) that mention Erdoğan or the AKP from 2002 to 2016. We end the analysis in 2016 because that is the year when democracy collapses in Turkey, and Erdoğan's rule transitions to autocracy.

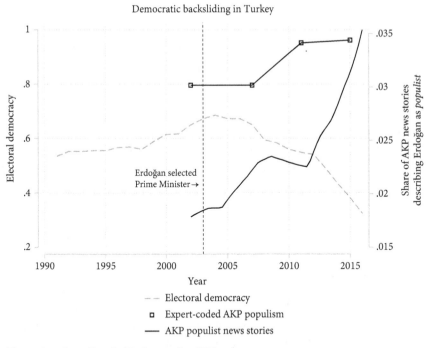

Figure 2.1 Populism in Turkey under AKP rule

decline in democracy that parallels a steep incline in news stories referencing AKP populism.[15] This suggests that journalists are more likely to use the term 'populist' to describe a leader or ruling party *after* democracy declines. And these journalistic impressions may even cloud experts' historical assessments of party populism.

The last trend shown in Figure 2.1—marked with small squares—is the expert-coded assessment of AKP populism. During the party's first election in 2002 the populism score is relatively high, at 0.8 on a (0,1) scale.[16] This assessment of AKP populism remains the same for the next election, in 2007, but then increases during the 2011 election. Notably, democracy started to decline quickly after the 2007 election; thus the rising populism score in 2011 may, in fact, reflect the decrease in democracy that occurred *prior* to the 2011 contest. This expert-coded assessment of AKP populism increases once more, though by a smaller margin, during the 2015 election, again possibly reflecting the decline in democracy between the 2011 and 2015 elections.

---

[15] Granger causality tests, reported in the online appendix, indicate that the lagged level of democracy predicts the share of news stories about the AKP that describe the party as populist but that the populism measure does *not* predict democracy levels.

[16] This variable aggregates multiple country experts' assessments of party populism for each party in each election year. We rescaled the variable so that the lowest score in the data set is 0 while the highest is 1.

38 THE ORIGINS OF ELECTED STRONGMEN

A systematic test of the possibility that changes in democracy presage populism scores, reported in the online appendix, uses all leaders in the data. The result indicates that changes in the level of democracy in the year prior to an election strongly predict changes in the ruling party's populism score from the prior election. This finding suggests that even expert-level assessments of populism, at least those used in the populism measure from the Varieties of Party project, are endogenous to democratic backsliding.

The patterns in this figure suggest that populism in Turkey, at least in part, reflects the downward trend in democracy. Explanatory concepts, such as populism and personalism, must be analytically distinct from the phenomenon they purport to explain, in our case, democratic backsliding. If 'populist' parties are simply those that we eventually observe subverting democracy, then the concept of populism (as an explanatory device) verges on tautology. Our measurement strategy elides this issue, as we discussed earlier in this chapter, by capturing information about leaders and their supporting party prior to the leader obtaining executive office; personalism, as we measure it, therefore predates a leader's observed behaviour or rhetoric once the leader assumes the top executive position.

To summarize, while there are many merits to studying populism, a study such as ours—which seeks to shed light on easily observable and measurable ways that features of leaders' support parties influence democratic erosion and related outcomes—focusing on party personalism has many advantages. As we show throughout the book, party personalism increases the chance of democratic decline, even beyond the influence of populism. Moreover, it does so through a clear set of causal pathways, for which we provide evidence throughout the chapters to follow.

2.3.2 Other Related Concepts and Measures

In addition to populism, there are other concepts and measures related to party personalism that are worth discussing. The first comes from the literature on the 'presidentialization of politics', which highlights the movement towards personalism in liberal democracies (Mughan, 1993, 2000; Samuels and Shugart, 2003; McAllister, 2007; Poguntke and Webb, 2007). This literature suggests that the declining importance of political parties is not restricted to presidential political systems, where party discipline is usually weaker and incentives for individual responsibility greater, but also occurs in parliamentary systems where leaders should, theoretically, not have a meaningful and unique identity from the perspective of voters. Our conceptualization of personalist parties also shares some aspects of work by Mughan (2000, 7), who notes that presidentialization is a 'movement over time away from collective to personalized government, movement away from a pattern of governmental and electoral politics dominated by the political party to one where the party leader becomes a more autonomous political force'. To be clear, presidentialization and personalization are not synonymous processes, yet understandings of how and why they differ depend on how scholars conceptualize them (Passarelli, 2015; Cross et al., 2018; Marino et al., 2021). We recognize the similarities between presidential and personalist political parties, but focus our attention on the latter for analytical clarity.

Personalist parties have some parallels to specific concepts and corresponding measures in the literature on political party and leadership characteristics. Research on party institutionalization, for example, highlights (among a range of factors) whether parties feature deep societal roots and organizational autonomy from their leader (Mainwaring and Scully, 1995; Mainwaring, 1998; Mainwaring and Torcal, 2006). In this way, personalist parties are similar to parties that are *not* institutionalized. Indeed, their organizational structures are typically 'light', with shallow and often fleeting grassroots networks (Kefford and McDonnell, 2018). This corresponds to insights by Janda (1980), who suggests that party institutionalization will be limited when party organizations function as leaders' personal instruments. Research on authoritarian regimes picks up on these themes, viewing party institutionalization as the process through which power is 'depersonalized' (Meng, 2020). We note, however, that not all poorly institutionalized parties are personalist even if personalist parties are typically poorly institutionalized.

Scholars use a number of approaches for measuring the components of party institutionalization, most of which emphasize legislative seat or vote share volatility (Powell and Tucker, 2014).[17] Others focus on specific features of party institutionalization. Mainwaring and Torcal (2006), for example, look at the depth of parties' societal roots using cross-sectional surveys of ideological voting. This strategy limits generalization, but they find evidence that personalistic links between voters and candidates tend to be weaker when 'party roots in society' are stronger (Mainwaring and Torcal, 2006, 22). Others use expert assessments of internal party characteristics (such as party branches and platforms), whether party members vote with their party, and whether the party emphasizes more clientelist or programmatic linkage strategies (Bizzarro et al., 2017). These data do not exist at the level of the individual party, however, but at the level of the party *system*, meaning the constellation of parties competing for power in a country at a particular moment in time. Finally, Meng (2020) assesses party institutionalization in autocracies by measuring the number of leaders for each authoritarian ruling party and calculating how long these parties endure following the exit of the leader who founded them. We focus on ruling parties in democracies and steer clear of measuring personalism as the strategy parties deploy when linking themselves to society or voters.

---

[17] This large literature includes, in addition, Kuenzi and Lambright (2001); Tavits (2005); Mainwaring and Torcal (2006); Lindberg (2007); Hicken and Martínez Kuhonta (2011).

40 THE ORIGINS OF ELECTED STRONGMEN

Our conceptualization of personalist parties is relevant to insights from the literature on 'political outsiders' and 'anti-system candidates', as well (Levitsky, 1999; Gunther and Diamond, 2003; Mainwaring and Torcal, 2006; Barr, 2009; Samuels and Shugart, 2010; Carreras, 2017). For example, leaders of personalist parties may promote themselves and their movement as challenging the traditional political establishment and politics as usual. Leaders such as Hugo Chavez of Venezuela (supported by the MVR) and Andrej Babis of the Czech Republic (supported by Action by Dissatisfied Citizens) would fit this characterization well. At the same time, these concepts are not synonymous (Levitsky, 1999; Barr, 2009; Kostadinova and Levitt, 2014). Importantly, being a political outsider or anti-system candidate is a characteristic of a political leader but is not indicative of the party organization that backs them.

For example, we may see elected leaders—who Carreras (2017, 366) defines as 'outsiders' who do not have extensive legislative or executive political experience— align with an established party when they run for office, just as we may see a political 'insider' break ties with an established party and run with the support of a party they themselves recently created. This was the case with Rafael Caldera of Venezuela, who was elected president in 1993. Caldera was a consummate politician, having already served as president (from 1969 to 1974) and helping found one of the country's main established parties, COPEI. Caldera defected from COPEI prior to the 1993 presidential election, however, creating a new party (National Convergence) from a coalition of small existing ones. He used this new party to serve as his electoral vehicle to launch him to power a second time. In this way, we can see how a political insider can still be supported by a personalist party.

2.4 Basic Facts and Features of Ruling Personalist Parties

In this section, we now introduce some basic facts and features of personalist parties using our measure of ruling party personalism. We begin by discussing the rising trend in party personalism in the past three decades.

2.4.1 Trends in Ruling Party Personalism over Time

Many observers have noted that we are in a period of global democratic decline. It is therefore useful to know whether trends in party personalism correspond. The left plot in Figure 2.2 shows the global trend in the level of democracy (dashed line) and the average age of democracies (in light grey) for the past three decades. During the 1990s, many countries transitioned from dictatorship to democracy, increasing the number of democracies in the world. Further, the average level

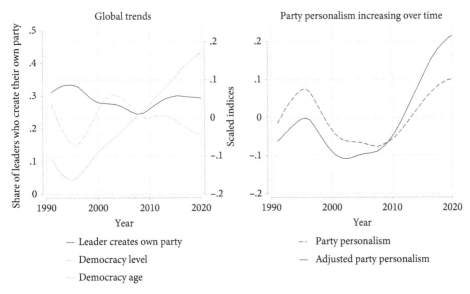

Figure 2.2 Party personalism time trend

of democracy *among democracies* also increased; this means that those countries that were already democratic became more so, on average, over the course of that first post-Cold-War decade. However, because many democracies in the 1990s are new, the average age of democracies does not start increasing until the late 1990s when fewer newer democracies enter the sample and countries that were already democracies grow older. During the mid-2000s, the average level of democracy *among democracies* starts to decline, a trend in backsliding that many observers have noted. The average age of democracies, however, continues to increase during this period because existing democracies grew older—for example, the democracy in Portugal is only fifteen years old in 1990 but forty-five years old by 2020—but fewer new democracies were born.

The left plot also shows, with a solid black line, the share of democracies led by a leader who created his or her own political party. Recall that this variable is one of the main indicators of party personalism. The global share of these leaders is highest in the 1990s, which makes sense once we consider the fact that many countries transitioned to multiparty democracies from dictatorships with no parties or a single, dominant one. Thus not only were many new democracies born in the 1990s but many new parties as well. In these cases, newly elected democratic leaders frequently played a significant role in helping to form new democratic parties, many from opposition organizations. That victorious parties will often be relatively new in newer democracies bears emphasis because, for this reason, our measure of party personalism will be higher in new democracies. Given the items we use to construct the measure, which incorporate pre-electoral information and not post-electoral behaviour, this is inevitable. Therefore, in applied analysis we must adjust for the *age of democracy* so that we can make comparisons that account for the fact that new democracies, mostly born in the 1990s, tend to have younger parties, which means fewer opportunities for leaders to have served in prior positions with their support party.

The right plot in Figure 2.2 shows both the average ruling party personalism scores over the past three decades, as well as the global trend in the *adjusted* personalism scores that account for the age of democracy.[18] Similar to patterns in new party creation shown in the left plot, unadjusted party personalism scores are relatively high in the 1990s, in part due to the newness of many democracies. The trend in unadjusted party personalism increases steadily, however, from the late 2000s onwards.

This pattern contrasts with the trend in the *adjusted* level of party personalism, which has risen substantially since 1991, with the largest increases in the past decade. In the early 1990s, adjusted personalism was below the sample average. But by 2020, personalism rises to roughly 0.2 standard deviations *above* the average. This indicates that ruling party personalism is growing substantially over time. Indeed, the rapid rise in (adjusted) party personalism in the right plot corresponds to the same time frame as the dip in democracy in the left plot. In short, incumbent party personalism has been rising in the past two decades, mirroring the global decline in the level of democracy.

2.4.2 Geographical Distribution of Personalist Parties

The dominant explanations for why some democracies endure while others fizzle rely on structural features of a country that tend to change slowly over time. Perhaps the most influential theory of democratic survival points to economic development (e.g., Lipset, 1959; Przeworski and Limongi, 1997). Others emphasize that older democracies are more stable than their young counterparts (e.g., Schedler, 1998, 94). While noting that consolidated democracies are more stable is certainly useful, this insight cannot explain why we have seen democratic backsliding in so many established democracies in the past decade.

Further, much of what we know about political parties and democratic stability relies on studies that focus on particular geographic regions. Those who point to reliable conservative parties to explain democratic endurance look to Europe (e.g.,

---

[18] The vertical scale is measured in standard deviations, with 0 set as the sample average. Adjusting for democracy entails partialing out the age of democracy from the ruling party personalism index and rescaling.

Ziblatt, 2017). And the predominant analyses of populism draw primarily from European and Latin American cases for evidence that populist leaders take aim at democracy (e.g., Weyland, 2001; Mudde and Kaltwasser, 2012; Berman, 2021).[19] Likewise, an older literature points to different electoral systems, which tend to cluster in the same geographic region, to explain democratic collapse (e.g., Linz, 1990). Presidents tend to rule in Africa and Latin America while prime ministers predominate in Europe and most of Asia. Even fine-grained differences in electoral rules often cluster by region, in part a reflection of colonial legacies.

The geographic clustering of cases in extant theories suggests that we should look closely at *where* party personalism arises. Is it a global phenomenon? Or is personalism the province of just one or a few geographic regions?

Table 2.2 shows the average level of the raw party personalism score for democracies across geographic regions. Ruling party personalism is highest in Eastern Europe and sub-Saharan Africa—regions where many countries transitioned to democracy since 1989. In contrast, party personalism is lowest in Western Europe and North America, home to the longest lived democracies in the world. This geographic variation in party personalism, however, matches the patterns seen in other relevant phenomena. Data on level of democracy, the age of democracy, and even GDP per capita demonstrate similar geographic clustering: Western European democracies have much higher democracy scores than African democracies; and the former tend to be much wealthier. Eastern European and Latin American democracies have similar democracy scores as well as levels of development but less democracy and wealth than Western Europe.

In short, geographic region tends to correlate with many phenomena that have been used to explain democratic stability. However, as we pointed out earlier, there are structural reasons why incumbent party personalism tends to be lower in newer democracies, which also tend to be poorer and have lower levels of democracy relative to their older counterparts. We measure personalism using the pre-electoral history of an elected leader with their party. In many new democracies, particularly those that transitioned from single-party rule or military rule in the 1990s, opposition political parties were often banned and, even if legal, had few resources. Thus, we are less likely to observe leaders who have had a long history with their support parties in new democracies simply because new democracies tend to have younger parties.

The final column of Table 2.2 shows the average *adjusted* level of party personalism by geographic region; the adjusted party personalism score accounts for the age of democracy when each leader is selected into power. With this adjustment, the geographic pattern for party personalism is not nearly as strong. In fact, incumbent parties in Western Europe have only slightly less party personalism, on average, than those in African democracies. And established democracies

---

[19] However, see Resnick (2014, 2017) on populism in Africa.

44 THE ORIGINS OF ELECTED STRONGMEN

Table 2.2 Party personalism is a global phenomenon

Region	Party personalism	Democracy level	Democracy age	GDP per capita	Adjusted party personalism
E. Europe and Central Asia	0.64	0.70	2.29	9.33	0.51
Latin America	0.55	0.70	2.80	8.89	0.47
Middle East and N. Africa	0.70	0.62	2.65	9.60	0.60
Sub-Saharan Africa	0.64	0.58	1.85	7.74	0.51
W. Europe and N. America	0.34	0.88	4.26	10.40	0.47
Asia and Pacific	0.59	0.61	2.55	8.83	0.51

Average values for democracies in each geographic region. Democracy age and GDP per capita figures calculated using a natural log scale. The adjusted party personalism score accounts for the age of democracy. Latin America includes Caribbean countries.

in Western Europe and North America have roughly the same level of adjusted personalism, on average, as democracies in Latin America. By this account, incumbent parties in the Middle East have the highest levels of personalism—largely driven by personalized parties in Lebanon and Turkey—but most of the other regions of the world have democracies with similar levels of party personalism. The larger point when examining the adjusted party scores is that personalism has a strong presence throughout the world and thus appears to be a truly global phenomenon.

2.4.3 Personalist Parties and Ideology

We assess how party personalism relates to party ideology for two reasons. First, it is useful to understand whether and to what extent incumbent party personalism overlaps with ideological measures of parties because it helps us better isolate the effects of party personalism in empirical analyses and more accurately interpret our results later in the book.

Second, understanding how party personalism relates to ideology has important theoretical implications. Numerous accounts of democratic stability point towards the ideological character of parties as a key causal factor that sustains democracy. For example, some argue that competitive conservative parties keep reactionary conservatives in check by restraining the redistributive impulses of left-wing parties that might spur authoritarian backlash among economic elites (Ziblatt, 2017), particularly if strong conservative parties sever the alliance between economic elites and the military (Middlebrook, 2000).

Indeed, one interpretation of the implications of redistributive models of dictatorship and democracy (e.g., Acemoglu and Robinson, 2006) is that if successful conservative parties can keep democracies from redistributing income and assets away from economic elites, these elites have less incentive to use the military to intervene to topple democracy in a coup. Understanding the extent to which party personalism reflects economic ideologies is therefore important for establishing evidence for our theoretical account of democratic erosion, which focuses on personalism in the ruling party rather than economic ideology or redistributive concerns.

We examine two measures of economic ideology from the Varieties of Party data set, the economic left-right ideology of ruling parties and whether incumbent parties espouse a welfare state ideology.[20] The left-right measure (v2pariglef) locates the ruling party in terms of its overall ideological stance on economic issues, while the welfare statist measure (v2pawelf) captures the extent to which the party promotes means-tested or universalistic welfare policies.

Figure 2.3 shows how these two ideological features of parties map onto our measure of party personalism. The horizontal axis displays the party personalism score while the vertical axis represents the ideology. Each plot also shows a blue horizontal line that marks the average ideological score for all ruling parties in the data. Both plots in Figure 2.3 show similar null results: there is no systematic mapping of economic ideology onto party personalism. Parties at both very high and very low ends of the party personalism distribution appear to be slightly more left-wing and welfare statist. However, most parties at the middle levels of party personalism sit at roughly the average level of economic ideology. We confirm this null result in additional empirical tests (not reported) that account for electoral rules, presidentialism, and the age of democracy, finding no statistical relationship between party personalism and economic ideology. In short, we find no evidence that incumbent party personalism is related to the ideological positioning of the ruling party, suggesting that empirical analysis using party personalism as a causal explanation for democratic decline is unlikely to be picking up the effect of partisan economic ideology.

---

[20] We use the Varieties of Party measure of ideology because it covers global samples of all ruling parties in our data set.

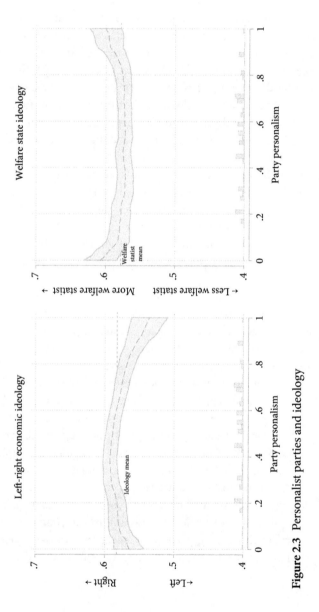

Figure 2.3 Personalist parties and ideology

2.4.4 Personalist Parties and Populism

Next, we return to a characteristic of parties that is potentially unrelated to economic ideological orientation but that nonetheless features prominently in recent accounts of democratic backsliding: populism. Populism is not only conceptually distinct from personalism as we discussed above, but the way researchers measure populism often conflates populism with the phenomenon we want to explain, namely democratic backsliding.

Earlier in this chapter, we used the example of Turkish President Recip Tayyip Erdoğan to illustrate how observers tend to increasingly view a leader as 'populist' *after* the government starts to undermine democracy. This issue arises, in part, because researchers typically assess populism using the observed rhetoric of party leaders or elites once in office. This rhetoric, in turn, may simply be the *post hoc* rhetorical justification leaders deploy when attempting to purge judges, circumvent term limits, or neuter opposition media. If this is the case, then populist rhetoric would be a by-product of democratic backsliding, not a cause. Our strategy for measuring party personalism elides this issue of conflating explanation and outcome by focusing on objective information about the leader and the support party from prior to the selection of the leader to the position of chief executive.

However, it is still instructive to examine the empirical overlap between party personalism and populism. We again turn to the Varieties of Party data because it is the only data set that covers a broad range of countries over the course of multiple decades.[21] The data are derived from surveys of country experts who specialize in the study of political parties, similar to the ones carried out for projects such as the Chapel Hill Expert Survey of European party positions. The *populism* measure from the Varieties of Party project, which is coded from each major party for each election, combines information from two variables: *How important is anti-elite rhetoric for this party?* and *Do leaders of this party glorify the ordinary people and*

---

[21] The other comprehensive global data on populism, from the Global Populisms project, defines populist parties as those with programmes, elite pronouncements, or academic citations that explicitly refer to the party 'making both the claim that the status quo elites are corrupt or malevolent, and that the people need representation as such' (Grzymala-Busse et al., 2020). However, this project does not specify whether coders record this information from before or after the party takes power and potentially moves to undermine democracy. Further, the project contains limited public documentation of the information collected to code populism or the coding decisions. Other party populism data sets—both those based on expert surveys, such as Chapel Hill Expert Survey (CHES) and the Global Party Survey (2019), or those based on elites' political speech such as Hawkins (2009)—have limited temporal and global coverage. One reason temporal coverage is limited in some of these data sets is that researchers did not start to record information about populism until the global wave of democratic backsliding had begun. For example, the CHES project started collecting information about party populism (anti-elite and corruption salience) for European parties in 2014, nearly a decade after the global trend in democratic collapses started to increase (see Chapter 4 for data documenting this). This suggests that the decision to systematically study populism in the first place may reflect observed democratic backsliding.

identify themselves as part of them? This operationalization captures key aspects of a seminal definition of *populism*: an 'ideology that divides society into two antagonistic camps, the "pure people" versus the "corrupt elite", and that privileges the general will of the people above all else' (Rooduijn and Pauwels, 2011; Mudde and Kaltwasser, 2012, 2017, 2018). Because this measure is taken for each major party in each election, it will capture changes in ruling parties' rhetorical strategies from one election to another.

First, we examine all leaders for all years in which they are in power during the sample period (1991–2020) to test whether this measure of party *populism* is correlated with our measure of party personalism.[22] We find a positive correlation: 0.28, which suggests that these two variables overlap to some extent even though this overlap is not substantial.

To further understand this relationship, it is important to clarify how the party populism data are generated. First, even though expert coders for the Variety of Parties data set are specifically instructed to code the level of populism for each party *prior* to each election, it is still possible that these experts' assessments of a party's *historical* character along this dimension is coloured by present features of the party. For example, experts were asked in 2019 to assess populism for Fidesz in Hungary for all elections since the early 1990s; and they may use information about the present level of Fidesz populism when doing so. This means that current manifestations of populism may influence assessments of historical populism. Moreover, once in power, leaders may strategically alter their behaviour to become more populist. For example, after an election, a leader might deploy anti-elite rhetoric to shape public opinion when facing legislative opposition. And if anti-elitist discourse helps leaders win elections, they may double down on anti-elitism once in office.

To examine whether the positive correlation for all years is potentially 'contaminated' by post-election information about how the leader behaves in office, we examine whether party personalism is related to the *initial* level of populism for each ruling party. We define the *initial* level of party populism as the first measure from the data for each party in the election year in which that party is first selected into office as the chief executive. For example, US President Donald Trump is selected chief executive in 2016 while Israeli Prime Minister Benjamin Netanyahu is selected (for a second stint in power) in 2009. In these cases, the level of populism rises once in office: the Republican Party's populism score rises from 0.69 (on a 0,1 scale) in 2016 to nearly 0.8 two years later; similarly, the Likud Party has a populism score of 0.35 in 2009 when Netanyahu was selected prime minister but this score more than doubles to 0.74 by 2018. These increases in party populism may reflect, in part, strategies to dismantle horizontal checks on their

---

[22] Correlation coefficients calculated from kernel regressions that allow for non-linear functional forms.

power. We therefore test the correlation between our measure of party personalism and the Varieties of Party populism measure for the years in which each new leader is selected as chief executive; for example, 2016 for Trump and 2009 for Netanyahu.

Last, we test the correlation between party personalism and populism while adjusting for the age of the democracy. As we discussed earlier, our measure of party personalism is best interpreted with this adjustment because new democracies born at the start of the sample period were likely to transition from autocracies, such as military *juntas* and single-party dictatorships, where opposition parties did not legally exist. Therefore, many new democracies in the 1990s also had new parties, which meant newly elected democratic leaders in these countries had no opportunity to partake in party politics before democratic transitions, artificially increasing the party personalism measure in new democracies.

Figure 2.4 reports results from these tests. The first correlation coefficient (ρ) shows the overlap between party personalism and populism for all years in the data (0.28). The next correlation coefficient examines only the first year in power for every leader; the correlation, while smaller, is still statistically significant (0.19). However, once we adjust for the age of democracy, the correlation coefficient is quite small (0.05) and not statistically significant. This suggests that once we account for the fact that new democracies are likely to have new parties and elected leaders in these countries do not have a prior opportunity to develop prior

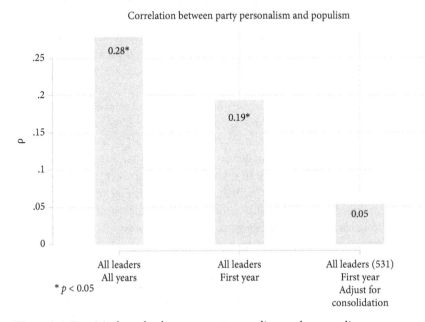

Figure 2.4 Empirical overlap between party populism and personalism

party activities, there remains little empirical overlap between populism and party personalism.

We will still consider carefully the extent to which party personalism and populist party rhetoric overlap in subsequent empirical analyses. We emphasize, however, that the leadership's use of populist rhetoric cannot in and of itself explain or cause democratic backsliding, though it may be a symptom of decline. Irrespective of the measurement issues that arise in capturing rhetoric systematically across time and space, rhetoric still requires human and organizational agents to act in concert to dismantle democracy. Words, by themselves, cannot do this. For this reason, our book focuses on the structure of power within parties to shape the behaviour of human agents who do the work of undermining democratic institutions.

2.4.5 Institutional Arrangements and Personalist Parties

We next look at institutional arrangements—specifically the type of executive in different political systems and electoral rules—and their relationship with personalist parties. Executive powers and electoral rules mostly vary across (and not within) countries, though occasionally some countries have altered their electoral rules or changed the executive powers of the leader. For example, after nearly a decade-long process, Georgians changed their constitution to move from a presidential to a mixed parliamentary system in 2018. The power of the government would no longer reside in the president's office; instead the prime minister would control the government. And Ecuador switched lower house electoral rules from proportional to majoritarian in 1998 and back again four years later. These types of major electoral system changes, however, are relatively rare.

Knowing whether certain executive powers or electoral rules aid the rise of ruling party personalism not only helps contextualize the observed phenomenon but also has important theoretical implications because a substantial literature on democratic survival points to presidential (indeed majoritarian) systems as unstable forms of government relative to their more parliamentary and proportional counterparts (e.g., Linz, 1990, Cheibub, 2007). Establishing whether presidential systems breed party personalism thus helps us understand not only where party personalism may be most likely to arise but also the pathway through which presidential systems breed instability.

Presidents and Prime Ministers. Presidential systems are democracies 'in which the executive is distinct from the legislative branch and considerable decision-making authority is granted to the executive' (Bell, 2016). As such, the president in these systems serves as the *de facto* chief executive rather than a figurehead. In contrast, in parliamentary systems the legislature is more powerful and the leader, or chief executive, is less autonomous from the ruling coalition in the legislature.[23] This delineation between presidential executives and parliamentary ones not only structures how party systems develop, with possible implications for the rise of incumbent party personalism, but also helps us identify the specific individuals we code as the 'leader' in each country when collecting the data for our party personalism measures—i.e., the pre-electoral history of the country's leader with the party that supports them in the election. In presidential systems we code the president as the 'leader', or chief executive, while in parliamentary systems we identify the prime minister as the leader.

Here we assess whether presidential systems are more likely to yield ruling parties with high levels of personalism. We do so by testing a regression model using only the first year of leaders' tenure in power because our measure of party personalism only varies between leaders. First, we test a specification without adjusting for the age of the democracy (reported in the left panel of Figure 2.B-1 in the Appendix to this chapter). The estimate shows that presidential systems, on average, have higher levels of party personalism than parliamentary systems. Next, we test a specification that adjusts for democracy age. The estimate for presidential systems is much smaller and not statistically different from zero. This suggests that once we account for the fact that party personalism tends to be higher in younger democracies, the level of party personalism is not systematically higher in presidential systems. And while there may be some evidence (from the first test) that presidential systems yield more personalist ruling parties, on average, than parliamentary ones, this factor is largely irrelevant when we look at variation over time within countries because presidential systems have so rarely changed to parliamentary ones (or vice versa) within the past three decades.

Electoral Rules. Next we examine electoral systems, focusing on the type of electoral rules used to select members of the lower house of the legislature (or simply the legislature in uni-cameral systems). Electoral rules structure both the number and size of parties as well as the extent to which democratic leaders depend on their own and other parties to pass legislation, select personnel, and execute laws. Electoral rules and the types of governments they tend to yield therefore have important consequences for the quality of democratic representation, redistributive politics, power-sharing, and even civil conflict (see, e.g., Lijphart, 1991, and Iverson and Soskice, 2006). Thus, electoral rules may not only shape whether personalist parties emerge and win power but may also help or harm democratic stability.

We group electoral systems into three broad categories: majoritarian, proportional, and mixed. We note that lower house electoral rules do *not* necessarily

---

[23] The data for this variable from Bell (2016) classify hybrid semi-presidential systems on a case-by-case basis, with most coded as parliamentary democracies. In our sample, fifty-six countries have presidential systems, forty-eight have parliamentary ones, and four countries (Armenia, Finland, Georgia, and Tunisia) switch systems during periods of democratic rule.

overlap with the distinction between presidential and parliamentary systems: while 26 per cent of presidential systems are also majoritarian so too are 21 per cent of parliamentary systems; 50 per cent of presidential systems are proportional, as are 58 per cent of parliamentary systems; and, finally, 23 per cent of presidential systems are mixed, as are just under 20 per cent of parliamentary systems. Again, we restrict analysis to the first year in power for each leader and test a series of regression models.

We report the results in the right panel of Figure 2.B-1 in the Appendix to this chapter. First, we test a bivariate specification and then adjust for the age of the democracy. Last, we adjust for an indicator for presidential executives (relative to parliamentary ones). None of the estimates for either *proportional* or *mixed* systems suggest that party personalism varies by lower house electoral rules.

Our final analysis of electoral rules and ruling party personalism focuses on a specific set of rules that provide incentives for politicians to campaign on personal attributes and develop personal reputations distinct from the party (Carey and Shugart, 1995). Electoral rules specifying that voters select parties rather than candidates on a ballot in conjunction with the power of parties to control nominations and the placement of candidate names on a ballot provide incentives for individual candidates to hew closely to the party label. In contrast, when parties have less control over the ballot and voters select individual candidates (and not parties), politicians have an incentive to invest in their personal reputations rather than in the party. Naturally, these types of rules could shape whether personalist parties—as we define them—emerge and win.

We therefore test a similar set of regression models as in Figure 2.B-1 but include an ordinal rank for the tiers of electoral rules with the greatest incentives for candidates to cultivate a personal (rather than party) vote.[24] We report the results of these tests in the online appendix, finding no statistical relationship between these electoral rules and our measure of party personalism.

To summarize, we find that incumbent parties in presidential or majoritarian systems are not systematically different in terms of personalism than their parliamentary or proportional counterparts. We find little evidence that electoral systems or rules breed higher or lower levels of personalism in incumbent parties, nor do electoral rules that cultivate a personal vote.

2.5 Why Do Personalist Parties Win Elections?

In the previous sections, we showed that, globally, ruling party personalism has been rising in democracies over the past three decades—and particularly since

---

[24] Data on electoral rules to cultivate a personal vote come from Johnson and Wallack (2012).

2010. We then demonstrated that many of the common structural factors that scholars have used to explain democratic survival and breakdown—such as presidential democracies being more fragile—are not strongly associated with party personalism.

However, there may be additional background factors that have shifted over time within countries that help explain the rise of personalist ruling parties in the past three decades. And these changing background conditions may also explain the origins of elected strongmen. For example, declining support for democracy as a political system might cause citizens to vote for new, personalist parties at the expense of traditional, established parties. Indeed, some argue that faltering mass public support for democracy explains the recent trend in democratic backsliding (Foa and Mounk, 2017; Claassen, 2020). If this is the case, then, personalist ruling parties might simply be a symptom of a deeper trend in public attitudes and thus not much help in explaining the origins of elected strongmen.

To assess this and other possible dynamic explanations for democratic demise that might also cause voters to support personalist parties, we examined whether trends in political polarization, public support for democracy, party system institutionalization, and economic growth are associated with ruling party personalism. The details of the tests are discussed in the Appendix to this chapter, along with the reported results.[25]

In addition to well-trodden explanations for democratic backsliding, we also look at campaign finance rules. In the next chapter, we demonstrate that personalist parties are likely to be financed by the personal wealth of their leaders or, if not the leaders themselves, a personal network of family and friends. By financing their own parties, we point out, leaders control key financial resources within the party, giving them more power over elites within it. Publicly financed campaigns, in contrast, allow parties to win power without the leaders of the party—and their personal networks—stumping up the cash to run a successful campaign. This common feature of personalist parties suggests that changing patterns in how parties—and their political campaigns—are financed may help explain why personalist parties win elections.

Dynamic explanations, such as rising polarization or declining support for democracy, require a test that isolates the trends in these factors over time within countries. When we conduct tests that compare time trends *within* countries, we find no evidence that rising polarization, declining public support for democracy, or collapsing party system institutionalization are correlated with ruling party

---

[25] Because the party personalism variable only changes for different leaders within countries, we limit these tests of selection into ruling party personalism to the first year of each leader's tenure in power and lag explanatory variables.

54 THE ORIGINS OF ELECTED STRONGMEN

personalism. Instead, we find a consistent pattern that personalist ruling parties are less likely to win power when political campaigns are publicly financed.

If neither well-known structural factors, such as presidentialism or economic development, nor dynamic shifts in public attitudes explain selection into ruling party personalism, this may leave readers wondering why we observe more leaders winning office backed by personalist parties in the first place. While it is beyond the scope of this book to provide a comprehensive explanation backed by both micro- and macro-evidence, we point readers to the existing (and abundant) literature discussed in Chapter 1 devoted to the broader trends that might explain rising political personalism more generally. This literature highlights two factors as particularly important—the changing media landscape and partisan dealignment—both of which we see as persuasive links to rising ruling party personalism. In fact, if changes in the media landscape, such as the rise of social media, that allow would-be strongmen to circumvent traditional ways of connecting with voters—through either print and television news or long-enduring party networks based on traditional social cleavages—then our initial finding linking ruling party personalism to changes in how successful campaigns are financed fits within the larger forces, including rising inequality that concentrates wealth and technological change, that might explain observed patterns of partisan dealignment.

2.6 Conclusion

We began this chapter by conceptualizing and measuring party personalism, which we define as: '*the extent to which parties are vehicles to advance leaders' personal political careers such that the leader has more control and power over the party than do other senior party elites in advancing policy and making personnel choices*'. In their most extreme form, personalist parties are those where the leader creates the party to support their candidacy in an executive election.

We then proposed a strategy for collecting data on party personalism that leverages the pre-electoral history of the leader and the supporting political party, allowing researchers to make inferences about how party personalism shapes outcomes for democracy in the post-election period, including analysis of leaders' behaviour once in office. This measurement strategy is important because it elides inference issues that arise when explanations for democratic backsliding are likely to result from the strategic behaviour of leaders once they are in power.

From there, we described the basic facts and features of personalist ruling parties, using our measure of party personalism. First, we demonstrated that party personalism has risen significantly in the last decade and is currently at its highest observed level in the period. Next, we demonstrated that party personalism is a global phenomenon that is not restricted to one or a handful of regions of the world. Importantly, we find that party personalism is more likely to arise in newer democracies than older ones, which is a function, in part, of the fact that parties in new democracies are often themselves quite young, leaving little room for leaders to have had a long history of political positions within the party prior to being selected that country's leader.

We then examined the ideological character of personalist parties. We found no strong association between ruling party personalism and either economic ideology or welfare statism. This suggests that party personalism is not related to long-standing ideological differences among parties that structured politics in much of post-World-War-II era, especially in developed democracies in Europe and North America, and in Latin America. Next, we showed that while party personalism correlates with party populism, this overlap is quite weak once we account for the age of democracy.

We also find little evidence to suggest that party personalism is simply an artefact of institutional arrangements. Indeed, the data patterns indicate that presidential systems do not necessarily have higher levels of incumbent party personalism than parliamentary ones, and formal electoral rules (even those that provide an incentive to cultivate a personalist vote) have no broad bearing on whether ruling party personalism emerges in democracies. At the same time, few countries have changed from presidential to parliamentary systems (or vice versa) or altered their electoral rules in meaningful ways in the past three decades. This means we can easily account for these institutional factors in empirical analysis by identifying patterns over time, holding constant differences between countries.

Last, we examined dynamic factors that might explain rising party personalism in democracies by looking at trends within countries over time. While countries that are new democracies and countries with relatively low levels of party system institutionalization are more likely to elect personalist ruling parties, shifts over time within countries in these factors are not associated with party personalism. Finally, we find little evidence that economic stagnation, declining public support for democracy, or rising political polarization are associated with ruling party personalism.

As we argue in the next chapter—and document in the sixth chapter—these dynamic factors are often endogenous to the strategic political choices personalist leaders make once in office. Indeed, incumbent moves to undermine democracy— the very things we observe as democratic backsliding—may cause citizens to become disheartened with democracy or polarize voters into opposing political camps. If this is the case, then common explanations of backsliding rooted in shifts in mass public attitudes and behaviour may, in fact, be symptoms rather than causes of declining democracy. With these insights in mind, we now turn to our central argument.

2.7 Appendix A: Measurement Model of Ruling Party Personalism

This Appendix provides details of the measurement used to construct the main explanatory variable in our analysis, ruling party personalism. Measurement models provide a principled way of aggregating multiple indicators of a similar concept, which may contain measurement error or temporal biases. We estimate a 2-parameter logistic (IRT-2PL) model, where i indexes each country, t indexes calendar years, and j indexes the eight items that we treat as observable indicators (with measurement error) of personalism.[26]

$$Pr(y_{j,i,t} = 1|personalism_{i,t}) = logit(\delta_j + \beta_j\theta_{i,t}) \tag{2.1}$$

In this equation, δ_j is the difficulty parameter; β_j is the discrimination parameter for item j; and the logit function is a logistic transformation of the data. The purpose of the equation is to estimate $\theta_{i, t}$, which is the degree of party personalism for each leader year. The difficulty parameter (δ_j) reflects the extent to which leaders, on average, are observed to have political experience that corresponds with one of the items, while the discrimination parameter (β_j) reflects the extent to which one item predicts another item. As detailed earlier in the chapter, we include eight binary observed indicators of party personalism: Create party; National appointment with electing party; National elected with electing party; Party leadership position with electing party; Local appointed with electing party; Local elected with electing party; Prior independent; and Party experience.[27] Each item is coded for information pertaining to the leader and the electing party.

Figure 2.A-1 plots the item information functions (IIF) for the eight items in the latent estimate of *party personalism*, or θ. The vertical axis measures the item discrimination parameter: higher values indicate more information in the latent estimate over a smaller range of θ values. The horizontal axis corresponds to the 'difficulty' parameter: larger values indicate items for which observations have a higher estimate of θ. If the model accurately estimates latent *party personalism*,

---

[26] To identify the model, we set Var(θ) to 1.

[27] The last item, Party experience, takes the value of 1 if the leader has served for more than ten years in a party (top two-thirds of the distribution for leaders who do not create their own party) that has been in existence for at least forty-five years (top half of the distribution for leaders who do not create their own party) prior to the leader being selected chief executive. These cutpoints in the observed distributions are, in one sense, arbitrary. But they are nonetheless chosen to provide information to distinguish leaders from each other (discrimination) at a point in the latent trait distribution (difficulty) where other indicators do *not* provide substantial information to distinguish leaders. This helps prevent lots of leaders from having the same personalism score at a medium-low part of the latent trait space. In other words, we do not want a measure of the concept of party experience that overlaps with the indicator of party creation (i.e., one that provides unique discrimination). And we want an indicator that helps discriminate cases at the low-medium end of the personalism scale (low-medium difficulty value).

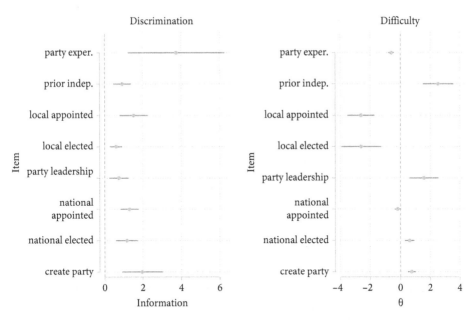

Figure 2.A-1 Item characteristic curves from the IRT model

more 'difficult' items are those for which an observation must be highly personalist to observe a 1 for this item. This parameter captures how well an item splits high and low *party personalism* cases at a particular point in the latent space.

The results indicate a mix of relatively high (locappt, natappt, and create) and relatively low (natparty, and priorindep) information items (vertical axis) as well as items that fall all along the latent space θ (horizontal axis). For example, leaders who previously held political office as independents register higher levels of party personalism (far right along the horizontal axis), while those who previously held appointed local positions with their electing party have relatively low levels of party personalism (far left along the horizontal axis). As shown in the plot, all estimated discrimination parameters are statistically significant at the 0.01 level with errors clustered by leader.

2.7.1 Internal Consistency and Reliability

To assess internal consistency and reliability we present two sets of tests. First we re-estimate the model as a linear combination of the items but drop one item at a time. This test examines whether the model is dependent on any one item when producing the latent estimate. All the leave-one-item-out estimates are correlated

Table 2.A-1 Split-sample reliability

Dimension	ρ*
Democracy age	0.98
Income	1.00
Party institutionalization	0.94
Population	0.99
Pre-/post-2005	1.00
Presidential/parliamentary system	0.97
Within/outside Africa	0.99
Within/outside Europe	0.98

* ρ rounded to nearest 0.01.

with the estimate from all seven items at 0.96 or greater and all leave-one-item-out estimates are correlated with each other at 0.94 or more. This suggests that the latent estimate is not highly dependent on any one particular item.

Second, we split the sample along various dimensions, re-estimate the IRT model for each half of the sample separately, and report how these split-sample estimates correlate with the full-sample estimate. This test assesses whether items capture a similar construct across diverse subgroups within the sample. We conduct this test along eight dimensions: presidential vs. parliamentary systems; high vs. low party system institutionalization; new vs. old democracies; high vs. low income countries; large vs. small population countries; two time periods (1991–2005 and 2006–20); within vs. outside Africa; and, finally, within and outside Europe. Table 2.A-1 reports the correlation coefficient from the split-sample estimates with the full-sample estimates. Each test yields a correlation coefficient (ρ) of 0.94 or higher, with some split-sample estimates nearly perfectly correlated with the full-sample estimate. These results indicate that the individual items intercorrelate in a similar way across very different geographic and temporal contexts. The conceptual construct, ruling party personalism, is measured similarly in new and old democracies, rich and poor ones, and in presidential and parliamentary ones.

2.7.2 Face Validity

One way to assess face validity is to examine the information captured in the items and the resulting latent estimates for each leader spell. The information used to code the data is contained in case narratives for each leader; the supplementary material for Frantz, Kendall-Taylor, Li, and Wright (2022) includes the leader narratives as a 550-page document with references. This original qualitative narrative contain information that is both objective and transparent; thus the best way for readers to assess face validity is to read the case narratives to examine the evidence.

A brief inspection of the data for Venezuela illustrates that the measure captures the underlying construct within the country. The estimated party personalism score for Carlos Andres Perez (0.16), who hailed from traditional parties is quite low, while scores for those who created their own parties to run for office, such as Rafael Caldera and Hugo Chavez (both 0.89), are relatively high. Further, Andres Perez held national elected (legislative seats) and national appointed positions (cabinet posts) with the party that backed his winning presidential bid in 1989 (AD, or Democratic Action), while neither Caldera (National Convergence in 1993) or Chavez (MVR in 1998) held similar posts with the parties that backed them for president, thus boosting their party personalism scores.

Expanding throughout the region, party stalwarts such as Michelle Bachelet (Chile) and Julio María Sanguinetti (Uruguay) have relatively low scores (0.21). Meanwhile, joining Chavez and Caldera with some of the highest party personalism scores in the region are Rafael Correa (Ecuador, 0.89), Alberto Fujimori (Peru, 0.89), and Nayib Bukele (El Salvador, 0.70). While this brief description only includes a handful of presidents from Latin America, we can make similar comparisons in other regions for all presidents and prime ministers.

2.7.3 External Validity

Next we illustrate convergent and divergent validity using external measures of similar and dissimilar concepts. Fortunately, the Varieties of Parties data contains a measure of a similar construct using country-expert coders: a variable, which we call V-Party personalism, defined as 'To what extent is this party a vehicle for the personal will and priorities of one individual leader?' Second, the Varieties of Democracy data contain a variable, which we call V-Legitimation, defined as 'To what extent is the chief executive portrayed as being endowed with extraordinary personal characteristics and/or leadership skills (e.g., as father or mother of the nation, exceptionally heroic, moral, pious, or wise, or any other extraordinary attribute valued by the society)?' While a distinct conceptual construct, this legitimation strategy should be correlated with ruling party personalism.

For divergent concepts, we turn to party system institutionalization and electoral democracy, again two indices from the Varieties of Democracy project. The former measures the extent to which political parties are institutionalized within the party system in a country. This variable is *not* measured at the party level but rather at the country level and thus pertains to the party system as a whole, not individual parties. Nonetheless, it should negatively correlate with party personalism because personalist ruling parties should be more common as party systems are less institutionalized. For example, parties created by leaders are unlikely to have the same linkage structures at the local level as less personalist parties.

Figure 4.1 shows how these four measures correlate with party personalism and the most concrete item associated with this concept, namely whether the leader

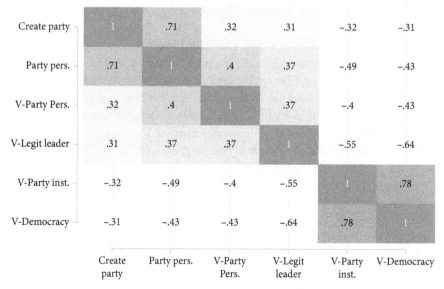

Figure 2.A-2 External validity tests

creates their own party (Create party). Party personalism and party creation are both positively correlated with V-Party personalism and V-Legitimation, demonstrating convergent validity. On the other hand, party personalism and creating a party are negatively correlated with party system institutionalization and the level of electoral democracy, demonstrating divergent validity (Figure 2.A-2).

2.8 Appendix B: Regression Results

The tests of government systems, electoral rules and ruling party personalism are reported in Figure 2.B-1. We restrict the sample to the first year in power for each of the 573 leader spells in 103 countries from 1991 to 2020. We estimate a linear model with standard errors clustered by country. The reference category in the left plot is parliamentary system; thus the estimate for *Presidential system* reflects the (conditional) difference in level of ruling party personalism between presidential and parliamentary systems. In the right plot, the reference category (shown in parantheses) is majoritiarian electoral rules. So the estimates for *Proportional* and *Mixed* reflect the (conditional) difference in level of ruling party personalism between these systems and majoritarian ones.

2.9 Appendix C: Selection into Ruling Party Personalism

To assess possible dynamic explanations for democratic demise that might also cause voters to support personalist parties, we examine whether political

WHAT ARE PERSONALIST PARTIES? 61

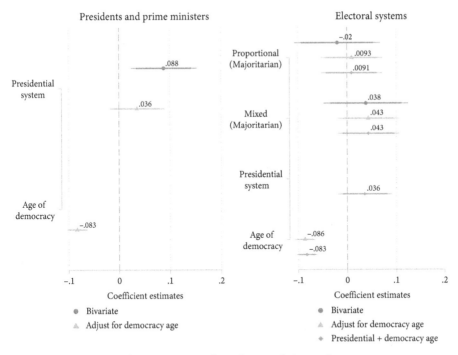

Figure 2.B-1 Personalist parties, presidentialism, and electoral systems

polarization, public support for democracy, party system institutionalization, and economic growth trends are associated with ruling party personalism.[28] We also examine whether political campaigns are publicly financed.

We test a country fixed effects model that compares time trends within countries; this test tells us whether changes over time within countries explain selection into ruling party personalism.[29] Because the party personalism variable only changes for different leaders within countries, we limit the test to the first year of each leader's tenure in power and lag all explanatory variables to assess selection into party personalism.

Figure 2.C-1 shows the results from tests that isolate variation in trends over time within countries. These models therefore test for potential dynamic explanations of rising personalism. The first specification excludes support for democracy because including this variable reduces the sample size substantially due to missing data. The second specification includes support for democracy, with a smaller sample (358).

---

[28] Polarization (v2cacamps) and party system institutionalization (v2xps_party) data are from the Varieties of Democracy data set. Public support for democracy is from Claassen (2020); and economic development data are from World Bank (2012). The public campaign finance data is the v2elpubfin variable from Coppedge (2021).

[29] We test a two-way (country, year) fixed effect linear model.

62   THE ORIGINS OF ELECTED STRONGMEN

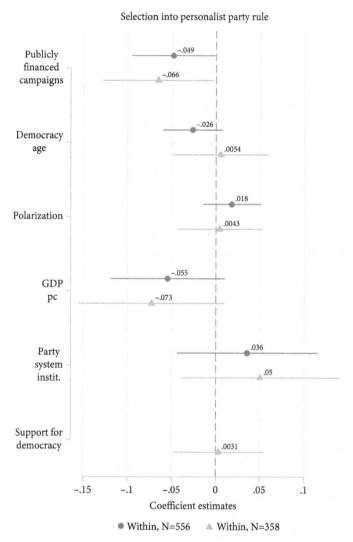

Figure 2.C-1 Selection into ruling party personalism

The results indicate that none of the variables are associated with selection into personalism—with the exception of publicly financed political campaigns. This suggests that trends in political polarization and citizens' support from democracy, for example, are unlikely to explain the observed rise in ruling party personalism.[30] Conversely, trends in how campaigns are financed may account for why personalist parties win elections to become the ruling party.

---

[30] See Frantz, Kendall-Taylor, Li, and Wright (2022) for similar results and further discussion.

3
The Argument

The instances where democratically elected leaders have gone on to dismantle democracy are well-documented. In cases across the globe—in countries that are geographically diverse and with dramatically different political, historical, and cultural contexts—this pattern of incumbent-led democratic decline has become common. Elected strongmen have emerged in countries as diverse as Peru under Alberto Fujimori, Hungary under Viktor Orban, and Venezuela under Hugo Chavez. In each of these cases elected strongmen undermined the democracies they governed. Sometimes, the extent of democratic erosion is less extreme. In Poland, and to a lesser degree in countries such as Slovenia and Czech Republic, democratically elected leaders presided over a process of incremental democratic decay, but stopped short of transitioning their countries to autocracy.

Despite the very different contexts in which this democratic decline is occurring, there is one factor these backsliding countries have in common: their elected leaders came to power with the backing of a personalist political party, in these cases one that they themselves had created. In some instances, these leaders pride themselves on being a political outsider before entering politics and creating the party that launches them to the top. In Peru, for example, Fujimori hosted a television show and served as a university rector prior to establishing Cambio 90 in 1989. Likewise, in Czech Republic, Prime Minister Andrej Babis made his fortune as head of chemicals company Agrofert before founding his party, Action by Dissatisfied Citizens (ANO), in 2011 and then becoming prime minister in 2017. Although his economic success meant that Babis was politically well connected, he was not a 'political insider' in the traditional sense.

But not all leaders that create their parties are new to politics. Many of them have more conventional political careers. Turkey's Erdoğan, for example, had long served in politics including as mayor of Istanbul before founding the Justice and Development Party (AKP). Together with his then-ally Abdullah Gül, Erdoğan created the AKP in 2001, the year before the party received the governing majority that paved the way for Erdoğan to become prime minister in 2003. Likewise, Senegal's Macky Sall was a long-time member of the Senegalese Democratic Party (PDS) and had previously served as prime minister, but left to create his own party, the Alliance for the Republic (APR), in 2008. Sall went on to win the election in 2012. Hungary's Viktor Orban too was a long-time politician and one of the founding members of the ruling party, Fidesz.

The Origins of Elected Strongmen. Erica Frantz, Andrea Kendall-Taylor, and Joseph Wright, Oxford University Press. © Erica Frantz, Andrea Kendall-Taylor, and Joseph Wright (2024). DOI: 10.1093/oso/9780198888079.003.0003

As we discussed in the last chapter, party creation is one of the strongest indicators of party personalism (and indeed all the parties referenced here rank high using our party personalism measure). This observed link between leaders winning office backed by parties they have created—and personalist parties more broadly—and subsequent democratic decline in the countries they govern raises an important question: is this relationship just anecdotal?

After all, there are cases where elected leaders entered power supported by a personalist party, and democracy did not erode. In France, for example, President Emmanuel Macron was launched into office in 2017 with the support of La République En Marche! (LREM), a party he created just the year before and one that was seen as a vehicle for his political career. And yet, the quality of democracy in France has not suffered. We show that the experience in France is an exception rather than the norm. Moreover, the case of France is quite instructive in that although Macron created LREM, the party is in many ways different from other personalist parties because it does not share the structural features that we identify in our explanation for why party personalism raises the risk of democratic backsliding.

As we elaborate in this chapter, personalist parties tend to be fundamentally different from other support parties in ways that are consequential for democracy. Importantly, personalist parties lack the *incentive* and *capacity* that non-personalist political parties have to constrain incumbent leaders and provide pushback on efforts to expand executive control. As a result, when leaders are elected to power backed by personalist parties, the chances that they will consolidate power grow, ultimately opening the door for democratic erosion.

After presenting our core argument, the rest of this chapter offers empirical evidence in support of it. Specifically, we offer a variety of tests consistent with our contention that party personalism lessens both incentive and capacity to challenge the leader. This chapter thus sets the stage for understanding the ways in which ruling party personalism harms democracy that we detail in the chapters to come.

3.1 The Argument

Our argument centres on the idea that personalist parties enable democratically elected leaders to undermine democracy. We emphasize the primacy of the incumbent's party for a variety of reasons. Parties organize elites and represent the most common and, often-times, last check on the leader's power. Standard theories of parties focus on how these organizations coordinate the behaviour and align the beliefs of citizens with those of elites (e.g., Aldrich, 1995). While we concur with this point, we note that parties are also key vehicles to coordinate elite actions; they help facilitate the collective action that is needed to push back on a leader's attempts to expand his or her power. Moreover, while other groups—such as opposition parties or civil society actors—can certainly play a role in challenging a leader, incumbent parties are particularly important: a leader's efforts to consolidate control have very little chance of success if key actors in the leader's party resist. For these reasons, we focus on features of the incumbent's support party as a first step to understanding the contemporary wave of democratic erosion from within.

3.1.1 Underlying Assumptions

Many political science theories assume from the outset that all leaders seek to maximize power (Bueno de Mesquita and Siverson, 1995). Democratically elected leaders are certainly ambitious and, by virtue of their candidacy, demonstrate that they want to win influence. But leaders almost certainly run for office in pursuit of more than just power: some want to shape policy while others may care more about the perks and privileges that come with political office.[1] Moreover, for those leaders intent on expanding influence, some may seek to do so within the confines of existing democratic norms and institutions, while history has shown that not all leaders' ambitions are so easily contained (Levitsky and Ziblatt, 2018). Some leaders will 'push back against democratic norms precisely because these norms tie their hands and limit their power' (Kingzette et al., 2021, 665). Yet, as observers, it is impossible to know which 'type' of leader we are dealing with *a priori*. To understand the true nature of leaders, we would need to identify—prior to observing their behaviour in power—the extent to which they are committed to democracy. The problem is, past experience is not always a good indicator of future performance.

In some instances, leaders do conform with expectations of their type. Consider, for example, United States Presidents Barak Obama and Donald Trump. We would have been right to assume that President Obama's background as a civil society organizer, constitutional lawyer, and respected academic presaged a deep and abiding normative commitment to democracy. In contrast, prior to coming to office President Trump had nearly ruined an inherited real estate empire despite receiving numerous bailouts from banks before becoming a semi-successful reality TV star who then kicked off his political career by proffering conspiracy theories. All of this perhaps indicated that Trump—when president—would have a weak commitment to democracy. Indeed, prior to his election, candidate Trump all but admitted that he would be a leader who would only like democracy if he won (Zengerle, 2016).

In contrast to the duo from the US, however, we can just as easily point to evidence of saintly leaders who turned sour once in office. Orban's political career

---

[1] Political scientists often call these perks *rents*, which are the personal and familial economic gains from corruption and market manipulation which the leader can obtain only by winning power. Some leaders may also seek to remain in power to retain legal immunity.

66 THE ORIGINS OF ELECTED STRONGMEN

in Hungary, for example, started with an impassioned pro-democracy speech in Budapest in 1989—a speech demanding free elections and the end of Soviet occupation (Lendvai, 2018). Orban also worked briefly for George Soros' Open Society Foundation and conducted research at Oxford University. During his student days in the 1980s he even made clandestine trips to visit leaders of the Solidarity movement in Poland. As a proponent of 'liberal economic, educational, and social policies', Orban would win election to parliament in 1990 as the head of the new, youthful party he helped establish, Fidesz (Lendvai, 2018). The early read on Orban's principled commitment to democracy would therefore have to be quite positive. However, nearly thirty years later, Orban would join the ranks of elected strongmen.

Turkey's Erdoğan offers another similar example. Back at the height of the US 'War on Terror', liberal pundits praised Erdoğan and his party, the AKP, as a shining example of how Islam and democracy could flourish together. *The Economist* (2004) hailed an Erdoğan trip to the White House in 2004, for example, remarking that '[a]lthough the Turkish prime minister and his Justice and Development Party have Islamist roots, they are proving in office to be of the liberal variety that believes in free markets and secular democracy'. And writing in a leading democracy journal after observing six years of AKP rule, one observer noted that '[t]he EU's October 2005 decision to commence accession negotiations with Turkey ... clearly constituted an approval of the AKP's performance according to metrics not of Islamization, but of democratization and Europeanization' (Dagi, 2008, 28). Even in 2011, after nearly a decade in power, the *Time Magazine* cover for its European edition declared that Erdoğan had 'built his (secular, democratic, Western-friendly) nation into a regional powerhouse' (Aydintasbas, 2015).

By 2013, however, the tide was turning. During the Turkish government's crackdown on the Gezi protests that year, the *Washington Post* (2013) declared that Erdoğan 'is offering unfortunate proof that it is possible to be both elected and authoritarian'. And by 2016, in the aftermath of the failed coup attempt to oust him from power, the covers of *Der Spiegel* and *Time Magazine* would both proclaim Turkey's elected prime minister a 'dictator', with *The Economist* following suit in 2017 and the French magazine *Le Point* in 2018.[2] After nearly two decades in power, Erdoğan too joined the ranks of elected strongmen. Again, the liberal reformer and shining star of democracy had turned sour.

As these examples illustrate, it is difficult to anticipate whether a leader will play by democracy's rules or break them. One might argue that aspiring politicians with anti-democratic inclinations will be more likely to create their own support party to begin with, a key indicator of party personalism. And yet, certainly not *all* leaders who create their own political party are intent on destroying

---

[2] *The Economist* (2017); *Le Point* (2018).

democracy. We simply cannot reliably assess a leader's 'type' without observing their behaviours once in office.

Further complicating matters, we cannot infer that the absence of a leadership power grab means that a leader *is* committed to democracy. Leaders who appear to be respecting democratic norms and institutions may only be doing so because they know they would be unlikely to succeed in undermining them. Put simply, leaders will be reluctant to pursue a grab for power if they assess that it would likely fail. (We return to this issue of a negative equilibrium outcome when we discuss term limit extensions in Chapter 5.)

For these reasons, rather than trying to identify a given leader's commitment to democracy *a priori*, we assume that some leaders will—for various context-specific reasons—seek to expand their power once they enter office. Our theory focuses on the conditions under which their efforts are likely to succeed.

We posit that party personalism is detrimental to democracy because leaders that enter office with the backing of these parties face less resistance to attempts to expand power than do those who assume office with the support of non-personalist parties. While all sorts of leaders may look for opportunities to consolidate control, the leaders of personalist parties are more likely to be successful in doing so. This paves the way for eventual actions that undermine democracy.

3.2 Executive Restraint in Incumbent Support Parties

We contend that political actors in personalist parties have less incentive and capacity to challenge a leader's attempt to expand executive power than do their counterparts in non-personalist support parties. There are a variety of reasons to expect this, which we will unpack in this section. We note that many of the pathways we identify below through which party personalism lessens resistance to a leader's efforts to expand executive power are overlapping and reinforcing. Not all of them will be relevant to all personalist parties, but their accumulation results in a situation permissive to executive overreach.

3.2.1 Incentive

The first element of our argument suggests that elites in personalist parties have less incentive to restrain their leaders relative to their counterparts in non-personalist parties. For one, the political fortunes of elites in personalist parties are more likely to be tied to those of the incumbent leader rather than to the party and its reputation. Elites in personalist parties—particularly those the leader creates—are often close associates of the leader and lack experience in politics,

68 THE ORIGINS OF ELECTED STRONGMEN

providing them with fewer prospects for maintaining a political career in the leader's absence. Of course, they are likely to have future career prospects outside of politics, but we assume that once in a position of political influence, elites would prefer to maintain it. This makes pushing back against the leader an unappealing proposition because it could cause the leader to exclude the non-compliant elites from the coalition. For many elites in personalist parties, the choice is keep silent or leave. Those who express dissent can be pushed out of the party, losing their ability to influence policies they care about. Either the elites become advocates for the leader or they lose clout.

Likewise, given that many personalist parties fizzle or dissolve following their leader's departure from politics, the elites that fill their ranks have strong incentive to keep the leader in executive office, making them more willing to tolerate (or even support) anti-democratic moves that enhance their prospects of maintaining control.

The lack of political experience of the party elites in personalist parties is in part the result of the fact that such leaders tend to fill their party ranks with family, friends, and other individuals who have direct and personal ties with them. Take El Salvador's President Nayib Bukele, whose ruling New Ideas (Nuevas Ideas) Party ranks relatively high on the party personalism scale. Bukele created New Ideas in 2017 as a vehicle to push his political career forward. The first president of the party was Federico Anliker, a childhood friend of Bukele's. Anliker was succeeded by Xavier Zablah Bukele, the president's cousin, who still maintains the position. Beyond the party leadership post, long-time friends and family members of Bukele fill a variety of other key posts within the party. These individuals lacked any direct political or government experience prior to their appointments (Labrador et al., 2019; Alvarado et al., 2020).[3]

Similarly, in Poland, Jarosław Kaczyński founded the Law and Justice Party (PiS) in 2001, along with his twin brother Lech Kaczyński, who died in a plane crash in 2010. Over time, Kaczyński filled the ranks of the party with loyalists— elites he had cultivated and who became tied to his success as leader. As Tworzecki (2019, 102) describes:

> Although for a few years after its founding in 2001—when it was still a moderate, mainstream party—PiS could accommodate within its ranks a number of moderate, mainstream politicians with national reputations of their own. Afterwards it became clear that Mr. Kaczyński insisted on treating the party as his personal property, the party was subjected to a process of negative selection, shedding its best and brightest and replacing them with more 'plebeian' cadres—people with

---

[3] Observers note that many New Ideas candidates running in the 2021 Salvadoran legislative elections were not 'new faces' but instead had held office as members of other parties. That said, we would expect defectors to personalist parties to be even less likely to publicly call out abuses of power by the leadership. See *Al Jazeera* (2021a).

THE ARGUMENT   69

little to lose and potentially much to gain from a fundamental transformation of the social, economic, and political orders in a manner that would discount meritocratic criteria in favour of political patronage and clientelism.

In Turkey, as well, the AKP's ranks were initially filled with political heavyweights such as Ali Babacan, Abdullah Gul, and Bulent Arinc, lending credence to the notion that the AKP was a representative party. Over time, however, Erdoğan shifted the makeup of the party's leaders, weeding out such experienced veterans. Particularly since the change from a parliamentary to a presidential system of government in 2018, the AKP's ranks grew filled with largely unknown political operators who were essentially Erdoğan sycophants (Alyanek and Kurt, 2021).

A similar picture emerges in Trump's Republican Party. As Robert Kagan describes:

> He [Trump] had to choose from an existing pool of Republican officials, who varied in their willingness to do his bidding. The GOP establishment hoped that the presence of 'adults' would restrain him, protecting their traditional agenda and, in their view, the country's interests, from his worst instincts. This was a miscalculation. Trump's grip on his supporters left no room for an alternative power center in the party. One by one, the 'adults' resigned or were run off. (Kagan, 2021)

The political careers of elites in typical personalist parties hinge on the leader's graces and, just as importantly, depend on the leader retaining power. This is consistent with research on dictatorships. Zakharov (2016), for example, shows in a theoretical model that elite subordinates who have poor outside options (i.e., low competence) will exert effort to keep the leader in power, even at the cost of receiving worse governance. In contrast, an elite subordinate not tied to the patron will exert less effort in prolonging the patron's tenure. This dynamic is exacerbated by the fact that personalist parties may not survive long after the leader's exit from politics. As such, supporting the leader (and not the party and its reputation) provides elites in personalist parties with their best option for a future in politics.

Elites in non-personalist parties, in comparison, have greater prospects of remaining politically relevant into the future, given that their parties have a reasonable chance of winning power again with a different candidate. They therefore have some incentive to uphold democratic norms and protect the reputation of the party so that it remains competitive in the future, advancing their own careers and influence in the process—whether the current leader remains in politics or not. Because elites in non-personalist parties have usually worked their way up the party ladder and secured their status within it, they can leverage this experience to create future political opportunities as long as the party, and not necessarily the leader, wins power later on down the road.

70 THE ORIGINS OF ELECTED STRONGMEN

Two examples highlight how non-personalist party elites are more likely to prioritize the reputation of the party over loyalty to the leader. In South Africa, for example, president and leader of the African National Congress (ANC), Cyril Ramaphosa, faced major corruption allegations in 2022. Some members of the ANC—a long-standing political party—called on Ramaphosa to resign given the harm his actions were inflicting on the party's reputation and future electoral prospects (*BBC News*, 2022).[4] Likewise, in the United Kingdom, the long-standing Conservative Party forced party leader Boris Johnson to resign in July 2022 after an ethics scandal around his leadership. Johnson sought to cling to power claiming that he had a 'colossal mandate' from voters. Members of his party, however, took a stand against his departure from accepted norms. More than fifty law-makers quit the government, with many invoking the reputation of the Conservative Party in their public statements. Health Secretary Sajid Javid captured the mood of many law-makers when he said Johnson's actions threatened to undermine the integrity of the Conservative Party (NPR, 2022). Both examples underscore how non-personalist party elites view the party and not the leader as the key to their continued political prospects, making them more likely than their personalist party counterparts to push back against a leader's abuses of power or deviations from democratic norms.

A second reason that personalist party elites have little incentive to hold the leader accountable stems from the fact that leaders backed by personalist parties tend to have substantial control over appointments and nominations. In many instances, leaders themselves directly control appointments and nominations, both to senior positions in the party and (once they are elected) to key positions in government. In non-personalist parties, in comparison, other actors (as well as rules) are influential in such decisions. As such, in personalist parties, securing favourable posts requires that party elites stay aligned with the leader. In the case of Hungary's Orban, for example, one observer noted to a journalist that the

> concentration of power in his [Orban's] hands is really incredible. He is the one who appoints members of the cabinet. He selects future MP candidates—so they depend on him. He selects members of the executive bodies of Fidesz. So he has no [limits] on him, either in the government or in his own party. (Buckley and Byrne, 2018)

Similarly, in the Czech Republic, Babis held significant control of party appointments, increasing his role relative to the rest of his ANO party over time. Based on the party's statutes, for example, regional coordinators supposedly had control over ANO lists for the 2013 elections. Yet, ultimately, it was Babis and his inner

---

[4] Although the party elite did not vote to remove Ramaphosa at the ANC Party conference in December 2022, the rhetoric used by ANC Party elites highlights the importance of the party and its reputation over that of the leader.

circle who selected the candidates for the top positions. In 2017, when Babis was re-elected party chair with 95 per cent of the votes, he further consolidated his control of candidate nominations, changing the party rules to give himself the 'right to intervene in selecting and ranking party candidates on candidates lists' (Guasti, 2020).

In sum, greater personalism in the party gives the leader substantial influence over key decisions, including those related to appointments and nominations. This is not lost on elites in personalist parties, who see staying in the leader's good favour as critical to their political careers.

3.2.2 Capacity

In addition to having less incentive to constrain the leader, members of personalist parties also have less capacity to do so. We contend that even if the elites within personalist parties prioritize normative values (or are otherwise motivated to restrain the leader), they may lack the capacity to rein the leader in. Work by Mainwaring and Perez-Linan (2014) emphasizes that elite normative attitudes about democracy are influential in determining whether democracy survives or falls. We concur, but argue that the impact of such attitudes is conditional on the capacity of elites to act. We posit that the relative weakness of personalist party organizations compared with non-personalist parties, the propensity for leaders to fund their parties, and the inexperience of the elites within their ranks account for the lack of capacity to constrain party leaders. We explain these dynamics in greater detail below.

First, personalist parties tend to be weak and superficial organizations, making it harder for party members to coordinate an effective challenge to the leader. Importantly, they often lack a local-level presence, limiting the chance that other actors outside the central party leadership will coordinate to constrain the leader. This matters because effectively pushing back against a power-hungry leader requires coordination. As Fjelde (2020, 142) writes, party breadth—such as active local-level networks—'facilitates information gathering ... upwards in the organization and [allows] for monitoring and information sharing from the top'. This sort of information transmission and coordination is critical to mobilizing support to challenge the leader. It suggests that a strong party infrastructure improves a party's capacity to serve as an internal counterweight to the leader.

An example from Burundi is telling. In the period leading up to the electoral crisis in 2015, then-President Pierre Nkurunziza launched his controversial bid for a third term, prompting a power struggle with the ruling party (the National Council for the Defense of Democracy—Forces for the Defense of Democracy, or CNDD-FDD). As Bouka (2015) documents, the weak and disorganized structure of the CNDD-FDD enabled Nkurunziza to push through with his effort to consolidate control, which eventually resulted in his tipping the country into dictatorship.

Conversely, an entrenched incumbent support party can help restrain a power-hungry leader. Experience from the US 2020 election illustrates this. There, then-President Trump sought to overturn the presidential election results in his favour, alleging fraud despite there being no evidence of foul play. Though many Republican Party elites at the national level did not push back against this power grab, particularly those with upcoming primary electoral campaigns, many local-level Republican officials spoke out, in key states such as Michigan and Georgia. Two state-level Republican leaders in Michigan asserted the victory of his competitor even after a personal visit from Trump; and key Republican electoral officials in Georgia directly contradicted Trump's false claims about election malfeasance and refused to adjust the vote tallies to give Trump the win. In this instance, the organizational depth of the Republican Party—particularly its strong local-level infrastructure—effectively constrained the leader.

The second factor explaining why personalist parties lack capacity is the fact that personalist leaders are more likely to fund their parties, either directly or through their personal networks. This diminishes the number of alternative centres of power within the party with the ability to influence the leader's choices, further hindering collective action potential. Leaders themselves or their personal networks of family and friends are often solely responsible for party funding. The leader's resource advantages not only dim prospects for collective action that might constrain their anti-democratic behaviour, but they also reduce the breadth of voices with the potential to have influence in the party.

Take the example of the Czech Republic where chemicals tycoon Babis created his party, the ANO. Babis declared early in the development of the ANO that he is 'the one who pays for it all' and that he would give it 'as much as will be necessary' (Bustikova and Guasti, 2019). Indeed, funding for the ANO came primarily from Babis and his companies through interest-free loans. In 2012 alone, Babis donated over one million euros to ANO. Babis' company, Agrofert, was involved as well. It not only provided financial resources and campaign funding to ANO but carried out the basic functioning of the party. Agrofert's financial director managed ANO's accounts; local firms within the Agrofert holding group lent ANO their offices for ANO regional branches; and company cars were emblazoned with the ANO campaign logo during the 2013 election campaign (Bustikova and Guasti, 2019). As such Babis was able to personalize the party. Hungary provides another example. As one observer notes, after Viktor Orban won the Fidesz Party presidency in 1993, he took 'control of party resources' and 'made his oldest school friend, Lajos Simicska, party treasurer' (Buckley and Byrne, 2018).

This contrasts with non-personalist parties, where party funding typically comes from a more diffuse set of backers, who often have different interests. This creates more space for competing ideas and power centres within the party. When party resources are controlled by a single individual or concentrated network linked to the leader, spheres of influence outside the leader's control shrink. Moreover, the resource advantages of the leader make collective action among those within the party more difficult.

Finally, elites in personalist parties are often inexperienced, as previously discussed. This means that they lack a history of repeatedly interacting with one another in the political arena. The opposite is true of their counterparts in other support parties, where working within the party and outside of it to negotiate and compromise is a normal occurrence. Their repeated interactions build trust among party members and facilitate coordination. The absence of this history in personalist parties, by contrast, creates challenges to collective action.

An example from French President Macron's first two cabinets illustrates how elites with prior political experience—both in government and in parties—can work together. Even though Macron created a new party (LREM) to launch his presidential bid and promised during his campaign a 'renewal' of politics, including a pledge to draw on the expertise of members of 'civil society' (Bucur, 2017, 343), the elites who served in his cabinet were largely selected from existing parties or, if they had never held a government post, they did have substantial experience advising government ministries in the past.[5] Bucur (2017, 350) notes that Macron's appointees were a 'mix of politicians appointed [who] had long elective careers at both national and local levels', and, if they lacked prior political affiliation, had 'senior civil service career paths' and 'considerable experience as advisers in ministerial cabinets'. In Macron's initial cabinet, only a handful of ministers (with less prominent portfolios) lacked prior political experience (Pommiers, 2017).

The politically experienced elites surrounding Macron not only included former members of traditional parties who had left established parties to join Macron's, but—once formed—Macron's government attracted support from traditional parties on the moderate left and right (Elgie, 2018, 24). Even though Macron's team worked together to push through his policy priorities, some of these elites were quick to leave the cabinet to protect their political reputations once Macron's approval rating started to slip. Just over a year into Macron's presidency, his first interior minister and most senior aide left the government to revive his mayoral career in Lyon, in the process distancing himself from Macron and his unpopularity (Deutsche Welle, 2018). This departure also suggests that the elites with substantial prior political experience had careers that were not tied closely to Macron or his tenure as president. In sum, even though LREM was a new party, the decision to fill its ranks with experienced political elites mitigated the risk that such personalist parties can pose for democracy.

---

[5] Prior to starting his own party, Macron had worked in the civil service and then private finance before he had joined President Francois Hollande's (Socialist Party) staff in 2012 and became deputy secretary-general at the Elysé, eventually becoming minister of economy, industry, and digital data in 2014 as part of a Socialist Party government.

74 THE ORIGINS OF ELECTED STRONGMEN

For these reasons, we argue that personalist parties have less capacity to restrain the leadership than do non-personalist parties. In the next section, we examine these expectations about party personalism using a variety of quantitative and qualitative evidence.

3.3 Empirical Patterns

Our argument about the detrimental effects of ruling party personalism on democracy rests on the idea that personalist parties are fundamentally different from their counterparts in other support parties in ways that increase the chance that we will see the deterioration of executive constraints and, ultimately, democratic decline. Specifically, ruling party personalism reduces the incentive and capacity of the party to push back against the leader.

In the sections above, we put forward a variety of overlapping and reinforcing reasons to expect this. First, elites in personalist parties have less incentive to challenge the leader because doing so would be dangerous for their political careers. Elites are more likely to lack political experience in personalist parties, meaning that they have few opportunities for a successful political career should the leader exit office. And further, leaders are more likely to control their access to key appointments and nominations in personalist parties. We also argue that it is more difficult for personalist parties to resist incumbent efforts to consolidate control than it is for non-personalist parties. Personalist parties tend to be organizationally weaker and more superficial compared to other support parties; they often lack a strong local-level network. The power structure is so centralized in the leadership that leaders in personalist parties are even more likely to directly control the party's financing.

With these insights in mind, we draw the following testable implications from our argument about personalist party elites' incentive and capacity:

1. Partisan elites should have less political experience as party personalism increases.
2. Leaders should have greater control over nominations as party personalism increases.
3. Local party strength should decline as party personalism increases.
4. Leaders should be more likely to fund the party as party personalism increases.

Finally, we test one implication of the argument for how leaders behave towards partisan elites when in power, examining the tenure of cabinet appointees. Cabinet appointees have considerable power to shape policy, select government personnel, and, in doing so, exert influence over citizens and elites alike. In presidential systems, cabinet positions are appointed by the executive and maintained only so long as members stay in the leader's good favour. In parliamentary systems—in the simplest terms—a majority of the parliament must agree to the cabinet's composition. Selection of cabinet members is therefore typically part of a bargaining process among representative parties. It reflects the outcome of a power-sharing agreement between parties and among coalitions within them (e.g., Riker, 1962; Laver and Schofield, 1998; Martinez-Gallardo, 2012). In both systems, however, cabinet appointees are ostensible political allies—the partisan elites with the most power over policy and personnel appointments.

Political leaders often seek out cabinet appointees who share their agenda for the country's political future. If appointees express too much resistance to the leader's proposed policies or if differences in opinions grow too wide, political leaders will try to replace such individuals with others who are more willing to fall in line. On the other hand, a high turnover of cabinet members is often undesirable from the perspective of a support party or governing coalition. If the leader's criticisms of appointees are deemed baseless, elites will often advise against replacing them. The hasty dismissal of a cabinet appointee may be politically damaging to the party or government, particularly if the individual has had a long history with the party or has a good reputation with the general public. Getting legislative approval of the appointee's replacement may also involve considerable political manoeuvring and rupture coalitions, and lead to long vacancies. Perhaps most importantly, turnover among cabinet members can disrupt the flow of policy; it limits the party's or coalition's ability to fulfil its agenda and is therefore politically risky.

Whether we see cabinet appointees frequently replaced will therefore depend on the extent to which executives face internal party constraints on their behaviour. In presidential systems or where the leader's party has the parliamentary majority, this constraint will come from within the ruling party. In parliamentary systems where the leader's party lacks a parliamentary majority, this constraint will come from within the governing coalition. In this latter scenario, where a cabinet appointee is dismissed for a baseless reason this would represent a breach of the bargain reached between coalition members and would suggest that the leader has a superior bargaining position.

In either instance, we should expect ruling party personalism to increase the frequency of replacements and decrease cabinet appointee tenures given the inability of these parties to constrain the behaviours of their leaders. That is, personalist parties enable leaders to frequently reshuffle their cabinet appointees, resulting in a shorter average appointee tenure. These expectations are consistent with research on dictatorships, which shows that replacement of the dictator's inner circle is more likely as power grows more concentrated in the leader (Geddes et al., 2018); and that cabinet reshuffling reflects the dictator's ability to alter elite power-sharing agreements (Kroeger, 2020). In short, we expect that cabinet member tenure should decrease as ruling party personalism increases, leading to a fifth testable implication of the argument:

76 THE ORIGINS OF ELECTED STRONGMEN

5. Appointed elites in the cabinet should have shorter tenures as party personalism increases.

3.3.1 The Political Experience of Elites

We begin by testing the first implication, where we examine whether more personalist parties have elites with less political experience. To do so, we turn to data from the Global Leadership Project (GLP) (Gerring et al., 2019). This project collects data on individual elites in national governments in the year 2013. The identity of elites and biographic information about them comes from country-expert surveys, which allows the definition of 'elite' to vary according to different country contexts. In most countries, the elites include legislative leaders, cabinet ministers, high-ranking executive staff, party leaders, court justices, and appointed leaders of powerful, but unelected, bodies, such as the central bank. For our analysis, we exclude rank-and-file legislators and focus on non-legislative elites and the legislative leader.[6] Because the definition of the 'elite' varies across countries, the number of officials considered 'elite' also differs by country.

The main advantage of the GLP data is that it includes information on *appointed* elites and, second, it is global, with elites from more than one or two regions of the world. For example, the sample we use includes elites from sixty-two democracies outside of Western Europe and North America; and the average number of elites per country is higher in most regions outside of Western Europe and North America. The main disadvantage of the GLP data is that it is cross-sectional so we must compare ruling parties in different countries rather than comparing more personalist to less personalist parties within the same country, a point we address below.

Crucially, the GLP data contains information on the political experience of these elites. This experience can include membership in a non-governmental organization (NGO), union, or interest group; local or municipal positions in government; being part of the party administration or youth branch; or having direct experience in politics as a prior member of parliament (MP) or minister. Additionally, almost 12 per cent of the elites in democracies (in 2013) had no prior political experience. We focus on two categories of political experience for elites: partisan experience (44 per cent of elites) and no experience (12 per cent of elites).[7]

In the test we report here, the analysis adjusts for the age of democracy, the level of democracy in the leader's first year in office, and the number of positions

---

[6] Many rank-and-file legislators (i.e., backbenchers) in the data set are members of opposition parties.

[7] The reference category in our analysis includes the following types of prior political experience: trade union; employers' organization; interest group; non- or inter-governmental organization; local government; and MP/minister.

considered as 'elite' in each country. We also account for differences in elite experience across different regions of the world. Adjusting for the age of the democracy and the level of initial democracy in the analysis is important because the data are for one year only (2013) and the test therefore leverages comparisons across countries. Thus there is only one leader per country in these tests.[8]

The left plot of Figure 3.1 shows how the likelihood of an elite having *party* experience varies with personalism.[9] For ruling parties with low personalism, partisans comprise over 50 per cent of elites, but this number drops to less than 30 per cent for highly personalist parties. That is, personalist parties have roughly 20 per cent fewer elites drawn from within the party than is the case with non-personalist parties.

We conducted a similar test, reported in the online appendix, for whether the elites had *no* political experience and find consistent results: more personalist ruling parties were 20 per cent more likely to have elites lacking political experience than less personalist ruling parties. These patterns support our contention that leaders backed by more personalist parties are less likely to select elites with prior party experience: elites in their parties are less likely to be drawn from the ranks of the party and more likely to have *no* prior political experience.

The right plot in Figure 3.1 makes a similar point using a slightly different way of measuring 'experience'. In this analysis, also drawn from the cross-country comparisons using the GLP data, 'experience' is simply measured in years, or length of time the member of the elite has spent in political office. The data thus reflect how long a member of the elite has held their current elite position. The figure shows how the average number of years of experience for a member of the elite— after adjusting for age of the democracy, initial democracy level, the number of elite positions, and geographic region—varies across levels of party personalism. It shows that the average number of years of experience for elites declines by over a year as ruling party personalism increases from its lowest to highest levels.

Our final tests using the GLP data examine elite experience along two dimensions of the ruling party: personalism and populism. This enables us to explore whether the finding that elites in highly personalist parties have less experience than their counterparts in less personalist parties is confounded by the empirical overlap between party personalism. After all, part of the ideology and strategy of populist leaders includes anti-elite rhetoric, which could translate into populist parties tapping candidates with less government experience. Indeed, one

---

[8] Additional tests reported in the online appendix adjust for other potential confounders, including: country wealth and population size; presidential system and electoral rules; the type of positions of the elite including how much power they each have; personal attributes such as age, gender, and education. These tests yield similar, statistically significant results.

[9] The figure shows rescaled partial probabilities drawn from a linear probability model with adjustments for age of democracy, initial democracy level, number of elite positions, and geographic region effects.

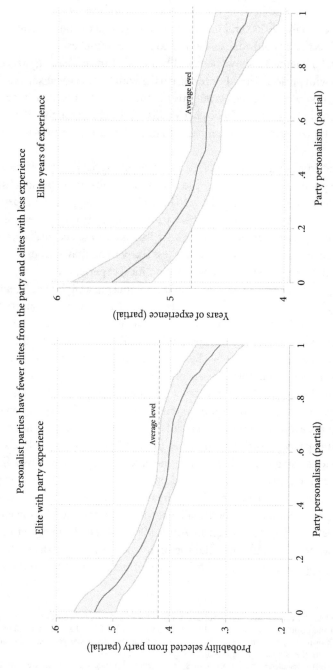

Figure 3.1 Elite political experience, Global Leadership Data

THE ARGUMENT   79

Table 3.1 Party personalism, party populism, and elite experience

	Marginal effect of party variable on:		
	Pr(Party experience)	Pr(No experience)	Years of experience
Personalism	−0.36*	0.20*	−1.26
	(0.16)	(0.09)	(0.67)
Populism	0.16	−0.06	1.07
	(0.15)	(0.07)	(0.57)

* Marginal effects estimates from specifications that adjust for democracy age, initial level of democracy, geographic region, and party populism or personalism. Estimates in first two column use logistic regression; third column uses a negative binomial count model and margins calculated as predicted count when changing variable of interest from 5 (low) to 95 (high) percentile of distribution.

interpretation of 'anti-elite' is simply running candidates from outside traditional governing networks.

We measure party *personalism* with our data described in the prior chapter; and we measure party *populism* using the Varieties of Party value for ruling party populist rhetoric in the year the leader was selected chief executive. This populism measure is the same as the one we used in the last chapter. Table 3.1 reports the marginal effects from this analysis. The first row shows that elites in personalist ruling parties are 36 per cent less likely to have prior party experience and 20 per cent more likely to have *no* political experience than elites in less personalist parties. Further, elites in parties with high personalism have roughly 1.25 years less experience than their counterparts in less personalist parties. The second row shows results for party populism which indicate the opposite or no pattern in these measures of elite experience. This analysis thus finds that party personalism—even after accounting for party populism—is associated with elites having less party and political experience. And we find some evidence that ruling parties with more populist rhetoric tend to have elites with *more* experience—precisely the opposite of what we find for ruling party personalism.

Partisan Candidate Surveys. Next we examine the expectation that elites in more personalist parties should have less political experience using data from the Comparative Candidate Survey (CCS). This data set contains surveys of partisan legislative candidates who hail mostly from Europe in the years between 2005 and 2013 (inclusive). The advantage of this data set is that it contains information from multiple parties in each country, including both opposition and incumbent parties. This allows us to compare more personalist parties to less personalist parties in the same country. The downside to this data set is that it is less global, containing data on partisan elites from only twenty-two countries—all in Europe save two, Australia and Canada.

The analysis of the CCS data differs from that of the GLP data in a number of important ways. First, the CCS data allows us to compare parties within countries using estimators that account for differences between countries, including different party systems, electoral rules, and levels of democratic consolidation. Second, the CCS data focus exclusively on partisan legislative candidates, not appointed elites in the government. Third, instead of relying on country experts, as in the GLP data, the CCS asks actual legislative candidates about their own political experience; we thus have data on elites generated by the elites themselves.

Finally, the CCS data query both ruling party and opposition party candidates. This means that we need a measure of party personalism for both ruling and opposition party candidates. The original data on party personalism we use throughout most of this book, however, only measures this concept in ruling parties. Therefore, for the CCS analysis, we turn to data on party personalism from the Varieties of Party project, which we call *V-Party personalism*.[10]

We examine two types of candidate experience: government experience and party experience. Government experience is simply the number of years since the candidate first started to serve in a government position, including local and regional government, irrespective of party affiliation.[11] Party experience, on the other hand, is the number of years since the candidate first served in any party position, including a local, regional, or national party office. Nearly 30 per cent of party elites held a local party office, while half held regional party positions, and 28 per cent held national party offices. Measures of government and party experience are therefore counts, so we estimate a count model that adjusts for the possibility that the data may be more dispersed in some countries than others.[12]

The left plot in Figure 3.2 shows results from a baseline model that models country-level differences in the dispersion of the count. The solid line in the left plot shows that elites, on average, have roughly seven years of government experience in parties with low levels of personalism, while elites in highly personalist parties have only four years of government experience—a more than 50 per cent decline in average government experience.

A second specification adjusts for additional potential confounders: candidate age, sex, and education level; the size of the party (measured as the party legislative seat share); whether the party was in government or the opposition; and institutional incentives to cultivate a personal vote. This latter factor accounts for electoral rules that vary by country and that shape candidate selection. The adjusted

---

[10] The Appendix to Chapter 2 shows that our measure of party personalism is highly correlated with the Varieties of Party measure. Frantz, Kendall-Taylor, Li, and Wright (2022) demonstrate that this strong, positive correlation persists across and within countries.

[11] Types of prior government experience include: mayor, in local government, regional government, local parliament, regional parliament, and national parliament.

[12] We estimate a negative binomial model, with a random dispersion parameter for each country. We check the finding by estimating negative binomial models with fixed dispersion parameters and, separately, count models with fixed country slopes—both with similar, significant results.

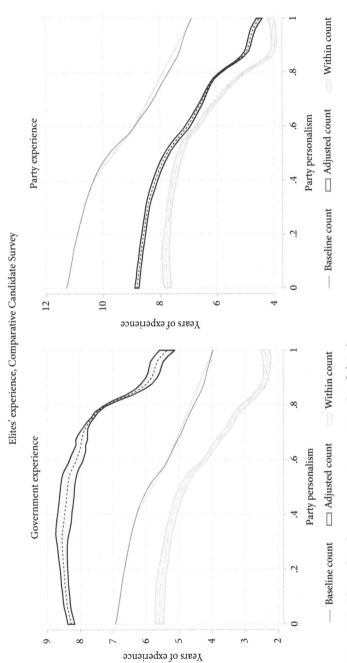

Figure 3.2 Elite political experience, Comparative Candidate Survey

count is shown in the short dashed line: elites in parties with low to medium levels of party personalism have over eight years of government experience while those in highly personalist parties have less than six years' experience—a nearly 30 per cent decline.

The third result shown in the left plot in Figure 3.2 is from a within estimator that not only adjusts for potential confounders but also models a separate country slope, thus accounting for all differences between countries such as party system institutionalization and democratic consolidation. This result, shown in the long dashed line, indicates that candidates from parties with low personalism have just under six years of experience but those in highly personalist parties have just over two years of experience.

Turning to the right plot in Figure 3.2, which shows the results for elites' party experience, we find similar patterns. In the baseline model, elites in low personalism parties have over nine years of party experience whereas elites in more personalist parties have only seven years of party experience. The other two estimates indicate even steeper relative declines in party experience. In short, evidence from the CCS indicates that elites from highly personalist parties have much less political experience than elites from parties with lower levels of personalism.

We again explore whether this finding is confounded by the overlap with party populism. Figure 3.3 shows the average years of government and party experience for candidates from high and low personalism parties; and then it compares this pattern to the average experience level of candidates from parties with high and low populism scores.[13] The left plot looks at government experience: candidates from highly personalist parties have, on average, two fewer years of government experience than candidates from low personalism parties. Dividing parties by their populism scores, however, shows that candidates from both low and high populism parties have roughly the same number of years of government experience. The right plot shows a similar pattern for candidates' party experience: personalist parties have candidates with less experience but populist parties do not. The raw data thus indicate that gaps in political experience result not from populism but rather from party personalism.

We then examine whether these patterns hold up in statistical tests by adjusting for the Varieties of Party measure of party populism in the models similar to those reported in Figure 3.2. The results that account for party populism are reported in the online appendix: we find that candidates from parties with high personalism have less government experience than those from parties with low personalism, consistent with the pattern in Figure 3.3. The same appears to be true of members of more populist parties, though the estimate is slightly smaller than the one for party personalism. The model of party experience, however, indicates that while candidates from more personalist parties have substantially less party experience

---

[13] Data on party personalism and party populism is from the Varieties of Party data set. High and low values demarcated by the in-sample median value.

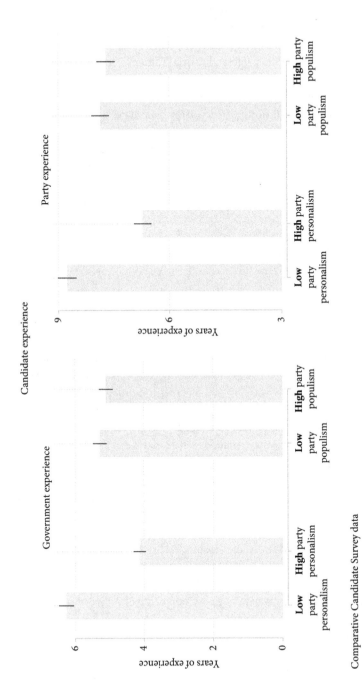

Comparative Candidate Survey data

Figure 3.3 Elite political experience by party type

than those from less personalist parties (again, consistent with the raw data pattern in Figure 3.3), the same is *not* true of more populist party candidates. Thus personalist parties tend to have candidates with both less government and less party experience, while candidates from populist parties tend to only have less government experience. This suggests that one difference between personalist and populist parties—at least in countries represented in the CCS—may be that elites in personalist parties lack experience of working together within the party itself, whereas both populist and non-populist party candidates appear to have ample experience as party members.

In short, all the tests of our first implication are consistent with the expectation that the political experience of elites decreases with party personalism. When elites have more political experience, their political careers are less likely to be tied closely to the political fate of the chief executive, thus providing them with a weaker incentive to condone anti-democratic behaviour on the part of the leader. Further, elites with substantial experience, particularly within the party, should have had more repeated interaction with other partisan elites, which constitutes a form of capacity that enables partisan elites to check the behaviour of their leader.

3.3.2 Party Nominations

We now turn to tests of party nominations to assess whether leaders are more likely to control nominations as party personalism increases. We test this implication in two ways. First we use a variable that assesses the process by which the party decides on candidates for the national legislative elections, employing a variable from the Varieties of Party data set (v2panom). This variable captures whether the party's nomination decisions are made by: national party leadership, local delegates, all party members, all voters, or a unilateral decision by the leader. We focus on this latter category, which we denote as *leader control over nominations*. We expect that in more personalist parties the leader should be more likely to control nominations than in less personalist parties.

The Varieties of Party data on party nominations is global; we therefore examine ruling parties in all democracies from 1991 to 2020. The unit of analysis is ruling party election year because the nominations data are coded for ruling parties for each election year (including legislative elections in presidential systems). To measure party personalism we employ our original measure of ruling party personalism introduced in Chapter 2.

The left panel of Figure 3.4 shows the pattern in the raw data using a local polynomial regression line, which can capture a possibly non-linear relationship between ruling party personalism and leader nomination power. The horizontal axis depicts party personalism while the vertical axis depicts the probability of leader nomination power. The dashed horizontal line at 0.08 shows that, on

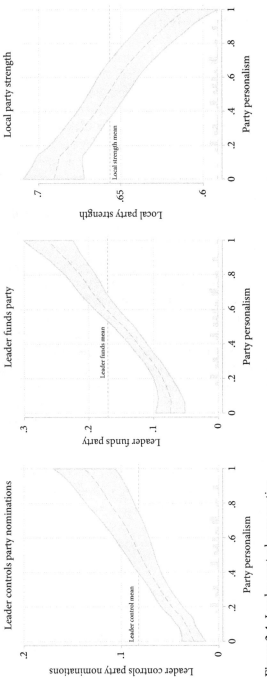

Figure 3.4 Leader control over parties

86 THE ORIGINS OF ELECTED STRONGMEN

average, democratic leaders control party nominations in about 8 per cent of cases. At low levels of ruling party personalism, however, only about 3 per cent of leaders control nominations; at high levels of personalism, in contrast, over 10 per cent of leaders control nominations.

We estimate a generalized linear model that adjusts for geographic region, five-year time period intervals, presidential (parliamentary) system, electoral rules, initial level of democracy when the leader first enters office, and democracy age. Importantly, initial level of democracy and democracy age adjust for different levels of democratic consolidation that might shape selection into more personalist ruling parties. This statistical adjustment yields a significant, positive association between party personalism and leader control of nominations, with an estimate suggesting that party personalism increases the chances of leader control over nominations by roughly 20 per cent.[14]

Next, we turn to candidate survey data from the CCS. Recall that this data set has information from surveys of candidates of all parties, but only for countries in Europe. The advantage of these data is that they allow us to compare personalist parties to other parties in the same country, including both ruling and opposition parties. We estimate a hierarchical probit model that adjusts for candidate age, sex, education level, party size, a time trend, and electoral rules that incentivize a personal vote. The estimate suggests that leaders of personalist parties are 25 per cent more likely to control party nominations than leaders of non-personalist parties. When we adjust for the level of party populism, using the populist rhetoric variable from the Variety of Party data set, the estimate is even stronger, indicating a 30 per cent increase in the likelihood of the leader controlling party nominations.

Thus using different types of data—both country-expert surveys of global parties from the Varieties of Party data set and partisan candidate surveys from Europe—we find that leaders are substantially more likely to control party nominations in highly personalist parties than in less personalist parties. Leader control over party nominations, we posit, indicates more power for the leader than other party elites. Whether we interpret party control over nominations as capacity or incentive, the implication remains the same: when leaders control nominations it should be more difficult for party elites to stand up to them when they usurp power and begin dismantling democracy from within.

3.3.3 Local Party Strength and Party Funding

We next turn to tests of local party strength and party funding, which we discuss jointly. We expect that parties with higher levels of personalism should have

---

[14] This result is reported in the online appendix. When adjusting for party populist rhetoric, we still find a positive estimate of 17 per cent.

weaker local party structures and should be more likely to be funded by the leader. Both features of parties indicate more relative power for the leader. To measure our key variables of interest here, we use data from the Varieties of Party data set, which aggregate country experts' ratings of various features of individual political parties.

To measure local party strength, we use the linear combination of two variables: the degree to which party activists and personnel are permanently active in local communities (v2paactcom) and whether the party maintains permanent offices that operate outside of election campaigns at the local or municipal level (v2palocoff). Higher values on this variable indicate *more* local party strength. We expect to observe that party personalism is associated with lower levels of local party strength.

To measure party funding, we use a variable for party funding sources (v2pafunds). For each election, expert coders record the major sources of party funds from among eight distinct categories: formal state subsidies; informal use of state funds by the ruling party; large-scale donations from individuals, companies, or civil society organizations (including trade unions); small-scale supporters' donations; candidates themselves; or the leader. We pinpoint this last category, the leader, which we denote as *leader control over party funds*. Our expectation is that parties are more likely to be funded primarily by the leader as party personalism increases.

The middle and right plots in Figure 3.4 show the relationship between party personalism and these two features of ruling parties. The horizontal axis in each plot shows the *party personalism* index while the vertical axis displays levels of the outcomes of interest (local party strength and leader control over party funds). The horizontal line in each plot shows the average level of the outcome variable, allowing visual comparison of how the outcome changes relative to the average as party personalism changes. The middle plots show that as party personalism increases so too does the extent to which the leader controls party resources, while the right plot shows that party personalism is associated with *less* local party strength. We corroborate these patterns using a generalized linear model that adjusts for geographic region, five-year time period intervals, a presidential (parliamentary) system, electoral rules, initial level of democracy when the leader first enters office, and democracy age, finding that party personalism increases the likelihood of leader party funding by 12 per cent but is associated with 25 per cent weaker local party structures. Further, we find no evidence that populist parties are more likely to be funded by their leader or to have weaker local party structures.

Next we compare ruling parties within countries rather than looking at patterns that might simply reflect differences between countries with distinct electorates and historical party development. We thus ask the question of whether more personalized ruling parties are different from less personalized ruling parties *in the same country*. This enables us to compare, for example, Rafael Caldera and Hugo

Chavez, two Venezuelan leaders with higher party personalism scores, with Carlos Andres Perez and Ramon Jose Velazquez, two leaders from the same country with lower party personalism scores. We pool these types of comparisons across all countries to estimate how party personalism bears on the features of parties we are interested in.[15] The plot in Figure 3.A-1 of the Appendix to this chapter reports the estimates for *party personalism* from this analysis. Consistent with the broad patterns shown in the prior figure, results from the 'within'-country comparisons indicate that personalist ruling parties are more likely to see the leader fund the party and control candidate selection and have local party groups that are quite weak.

3.3.4 The Duration of Cabinet Appointee Tenures

Finally, we look at the duration of cabinet appointee tenures, which provides insight into how elected leaders control allied elites who have the most policy and personnel control. We expect ruling party personalism to increase the frequency of replacements and decrease cabinet appointee tenure given the inability of these parties to constrain the behaviours of their leaders. That is, personalist parties should enable leaders to frequently reshuffle their cabinet appointees, resulting in shorter average appointee tenures.

We examine this proposition using global data on individual cabinet members from the WhoGov project (Nyrup and Bramwell, 2020). These data leverage biographical information about individual cabinet appointees on an annual basis for most countries in the world from the 1960s up to 2016.[16] We employ the data for our sample of democracies from 1991 onward. The data include a measure of the *tenure* (in years) of each cabinet member, which reflects the number of continuous years the cabinet member has been in the cabinet up to the observation year. The average tenure for each chief executive year is the mean value for all cabinet members in a given year for a particular leader.

First, we look at whether leaders who create their own party have cabinets with shorter tenures. Recall that a ruling party created by the leader is, according to our approach, one of the strongest indicators of party personalism. We adopt three ways of delineating the concept of elites in the cabinet, all derived from the WhoGov data. The first category of elites includes both ministerial appointments and additional appointed elites in positions of power in the government, even if their remit is not technically a ministry. This group of elites would include—in

---

[15] We report results from a country fixed effects linear estimator that adjusts for initial level of democracy, democracy age, and time period.

[16] WhoGov data is collected for July of every year, representing the configuration of the cabinet in that month for each country year.

addition to cabinet members—prime ministers, presidents, vice presidents, and vice prime ministers. Following the WhoGov designation, we call this group of ministers and elites the *core*. The second group comprises all *cabinet ministers* but excludes deputy and junior ministers. And a third group includes *all appointees*, including core and cabinet members as well as other appointees. These other appointees vary by country and may include, for example, the ambassador to the US, the permanent representative to the United Nations (UN), or the central bank chief.

Figure 3.5 shows the average tenure of elites for each of these three groups, based on whether the leader created the ruling party. The vertical axis delineates the average tenure of elites, measured in years. And the horizontal axis groups the observations into two categories: democratic years in which the country has a leader who created their own party and those with a leader who is selected by a pre-existing party. For example, in the left plot for core appointees, the average tenure is about 3.86 years for cabinet members when the leader is chosen by an existing party; it drops to 3.08 years, however, when the leader creates their own party. Substantively, if leaders create their own party, it amounts to a 20 per cent decrease in average cabinet member tenure. The same pattern, shown in the middle and right plots, holds for ministerial appointments and all appointees.

Next, we conduct a series of econometric tests for the average tenure of the core elite. These tests, reported in the Appendix to this chapter (Figure 3.A-2), adjust for the age of the democracy, which correlates with party personalism, a time trend, and the length of the leader's tenure as chief executive. This latter variable acts as a proxy for how well the leader has consolidated power during their tenure, as longer lasting leaders may have less accountability and thus more power. As Lewis (1972) notes with respect to cabinet member turnover in non-democracies, long-established leaders 'seem to experience slow rates of turnover, although they may go through an early period of high turnover as the "agitators" or "professional politicians" are edged out. When replacements are made, the tendency is to seek older men of long proven loyalty, rather than to recruit from younger generations' (87).

Other specifications also adjust for the number of parties in the cabinet and the number of positions defined as being in the 'core' elite, akin to the number of cabinet positions.[17] We also account for the electoral cycle because the frequency of elections differs across countries; and leaders are more likely to reshuffle cabinets just after an election. For example, average cabinet tenure drops substantially in the year after an election, presumably because the leader often selects new appointees at this time. And finally, we test specifications that account for

---

[17] Tests reported in the online appendix report similar results for all appointees, not just core appointees, as well as just cabinet members.

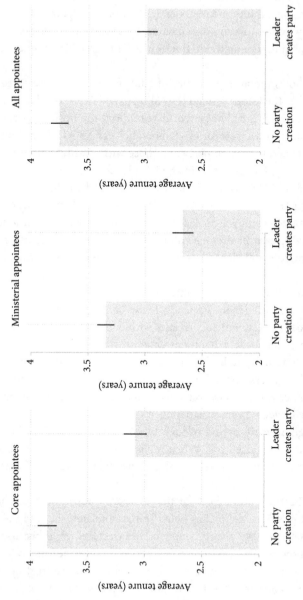

Figure 3.5 Leaders who create their own parties appoint elites with shorter tenures

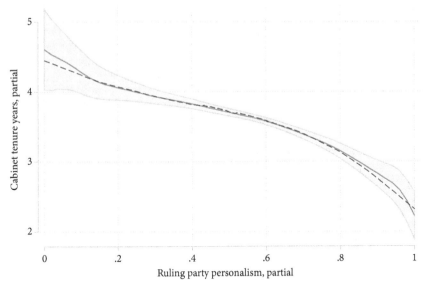

Figure 3.6 Personalist parties keep cabinet members on a short leash

country fixed effects. These latter tests account for all differences between countries, including electoral system and party system distinctions. In all of these tests, we find that party personalism shortens average cabinet tenures.

Figure 3.6 shows the partial regression result for average tenure, which offers the relationship between party personalism and the outcome of interest after adjusting for covariates.[18] At low levels of ruling party personalism, average cabinet tenure is over four years, while at high levels of party personalism it drops to just over two years—a nearly 50 per cent decrease in average tenure. This indicates that ruling party personalism is associated with substantially shorter cabinet tenures for these elites.

As we noted earlier, in presidential systems or where the leader's party has the parliamentary majority, constraints from cabinet elites will come from within the ruling party. In contrast, in parliamentary systems where the ruling party is a minority party forced to govern with coalition partners, cabinet tenures will reflect bargaining between parties and not just the power of the leader relative to other elites within the ruling party. The empirical implication of this logic suggests that we should find stronger evidence that ruling party personalism decreases cabinet tenure in presidential systems and parliamentary systems with a ruling party majority.

---

[18] Covariates include: time effects; age of democracy (log); leader tenure effects; the election cycle; the number of parties represented in the core elite; and the number of elite positions.

92   THE ORIGINS OF ELECTED STRONGMEN

When we split the sample into two groups, the first comprised of all presidential executives plus parliamentary leaders with ruling majorities, and the second comprised of minority parliamentary leaders, we find that party personalism only reduces average cabinet tenures in the former, as expected. And when we look at all parliamentary cases—majority and minority ruling parties—we find that ruling party personalism only decreases cabinet tenures when the ruling party seat share passes a threshold of roughly 40 per cent of seats.

In short, the evidence indicates that leaders backed by more personalist parties have cabinet appointees with shorter tenures than their counterparts backed by less personalist parties. This evidence is consistent with Meyer-Sahling and Toth's (2020) study of elite turnover in Hungary, which shows that state administration retention rates dropped significantly with the second Orban government, starting in 2010. Leaders face fewer constraints on their behaviour from elites as party personalism grows.

To summarize, we find evidence consistent with the contention that ruling party personalism weakens the incentive and capacity of the party to push back against consolidation of power on the part of the leaders. The pathways we identify linking party personalism with party features such as leadership control of funding and nominations, elite inexperience, and shallow local branches are not independent (or necessary conditions in and of themselves), but rather they work with one another in reinforcing ways. We suggest that elites in personalist parties have less reason to voice concern with the leader's agenda because their career prospects require that they stay in the leader's good favour. This is reflected in the fact that as party personalism increases, elites have less political experience (limiting their political career opportunities should they fall out with the leader) and leaders have greater control over party nominations. Moreover, we find evidence supportive of our argument that personalist parties have less capacity to constrain incumbent actions. The data show that as party personalism increases, the party's local presence is likely to be weaker, and leaders are more likely to personally be the party's source of funding.[19] Finally, to provide evidence that personalist leaders control elites and thus effectively discourage them from challenging the leader's agenda, we demonstrate that cabinet appointee tenures are significantly shorter when the leader's support party is personalist. These factors limit the party's ability to coordinate and mount an effective challenge against the leader. The evidence provided here illustrates that personalist parties differ from other support parties in important ways that have serious consequences for constraints on the leadership.

---

[19] Further, we find little evidence that party populism is associated with these features of parties.

3.4 Conclusion

This chapter laid out the theoretical foundation for understanding the role of parties in the story of contemporary democratic backsliding. In it, we argued that personalist parties are harmful for democracy, such that when leaders are elected to power supported by such parties, the chance that executive constraints will weaken escalates, ultimately paving the way for democratic erosion. Party personalism, we argue, is the origin of elected strongmen. We put forward two reasons for this relationship. First, elites in personalist parties have less *incentive* to push back against the leader's attacks on democracy. Because they are often close friends or family members of the leader who lack substantial political experience, they see their futures as tied to that of the leader, making resisting the leader a risky career move. This is amplified by the fact that the leader is more likely to control whether they receive choice nominations and appointments.

Second, personalist parties have less *capacity* to push back against a power-hungry leader. They are organizationally weaker than other support parties, complicating their ability to effectively coordinate a challenge to the leader. Because the leader is more likely to personally fund them, there are fewer voices with influence who could speak out against the leader's actions.

We provide a variety of evidence consistent with these claims. We show that personalist parties are fundamentally different from other support parties, in line with the implications of our argument. With greater party personalism, elites are less likely to have political experience, leaders are more likely to control nominations, the party's local presence is more likely to be limited, and the party's funding is more likely to come from the leader. Moreover, we offer evidence that cabinet appointee tenures are more likely to be shorter with ruling party personalism. This is because personalist leaders have greater control over elites and can effectively sideline and rotate them to ensure compliance with their agendas. These features of personalist parties make members less motivated and capable of resisting consolidation of power in the executive, paving the way for democratic deterioration from within.

In the chapter that follows, we provide evidence directly linking ruling party personalism with democratic backsliding to demonstrate that personalist parties explain the rise of elected strongmen. After demonstrating a global pattern linking ruling party personalism to declines in democracy and democratic collapse, we show how ruling party personalism weakens horizontal, institutional constraints on the leader in Chapter 5. We then turn to the social pathways through which ruling party personalism weakens democracy—by increasing social polarization and altering citizens' norms about acceptable democratic behaviour—in Chapter 6.

3.5 Appendix A: Regression Results

Figure 3.A-1 reports the estimates for *party personalism* from Ordinary Least Squares (OLS) fixed effects regressions of three outcomes discussed in the main text: candidate nominations, local party strength, and party funding. The global sample from 1991 to 2020 covers all election years. The horizontal axis lists each of these three internal party features. The vertical axis displays the estimated marginal effect of *party personalism* on the respective outcome.

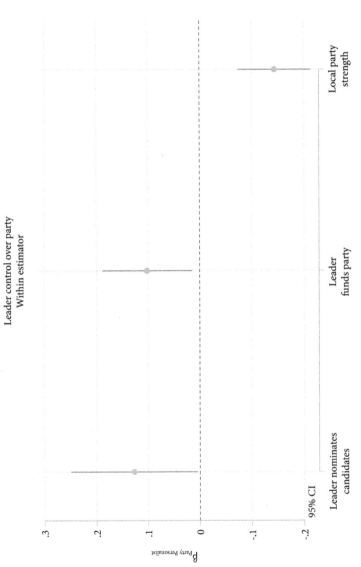

Figure 3.A-1 Within-country comparisons of leaders' control over parties

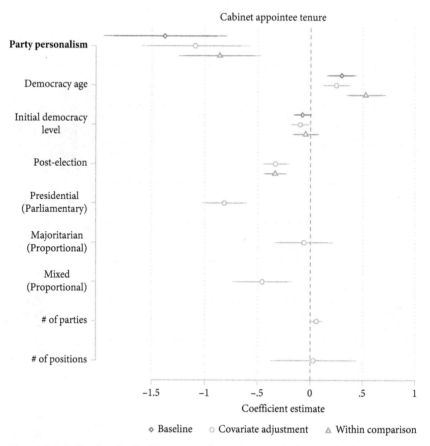

Figure 3.A-2 Leaders backed by personalist ruling parties have cabinet members with shorter tenures

4

The Evidence

We begin this chapter looking at Senegal, a country often lauded as one of the most stable democracies on the African continent. Yet, as with many seemingly robust democracies around the globe, its democracy appears to be under threat. As *The Economist* wrote in 2019, 'Whereas many in the neighborhood have rigged their elections, Senegal's have generally been seen as relatively fair, making a recent lurch away from openness all the more worrying' (*The Economist*, 2020b).

The troubling developments in Senegal began under the tenure of its current leader, Macky Sall. Prior to coming to power, Sall was a long-time member of the Senegalese Democratic Party (PDS). The PDS won the 2000 presidential election, wresting power from the Socialist Party, which had ruled since independence. Sall held various leadership positions within the PDS, including regional party chief, member of parliament, cabinet minister, and, eventually, the PDS leader in parliament (i.e., prime minister). He even directed the winning presidential campaign of Abdoulaye Wade, the PDS leader, in 2007. In 2008, however, President Wade backed a proposal to limit the legislative assembly leader's term to one year, which effectively sidelined Sall. In response, Sall left the ruling PDS and created his own party, the Alliance for the Republic (APR). In 2009, Sall was elected mayor of a small city in his home region with the backing of the APR. Then, in the next presidential election in 2012, Sall ran as the APR candidate, placing second in the first round of the election; and then defeating the incumbent—and Sall's former mentor—Wade in the second round.

Seven years later, when Sall was up for re-election, he barred the two leading presidential candidates from competing against him. With his strongest opponents sidelined, Sall easily won the first round of the election and avoided a run off. Shortly after re-election and with the backing of his legislative majority, Sall abolished the powerful position of prime minister (a post he had once held) to consolidate power. He then started to lay the groundwork for abolishing presidential term limits to allow himself a third term.

Nearly all measures of democracy—including those from the Varieties of Democracy and Freedom House—mark a sharp decline in democracy in Senegal from 2019 to 2020. Indeed, Freedom House moved Senegal from the 'Free' to 'Partly Free' category as a result of the flawed 2019 presidential contest (Freedom House, 2020). And in 2021, Sall repeated the trick, jailing another popular opposition leader, Ousmane Sonko. This time, the streets erupted in protest, in part

---

The Origins of Elected Strongmen. Erica Frantz, Andrea Kendall-Taylor, and Joseph Wright, Oxford University Press.
© Erica Frantz, Andrea Kendall-Taylor, and Joseph Wright (2024). DOI: 10.1093/oso/9780198888079.003.0004

because Sonko drew support from many urban youths who were attracted to his populist campaign appeals (Lu, 2021).

Sall, a democratically elected leader who created a political party as his own personal electoral vehicle, has now presided over one marred election and—though he announced in 2023 that he will not seek a third term in office—concerns over the future of democracy in Senegal remain, particularly given that Sonko is likely to be ineligible to run in elections slated for 2024 due to a recent jail conviction. Sall's moves to imprison opponents such as Sonko were rubber stamped by a compliant court and large legislative majorities. We argue that this is not coincidental. Ruling party personalism helps leaders weaken constraints on their rule, ultimately paving the way for democratic erosion. This vulnerability to backsliding occurs because personalist parties lack the incentive and capacity to push back against leaders when they attempt to consolidate power. In this way, the uptick in incumbents backed by personalist parties witnessed across the globe helps us make sense of the contemporary wave of democratic backsliding we are undergoing.

This chapter offers two case studies from El Salvador and Hungary that detail the full arc of our argument. Through these case studies, we substantiate the main points we put forward in Chapter 3, linking ruling party personalism to the deterioration of democracy. Next, we offer empirical tests evaluating the relationship between personalist parties and the deterioration of democracy worldwide in the past three decades. While the previous chapter provided a range of tests consistent with the argument we propose, the current chapter offers a more direct evaluation. We give concrete evidence that when leaders are elected to power backed by personalist parties, the chance of democratic backsliding rises.

Party personalism undermines democracy on a variety of fronts. First, we show that ruling party personalism negatively affects two components critical to the quality of democracy: freedoms of expression and association. Repression of these two freedoms—which we refer to collectively as political civil liberties—is a telltale indicator that democracy is under threat. Consistent with our argument, we find that ruling party personalism leads to a reduction in political civil liberties. We then look at democratic backsliding more broadly. We find that the election of leaders backed by personalist parties elevates the risk of democratic decline, whether it is measured incrementally, sharply, or by total democratic collapse.

Further, the evidence that party personalism undermines democracy is consistent across different modes of democratic collapse. Both military coups and incumbent power grabs are more likely when the leader rules with a personalist party. We then show that party personalism matters most when ruling parties have legislative majorities; under these conditions opposition parties are too weak to stop leaders so the ruling party becomes the most consequential constraint on executive-led power grabs. The overall message to emerge is clear: ruling party personalism is detrimental to the health of democracy.

Our findings are consistent with existing research tying weak new political parties with democratic backsliding, many of which are often personalist in nature. Grillo and Prato (2023), for example, find in their formal model that programmatically weak political parties increase the chance of democratic decline. When citizens are uncertain about politicians' policy positions—as is the case with programmatically weak parties—it is easier for opportunistic leaders to get away with a power grab, even when citizens intrinsically oppose one. Likewise, observers have suggested that the rise of new political parties is particularly troublesome for democracy (Haughton and Deegan-Krause, 2021). While new parties often do not remain popular long, they are harmful to democracy, nonetheless. As Deegan-Krause and Haughton (2021) write, 'New parties disrupt established parties' cozy networks—and those entrenched networks maintain democratic norms.' Here we show that the key feature of weak, often relatively new, parties that is so destructive for democracy is not newness, but personalism. Indeed, in our empirical tests, we find that party personalism—not the age of the ruling party or even the newness of the democracy—explains declining democracy.

4.1 Case Studies

The deterioration of a democracy is nearly always a complex process. As such, the argument we propose linking ruling party personalism with democratic backsliding is nuanced and layered. To provide a real-world context for understanding our central points, we begin this chapter with two case studies that illuminate the full arc of our argument. The first focuses on El Salvador, where the election of a leader—Nayib Bukele—backed by a personalist party in 2019 eroded that country's democracy but has yet to topple it. The second covers Hungary, where the same processes began with Viktor Orban's re-election in 2010, but ultimately gave way to democracy's complete demise in 2018. Both countries had experience of autocratic rule—various military regimes governed El Salvador throughout much of the post-World-War-II period, while a communist party governed Hungary for nearly all of the same period—and both democratized around the same time—El Salvador in 1994 and Hungary in 1990.

That said, there are many differences between the two cases. El Salvador is a substantially poorer country than Hungary and has a more violent past, with its democratization coming on the heels of a protracted and bloody civil war. While corruption is a major issue in both countries, violent crime is a persistent problem in El Salvador and criminal gangs hold considerable political influence. In Hungary, by contrast, economic issues are at the forefront, often sparking tensions over admitting refugees seeking asylum. The support parties of Bukele and Orban also differ in important ways. While both parties are highly personalist (according to our data) and were founded by their leader, Bukele's party was far newer than Orban's at the time of the onset of democratic backsliding. It was also highly personalist from its infancy, whereas Orban's party grew more personalist over time.

Predominant theories of democratic survival point to structural features of political systems to explain why democracy endures in some countries but not others. For example, perhaps the most prevalent theory of democratic survival simply posits that longer lived democracies are the least likely to collapse, meaning new democracies tend to be more unstable (Dahl, 1971). Indeed, one hallmark analysis of democratic survival suggests that once democracies have survived at least twenty years, they have fully consolidated and thus are very unlikely to collapse (Svolik, 2008). At the time when the elected strongmen in El Salvador and Hungary came to power, democracy in these countries had reached that milestone, suggesting that these democracies are among the *least likely* to falter. Even so, in our data set of post-1990 democracies, the median age of democracy is about twenty years. Thus despite being among the least likely cases of democratic collapse, El Salvador and Hungary are nonetheless roughly representative of post-Cold-War democracies.

Scholars have suggested other factors as well, such as whether the country has a presidential system or was ruled in the recent past by the military, to explain democratic survival (e.g., Linz, 1990; Cheibub, 2007). By these metrics, Hungary's democracy—with a parliamentary government and no recent history of military rule—should have been less likely to collapse than El Salvador's, where presidentialism rules and the military only retreated to the barracks in the mid-1990s. But, so far, this has not been the case: by 2020, Hungary's democracy had declined to a lower level than El Salvador's, by most observers' accounts.

Likewise, liberal theories of democracy posit that democracies embedded in the global economy and with close social and economic ties to Western democracies should be unlikely to collapse (e.g., Whitehead, 2001; Levitsky and Way, 2010). Yet, both El Salvador and Hungary sit in close proximity to and are highly integrated into huge economic markets dominated by Western democracies, namely the US and the European Union. Thus according to liberal theories, these two cases should, again, be of the least likely cases for democratic backsliding.

As this discussion makes clear, predominant theories of democratic survival largely fail to explain why we have observed steep declines in democracy in these two countries in the first place. That Hungary's democracy has declined even more than El Salvador's is further evidence that is inconsistent with these arguments. We argue, in contrast, that highly personalist ruling parties in El Salvador and Hungary paved the way for democratic decline in each. In what follows, we describe the processes that transpired in both countries, carefully marking the chronological and causal ordering of the events that led to backsliding.

4.1.1 El Salvador under Nayib Bukele

When Nayib Bukele won the presidency in El Salvador in 2019, he was the first candidate to win since 1994 who was not from one of the two major parties, ARENA (Alianza Republicana Nacionalista) and FMLN (Frente Farabundo Martí para la Liberacíon Nacional). While Bukele was a member of FMLN when he held political office prior—as mayor of Nuevo Cuscatlan (2012–15) and San Salvador (2015–18)—the party expelled Bukele in 2017 for fostering divisions within it (Melendez-Sanchez, 2021). Bukele created his own political movement, New Ideas (Nueva Ideas), that same year as a vehicle for contesting the 2019 presidential election. New Ideas failed to qualify with the country's Electoral Tribunal, however, and Bukele eventually jumped onto the ticket of GANA (Grand Alliance for National Unity) in order to run. On taking power, Bukele aligned himself again with New Ideas, the party with which he has governed ever since.

Bukele's victory at the polls is attributed to citizen frustrations with the traditional party establishment (ARENA and FMLN), which had dominated Salvadoran politics since the end of the country's civil war in the 1990s (*Al Jazeera*, 2021b). As early as 2015, research on partisan dealignment indicated that conditions in El Salvador favoured the emergence of a new party (Carreras et al., 2015). And in 2018, just prior to Bukele's rise to power, 78 per cent of Salvadorans reported that the country's political parties did not represent them (Melendez-Sanchez, 2021). The traditional parties had proven incapable of handling the country's serious problems with crime and corruption, issues that were front and centre of Bukele's platform (Associated Press, 2019).

Despite running without the organizational might of one of the two major parties, Bukele was able to mobilize support for his candidacy through his savvy use of new media. As one scholar put it, 'Bukele is a master of using Twitter and Facebook to communicate directly with voters, control his personal image, and shape the political narrative around him' (Melendez-Sanchez, 2021, 23). Bukele's sophisticated social media operation essentially served as a replacement for traditional party building, enabling his quick rise to power.

Once in office, Bukele has relied primarily on family members and close friends to govern, as discussed in Chapter 3. For example, Bukele's cousin is currently the head of New Ideas, his uncle is the commerce secretary, the father of his godson runs the export promotion agency, and his childhood friends control the port authority and the agriculture ministry. *The Economist* summarized this in 2020, writing that Bukele 'entrusts power mainly to members of his family' (*The Economist*, 2020a). Another critic notes that '[a]lmost no one in his cabinet has any political experience or knowledge of public administration. Bukele has chosen loyalty over governing capacity' (Dada, 2020, 105).

Bukele's centrality to New Ideas is such that the party and Bukele have become synonymous. As an extreme example of this, New Ideas markets itself with the letter 'N' for Nayib and little else (Barrera, 2021). Prior to the 2021 legislative elections, interviews with citizens intent on voting for New Ideas candidates revealed that many did not know the names of the candidates they planned to vote for; their votes were simply based on their support for Bukele (Barrera, 2021). While voters' identification with a party often determines how citizens vote, in Bukele's case, the leader of the party—not the party itself—is the key component of partisan identification.

Bukele's attacks on constraints to his rule began shortly after he took power. On some levels his actions were unsurprising, as he had exhibited some authoritarian inclinations prior to the 2019 presidential election (Melendez-Sanchez, 2021). In 2018, for example, he claimed that electoral authorities planned to rig the 2019 election and refused to participate in candidate debates. On election day in 2019, in violation of electoral law, he gave a televised speech to mobilize voters. That said, few observers expressed concerns for the future of democracy in Salvador upon Bukele's victory.[1] Even *The Economist* magazine—which would later flag his anti-democratic behaviour in office—hailed Bukele as a 'rising political star' prior to his presidency (*The Economist*, 2018).

The tide turned, however, starting in February 2020, when Bukele ordered security forces to take over the opposition-controlled legislature for a day in a last ditch attempt to gain legislative approval for his security funding request. After entering the legislative assembly building, with troops at his side, Bukele sat in the president of the legislature's seat and announced, 'I think now it is very clear who is in control of this situation' (Melendez-Sanchez, 2021, 21). Though the action was later ruled unconstitutional, it nonetheless sparked alarm among international democracy watchdog groups (Neuman, 2020).

That same year, Bukele's finance minister was forced to resign because he would not freeze the salaries of those legislators who had opposed Bukele's funding request (Freedom House, 2021c). Bukele also sought to bypass the legislature as part of the country's response to the onset of the COVID-19 pandemic, by issuing an emergency decree, which was later blocked by the country's Supreme Court. Bukele refused to submit mandatory COVID-19-related spending reports to the legislature in 2020 as well. This prompted the resignation of five members of the oversight committee, who claimed that the government was sidelining it when making spending decisions.

By the time of the 2021 legislative elections, civil society groups expressed concern that if New Ideas were to perform well, it would speed up the process of democratic backsliding that Bukele had already begun (*Al Jazeera*, 2021b). That said, Bukele remained tremendously popular, with polls suggesting his approval rating was as high as 90 per cent prior to the election (Navia and Perello, 2021). The party won by a landslide, securing a supermajority in the legislature. Not only

---

[1] See, for example, Freedom House (2021a).

did New Ideas win fifty-six of eighty-four seats in the unicameral legislature, but it won a plurality of seats in each of El Salvador's fourteen departments (legislative districts). As one expert commented, 'For the first time in El Salvador's democratic history, one man could legislate alone' (Melendez-Sanchez, 2021, 19).

Bukele wasted little time dismantling constraints to his rule. In May 2021, only hours after the new legislators had been sworn in, he used his control over the legislature to dismiss the country's attorney general and all five judges of the Constitutional Court, the country's highest court (Freedom House, 2021c). By the next morning, the legislature had replaced these individuals with Bukele loyalists. These moves represented a 'major blow to horizontal accountability' in El Salvador (Melendez-Sanchez, 2021, 19) and raised concerns among human rights groups and judicial experts (*Al Jazeera*, 2021b).

A number of Bukele's actions throughout 2021 further contributed to his consolidation of power (Freedom House, 2021c). For one, the Constitutional Court—now full of Bukele supporters—issued a ruling enabling the president to serve two consecutive terms, paving the way for Bukele to run for re-election. Bukele also announced a 'purge' of the judiciary, forcing out nearly a third of all judges and prosecutors who were over 60 years old or who had served more than thirty years. Bukele changed the process for appointing and reassigning judges, as well, so that it is now largely arbitrary. He issued a number of executive decrees, which weakened the ability of the government to ensure transparency and prevent official misconduct. And, on top of this, there are reports that the government and legislators allied with New Ideas regularly restrict opposition legislators from accessing key information, such as drafts of legislation. Instead, laws are drafted by Bukele and his inner circle of advisors, with the legislature effectively functioning as a rubber stamp.

This evidence indicates that Bukele systematically dismantled two of the main institutional checks on his power, namely the judiciary and the legislature. While the data for our empirical analysis in this chapter and the next only extend to 2020, newly released data that cover the year 2021 show that judicial constraint on the executive has fallen by over 50 per cent from the year of Bukele's election (2019) to 2021.[2] The decline in legislative constraint in the data is nearly as steep, falling from 0.78 to 0.32 (on a 0–1 scale) from 2020 to 2021.

Bukele has coupled these actions with extremely harsh rhetoric with respect to his opponents. He stated on Twitter, for example, that 'ARENA and the FMLN aren't trash, they are worse than that' (Navia and Perello, 2021). He has also repeatedly launched personal attacks on social media and during press conferences against journalists (Melendez-Sanchez, 2021). And he has not shied away from threats of violence, having ordered police units to follow opposition legislators in

---

[2] Varieties of Democracy Core Data (2022). The judicial constraint index falls from 0.59 to 0.08 from 2019 to 2021.

2020 (Melendez-Sanchez, 2021). Bukele has sought to reframe Salvadoran politics into an 'us versus them' narrative, painting his critics as 'disgusting' (Vida, 2019).

Despite Bukele's anti-democratic tendencies, he remains hugely popular in El Salvador.[3] There are signs of this popularity fraying, however. Large-scale protests against his rule have been infrequent, but they erupted for the first time in late 2021 in response to Bukele's cumulative power grabs (Kiratas, 2021). Bukele ratcheted up the tension in response, changing his Twitter profile name to 'Emperor of Salvador' (*News Wires*, 2021). For most of the population supportive of Bukele, his actions appear to have shifted their perspective of what acceptable behaviours look like in a democracy. As an indicator of this, polls suggest that after Bukele dismissed the attorney general and the high court judges, 70 per cent of Salvadorans supported him in having done so (Melendez-Sanchez, 2021). That said, the most recent data on political polarization, which we discuss in detail in Chapter 6, indicates that social polarization into opposing political camps had risen in 2021—Bukele's second full year as president—to its highest level since the end of the civil war. However, with his supporters tolerant of anti-democratic behaviours, the likelihood of Bukele facing accountability from below in the years to come (in the off-chance that elections remain democratic) seems low.

El Salvador's democracy has clearly experienced decline in the short time since Bukele took power, but by most accounts the most recent electoral contest in 2021—while imperfect—was free and fair and a reflection of 'the popular will' (Freedom House, 2021c). As one observer put it, however, 'Bukele looks set to forge ahead with his trademark style of demonizing the opposition and undermining the country's young democratic institutions' (Navia and Perello, 2021). By most assessments, the future for democracy in El Salvador looks bleak.

4.1.2 Hungary under Viktor Orban

Viktor Orban first became prime minister of Hungary in 1998 with the support of the Fidesz coalition. Orban was a founding member of Fidesz, a political movement established in 1988 that eventually became a political party in 1990; he was elected its chairman in 1993. Orban's first stint as prime minister lasted until 2002, when Fidesz lost that year's elections. Notably, however, there were no changes in the quality of Hungary's democracy during his tenure, which remained high.[4]

The defeat was a learning moment for Orban, however, who 'recognized that political success in Hungarian politics requires strong leadership and absolute

---

[3] Support for democracy has typically been relatively low in El Salvador, according to surveys from Latinobarometer (Latinobarometer, 2022), but this has never previously led to an onset of democratic backsliding, suggesting that Bukele was not elected to power in the first place for this reason.

[4] See, for example, the country's Freedom House scores during the period.

control over the party' (Metz and Varnagy, 2021, 324). In response, Orban neutralized or sidelined any autonomous centres of power within the party and reformed the party constitution to give him a tighter grip on its leadership (Metz and Varnagy, 2021). These changes gave Orban control over the selection of local party leaders in each constituency, all party parliamentary candidates, and the leader of the party's parliamentary group (Hlousek, 2015; Korosenyi et al., 2020). The result was a top-heavy party structure with Orban at the helm, such that 'the government, the party, and the leader are ultimately inseparable' (Metz and Varnagy, 2021, 325). Put simply, 'Since then it is Orban who has a party, rather than that Fidesz has Orban as its leader' (Korosenyi et al., 2020, 29).

Fidesz was victorious again in the 2010 elections, making Orban prime minister for a second time, only this time with a party over which he now had full and total control. Orban's return to power, however, was seen more as a result of frustration with the Socialist Party—which had overseen the 2008 financial crisis and was at the centre of a number of corruption scandals—than as backing of Orban and his agenda (Beauchamp, 2018). Importantly, although Fidesz had secured a constitutional majority in parliament, most observers at this time deemed Hungary's democracy secure and consolidated, and few saw this development as a red flag (Mounk, 2018a). If anything, at this time Orban was viewed 'first and foremost an anti-communist reformer' (Laczo, 2020).

In the years to come, however, Orban slowly chipped away at constraints to his rule, eventually pushing the country to authoritarianism.[5] He leveraged Fidesz's constitutional majority to change the rules of government in ways that radically enhanced his control (Bernhard, 2021).[6] Constitutional reforms were the first step in this process. With Fidesz commanding a two-thirds parliamentary majority, Orban pushed through policies of his choosing, amending the constitution twelve times and changing fifty separate provisions just during his first year in office. Most of these changes weakened institutional checks on the government, setting the stage for Orban to further consolidate power.

One of Orban's first targets was the Constitutional Court, the body charged with ensuring the constitutionality of laws. The government changed the nomination process for judges to the court, such that Fidesz could essentially nominate judges without the backing of other parties. Next, it limited the jurisdiction of the court so that it no longer had influence over fiscal issues, including the ability to review the budget or tax laws. It also changed the size of the court, so that it could stack

---

[5] The changes referenced in what follows here come from Bankuti et al. (2012) unless otherwise noted.

[6] As many observers have pointed out, Fidesz's parliamentary dominance following the 2010 elections was largely 'a mistake of constitutional design' (Bankuti et al., 2012, 1). Rules designed to prevent a fractured parliament and a rigid constitution meant that Fidesz—with only 53 per cent of the popular vote—received 68 per cent of seats in parliament. With this two-thirds supermajority, it had the power to amend the constitution.

it with judges who were loyal to Orban. By 2012, the court still existed but it was largely impotent.

Orban also took action to limit the influence of the Election Commission, the body tasked with overseeing elections and one that was designed to be politically diverse. The government ended the mandates of some of the body's members early and replaced them with Fidesz loyalists. With a majority of Fidesz supporters on the commission, the party now had substantial influence over election monitoring, as well as proposals for referendums.

Beyond stacking the electoral deck to favour Fidesz, Orban took aim at independent media outlets. In 2011, the government passed laws that restructured the state's regulatory agency, the Media Authority, and established a body (the Media Council) tasked with monitoring the media and levying fines on outlets. Both of these groups were now staffed by Fidesz loyalists. These changes paved the way for Fidesz to pass a new constitution later that year, absent any input from other institutional actors. The new constitution, which went into effect in 2012, significantly weakened checks on the government. While under the old constitution, any citizen could challenge the constitutionality of a law, under the new system they could only do so if they had been personally affected by it. The new constitution also reduced the independence of the courts, changing the process of selecting judges so that it was essentially in the hands of a Fidesz loyalist. Rule changes also gave Fidesz greater control over the assignment of cases, giving it 'extraordinary power' over judicial affairs (Bankuti et al., 2012, 9). The new constitution lowered the judicial retirement age from 70 to 62, as well, creating a large number of new judicial vacancies that Fidesz quickly filled with its loyalists.

In addition to these changes, institutional democracy watchdogs were removed, and the human rights, data production, and minority ombudsmen positions were combined into one (Scheppele, 2011). The powers of the state audit office and the public prosecutor were expanded, with both run by Fidesz allies appointed to lengthy terms of office. In the case of the state audit office, the new head was a former Fidesz legislator with no professional auditing experience.

Electoral reforms also enhanced Fidesz's dominance, while increasing Orban's importance in the party. Election districts were gerrymandered in ways that favoured Fidesz, and the number of constituencies reduced from 176 to 106. This generated competition among Fidesz politicians to try to secure the party's nomination, increasing the value of loyalty to Orban, who personally controlled nominations. As Korosenyi et al. (2020, 50) wrote, 'all MPs are indebted and accountable to Orban himself'.

The accumulated effect of these changes was a political system tightly controlled by Orban, such that by the time of the 2014 elections, the government had 'effectively weakened many important countervailing power centers that provide horizontal accountability' (Bernhard, 2021, 599). To no one's surprise, Fidesz was victorious in the 2014 contest, and the 45 per cent popular vote share it received was sufficient to guarantee it a constitutional majority again (Mudde, 2014). Despite the fact that Fidesz had many advantages, most observers considered the elections democratic, albeit flawed, particularly in terms of being unfair.

The stage was set, however, for Orban to further push Hungary towards authoritarianism. Orban even seemed aware of this. He famously stated in a 2014 speech that 'a democracy does not necessarily have to be liberal' (Plattner, 2019). His dominance within Fidesz—in particular his continued control over appointments within the party—all but ensured that he would face little push-back for such statements, or for any actions in line with it. Orban subsequently escalated existing efforts to dominate the media landscape and silence his critics, either by buying media outlets or by banning them. In 2016, for example, the leading daily newspaper in the country (*Nepszabadság*) was closed after uncovering scandals involving members of Fidesz, and it was later sold to an Orban ally. By 2017, the government and Fidesz allies owned 90 per cent of all media in the country and all of its regional newspapers (Beauchamp, 2018).

Orban also intensified his illiberal rhetoric during this time—particularly xenophobic statements with respect to migrants—which he followed through with anti-migrant actions (Freedom House, 2017b). As one observer wrote, 'Orban saw a political opportunity in rising public anxiety about migration' (Beauchamp, 2018). He used the issue as a basis for ratcheting up efforts to divide Hungarian society into two camps: Fidesz and the enemy it is at war with (Vidra, 2019). The macro-data on political polarization we analyse in Chapter 6 reflect this trend: during Orban's second stint as prime minister, polarization has been higher than during any other years in the country's post-communist period.

By 2017, surveys revealed that a majority of citizens thought that polarization was getting worse in Hungary and that the country was headed in the wrong direction (Zrt, 2017). Only 24 per cent of citizens thought that rule by a strong leader would be a good way to govern the country, while 78 per cent expressed support for representative democracy (Wike et al., 2017).

Despite this ostensible support for democratic governance and distaste for authoritarianism, however, polls prior to the 2018 elections revealed that 40 per cent (a plurality) of voters supported Fidesz, the party's highest polling numbers since 2011 (Reuters Staff, 2017). The polarization that Orban and Fidesz had intensified since returning to power in 2010 led to a situation in which voters—even if supportive of democracy in theory—'are voting more against the other candidates than they are for their own candidate' (Heil, 2022). Rather than punishing Orban for his efforts to consolidate control and degrade democracy, fear of the opposition gaining power had created a situation in which defections from Fidesz were rare.

108   THE ORIGINS OF ELECTED STRONGMEN

While some remnants of democracy remained in the years that followed the 2014 elections—including Fidesz's loss of its constitutional majority in 2015 by-elections (Szakacs and Than, 2015)—they had vanished by the time of the 2018 elections. Fidesz won back its supermajority with an electoral playing field so tilted in its favour that international monitors concluded the elections were unfair; there was also some evidence of fraudulence (OSCE, 2018; Santora and Bienvenu, 2018; Goat and Banuta, 2019). The low quality of the contest marked the end of democracy in Hungary in the eyes of many and the start of its authoritarian rule under Orban (Mounk, 2018a; Freedom House, 2019).

These case studies illustrate how our argument plays out in various real-world ruling parties, highlighting the pathways by which incumbent party personalism can undermine democracy. We provide empirical evidence linking personalism to these pathways in the chapters that follow. Before doing so, we first offer direct evidence demonstrating that personalist ruling parties' harm democracy.

4.2 Ruling Party Personalism and Democratic Backsliding

In the rest of this chapter, we offer empirical tests that directly evaluate the impact of ruling party personalism on democratic backsliding. As discussed in Chapter 1, the core component of any healthy democracy is the freeness and fairness of its elections. We therefore see electoral integrity as a necessary condition for democracy. In addition to this, freedoms of association and expression are important, primarily for guaranteeing the quality of democracy. Given the multi-faceted nature of democracy, in this section we examine a range of related measures. Specifically, we examine how ruling party personalism shapes government repression of political civil liberties (i.e., repression of freedoms of association and expression), democratic decline (i.e., a decline in political civil liberties and the freeness and fairness of elections), and democratic collapse (i.e., a transition from a system with electoral integrity to one without it). We discuss all these measures in greater detail in what follows. Taken together, the evidence we provide indicates that ruling party personalism boosts the risk of democratic backsliding, regardless of how the latter is measured.

4.2.1 Repression of Political Civil Liberties

We first look at how ruling party personalism influences repression of political civil liberties, which encompass two components of democracy critical to its quality: freedoms of association and expression. Generally, governments in democracies are much less likely to repress their citizens than autocratic governments are (Davenport, 2007). However, many citizens in democracies still face state repression

(Davenport and Inman, 2012, 622). In fact, even during the 1990s when democratic transitions from authoritarian rule reached their peak, observers noted a rise in 'illiberal democracy'—democracies where elections were competitive and relatively fraud free but where governments nevertheless failed to respect basic political civil liberties (e.g., Zakaria, 1997). Indeed, a long history of political thinkers, such as James Madison and Alexis de Tocqueville, have raised concerns that democratically elected leaders may eventually use the state to undermine the protection of individual liberties, yielding a 'tyranny of the majority' where the state curtails freedom of association and expression.

Zakaria (1997) noted that majoritarian tyranny might result from introducing competitive elections with free participation in countries that lacked a virtuous 'liberal' tradition. Democratic transitions, marked ostensibly by the introduction of multi-party elections, could undermine the deepening of democracy if constitutional liberalism did not precede competitive and participatory elections. Likely, the fear that competitive democracy would yield systems disrespectful of political civil liberties pertained most to newly transitioning countries in Eastern Europe and to some extent in Africa, Asia, and Latin America. At least in the 1990s, Zakaria did not voice concern about the rise of 'illiberalism' in *consolidated* democracies. And early American critics of majoritarian democracy, such as Madison, were undoubtedly focused on new democracies, indeed new nation-states as well.

However, in the past two decades, we have seen disrespect of political civil liberties not only in new and unconsolidated democracies but also in some of the most long-lived democracies in the world, including India and the United States. Further, the threat of repression of such liberties did not necessarily arise in the early phases of democratic consolidation in countries that transitioned from autocratic rule in the 1990s. In Hungary, for example, observers grew concerned with Orban's undemocratic actions during his second stint in power—beginning a full two decades after the transition from communist rule—but not his first, as discussed earlier in this chapter. And recent repressive turns in Benin, Poland, the Philippines, and Turkey transpired two decades or more after their transitions from autocratic rule. Indeed, in all these countries, democracy had endured past the two post-transition electoral turnover thresholds—once seen as the hallmark of a consolidated democracy—before seeing the attacks on individual liberties that drew observers' attention. In short, trampling of political civil liberties may be a key precursor to further democratic decline.

In late 2016, for example, when the Polish governing party pushed through laws to re-form the judiciary to its liking, protesters took to the streets in their thousands and the government responded with repression. Amnesty International (2017) details how the police routinely detained peaceful protesters and surveilled, monitored, and pressed unlawful charges against journalists. The report clearly indicates that government forces blocked peaceful assembly, harassed the media, and prevented political expression. In a political confrontation between the ruling party and opposition groups, the former used the state apparatus to violate the political liberties of the latter. Harassing protesters violated their freedom of assembly; and jailing journalist violated their freedom of expression.

In this instance, the leadership pushed through actions that repressed political civil liberties as a means of securing its political goals. As we show in this section, the fact that levels of personalism in the ruling party in Poland were also relatively high is not coincidental.

To look at the impact of ruling party personalism on repression of political civil liberties, we use data from Varieties of Democracy (v2x clpol). This measure captures government repression of freedoms of association and expression, specifically government censorship of the media, repression of discussion for individuals as well as academic and cultural expression, and repression of political organizations such as political parties and civil society groups. We flip the scale so that higher values correspond with more government repression of civil liberties.

Our baseline empirical test accounts for age of democracy and the initial level of democracy in a country when the leader was first selected.[7] The age of democracy and the initial democracy level capture the relevant variation in democratic consolidation, which is important when using our measure of party personalism (as outlined in Chapter 2), but they also reflect a predominant explanation for democratic survival.

Using this baseline specification, we then test a series of potential confounders related to political parties. First, we add an index for new ruling parties and, second, a measure of party *system* institutionalization.[8] Finally, we adjust for party populism, which many observers have suggested is the root cause of rising illiberalism in democracies (e.g., Galston, 2018).

The plot in Figure 4.A-1, in the Appendix to this chapter, reports the results. Estimates for the average marginal effect of ruling party personalism on repression of political civil liberties are positive and statistically significant across specifications. Substantively, the estimates indicate that ruling party personalism increases government civil liberties repression by roughly one-half of a standard deviation, which is equivalent to the increase in government repression in the US during the first two years of the Trump presidency or the rise of repression during the first full year of the Chavez presidency in Venezuela. To probe this result further, we re-examined the data but excluded the year 2020, when many democratic governments issued sweeping lockdown orders as a necessary public health strategy to

---

[7] We include two lags of the outcome variable to purge the model of serial correlation and partial out country fixed effects that capture variation in electoral systems, presidentialism, and cross-country differences in level of economic development and inequality. All specifications include a common time trend. We report cluster-robust standard errors.

[8] The new parties' index is simply the inverse of the square root of party age. The party system institutionalization index is from Bizzarro et al. (2017).

combat the Covid-19 pandemic; and we find robust support.[9] In short, the evidence indicates that ruling party personalism increases government repression of political civil liberties in democracies.

In 2014, the Hungarian prime minister proudly declared that he would lead an 'illiberal state' focused on upholding the rights of a 'community', and that his government would, in turn, 'organize', 'strengthen', and 'develop' itself at the expense of individual liberty.[10] True to Orban's word, Hungarian democracy has suffered. When Orban was elected for a second time in 2010, Hungary ranked among the world's 'liberal democracies'. Within a year, one classification of political regimes would remove the 'liberal' title and simply call Hungary an 'electoral democracy'. And by 2018, Hungary would descend to being ranked an autocracy, though one that still held elections, making it an 'electoral autocracy'. Illiberal democracies have grown in number over the past two decades, and, as we demonstrate in this chapter, the rise of personalist political parties lies beneath this trend.

4.2.2 Democratic Backsliding Broadly

We now turn to tests of ruling party personalism's impact on various broader indicators of democratic backsliding. To preview the basic findings: personalist parties increase the chance of democratic backsliding, regardless of whether we conceptualize it as a subtle decline, a sharp decline, or full democratic collapse. To show this, we operationalize the concept of democratic backsliding in three related ways because there are strengths and weakness to different measurement strategies (e.g., Collier and Adcock, 1999; Munck and Verkuilen, 2002).

Democratic Decay. The first measure of democratic backsliding captures any movement in the level of democracy, which for expositional purposes we refer to as *democratic decay.* We measure the level of democracy using the Varieties of Democracy polyarchy score: v2x polyarchy (Coppedge et al., 2021). This measure aggregates indicators of free and fair elections, freedom of association, and freedom of expression. Here we are looking at any deterioration in the quality of democracy, even if small.[11] Figure 2.2 showed that the average level of electoral

---

[9] Additional tests reported in the online appendix include: interactive fixed effects; specifications that include (separately) fifteen potential observed confounders; and tests that use party creation—rather than the full party personalism index. All tests yield consistent results.

[10] Eva S. Balogh posted the English translation of the speech by Orban on 26 July 2014, which can be found at Hungarian Spectrum: https://hungarianspectrum.org (accessed 24 May 2022).

[11] Vaccaro (2021, 680) shows that this measure of democracy has superior distributional properties than other measures of democracy because it can 'distinguish between different degrees of democracy at the high end of the scale'. Because we sample democracies—all of which have relatively high levels of democracy compared with dictatorships—we want a continuous measure of democracy that captures degrees of democracy at the high end of an overall scale.

democracy among countries coded as democracies has declined since the mid-2000s. This measure therefore reflects the global trend in eroding democracies in the past two decades.

Democratic Erosion. The second measure captures only large, negative changes in the level of democracy, which we refer to as *democratic erosion*. We define this outcome as a 10 per cent (or more) decrease in the level of democracy from the initial level inherited from each leader's predecessor (using the same democracy data above).[12] This variable captures steep declines in democracy irrespective of whether the country scores as being highly democratic when the leader first enters office (Polish President Andrjez Duda) or the country was at intermediate levels of democracy (President Gloria Macapagal Arroyo of the Philippines) the year the leader comes to power.

We model this binary outcome using survival techniques and examine all years for each ruler up to and including the first year of the steep democratic decline. For example, Ecuadorian President Correa was elected in 2006, with 2007 being his first full year in office. Ecuador's democracy score decreases by 10 per cent by 2010, however. So we treat 2010 as the year of democratic erosion and exclude the latter years of his presidency from the analysis (2011–17). In other countries, the steep decline occurs during the first full year of leader's time in power, as was the case in Venezuela under Chavez in 2000.

Using this measure we identify thirty-two leaders who erode democracy—or who preside over a steep democratic decline while in office. Of these, in roughly half the cases this decline occurs in the first three years a leader holds executive office while in the other half of cases it occurs in years four to nine. This means that steep declines in democracy can occur at any point during a leader's tenure—not just at the end or the beginning. The majority of democratic declines occur in newer democracies that have survived only twenty years or less, though nearly 30 per cent occur in relatively consolidated democracies that have lasted longer than two decades. Democratic erosion is thus not simply the province of new or unconsolidated democracies.

Democratic Collapse. Lastly, the third measure captures *democratic collapse*, an event marking the transition from a democratic system to an autocratic one. We measure this using our own updates to the Geddes et al. (2014) autocratic regime data, which assess the start and end dates of both democratic and autocratic regimes. This measure captures the moment in which free and fair elections fail to determine the selection of the leadership, either because the new leadership has achieved power through force or because electoral contests became so

---

[12] To ensure results are not sensitive to the 10 per cent threshold, we test models with varying thresholds (8 per cent to 15 per cent), with similarly significant results. The 10 per cent threshold is consistent with the operationalization of 'liberalization' episodes under autocratic rule, as developed by Wilson et al. (2022); thus 'democratic erosion' as we operationalize the concept is the converse of 'liberalization under autocratic rule'.

non-competitive that opponents no longer had the ability to effectively compete in them.

We record thirty-five instances of democratic collapse from 1991 to 2020. Again, roughly half of these occur during a leader's first three years in office, while the other half occur afterwards. Similarly, roughly three-quarters occur in the first two decades of a democracy, while one-quarter occur after a democracy has survived at least twenty years. These descriptive patterns underscore the well-studied fact that newer democracies are more fragile than older, established democracies. But, again, democracy collapse does occur in some consolidated democracies. Finally, democratic decline and collapse, as we have measured them, are global phenomenon: roughly one-third of democratic declines and collapses occur in Africa, while nearly one-quarter occur in Europe, and another 20 per cent in Asia. Only 16 per cent occur in the Americas.

To understand how these three measures are related, we highlight a few examples. Some leaders rule when a steep decline (or democratic erosion) occurs as well as when the democracy collapses—even if these happen in different years. For example, Hugo Chavez was the Venezuelan president in 2000 when the steep decline occurred as well as in 2005 when we code democracy as collapsing. In other cases, the steep decline (erosion) and collapse occur in the same year and reflect the same political event, for example the Thai military coup in 2006 that ousted Thaksin Shinawata. For both Chavez and Shinawata, the overall democracy level saw a further decline in almost every year they were in power, though increasingly so in some years than others. Still other leaders have presided over a steady erosion of democracy that culminates in a steep decline but without the democracy collapsing completely. For example, the democracy score in Ecuador declines in more than half the years Correa is president and we record a steep decline in 2010; but the democracy fell short of collapsing. And, finally, in still other cases democracy declines but not so steeply as to register a steep decline (erosion) or collapse. For example, US democracy scores fell from 0.89 in 2016 to 0.81 by 2020; similarly, democracy in South Africa decreased from 0.78 to 0.73 when Jacob Zuma was president but South African democracy has neither faced a steep decline nor collapsed.

Descriptive Patterns. To begin the analysis of these measures of democratic backsliding, we show how the three outcomes vary by party creation, which is one item in our measure of party personalism and perhaps the most straightforward way to capture it. Recall that this binary indicator measures whether the chief executive created the support party; conceptually it captures whether the leader picks the party or the party picks the leader. Figure 4.1 shows difference of means tests illustrating the central finding. When leaders create their own parties, democracy levels are lower, and the chances of democratic erosion and collapse are higher. No matter how we measure democracy, a strong pattern remains: leaders who create their own party are more likely to undermine democracy.

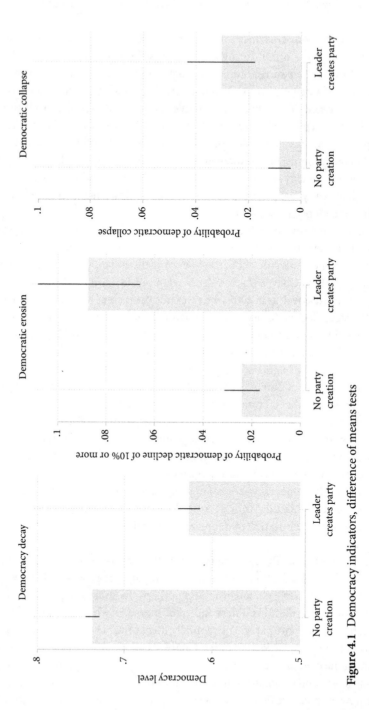

Figure 4.1 Democracy indicators, difference of means tests

Next we unpack the data patterns to illustrate how this basic indicator of party personalism—creation of the support party by the leader—harms democracy along various dimensions of parties. This exercise helps us to isolate the effect of ruling party personalism to distinguish it from other party-related concepts that might also impact democracy. Again, we look at three additional measures of parties: party populism; the age of the ruling party; and party system institutionalization. The democratic backsliding literature points to these features of parties to explain why democracy is declining. Here we distinguish empirically how the leader creating a party is correlated with democratic collapse by dividing democracies into high and low groups for each of these additional measures. For example, using bivariate difference of means tests, we examine whether creating a party is correlated with democratic collapse in the group of ruling parties that score high on populism and among ruling parties that score low on party populism. We conduct the same comparisons for young and old ruling parties as well as for party systems with low and high system institutionalization.

The top panel of Figure 4.2 groups democracies into those with ruling parties that score low on populism and those that score high.[13] Among low populism ruling parties, the probability of democratic collapse is nearly zero (0.2 per cent) when the leader did not create the party; but when a non-populist party has been created by the leader the chances of collapse rise to 2.7 per cent. Next, among populist parties, shown in the top right plot, the probability of collapse when the leader has not created the ruling party is just under 1.5 per cent, but this figure more than doubles, to 3.2, when the leader has created the party. Thus irrespective of whether the ruling party is populist, when a leader creates the ruling party, the chances of democratic collapse rise substantially.

The middle plots in Figure 4.2 show the data pattern for young ruling parties—those that had existed for ten years or less when the leader was elected into executive office—and older, more established ruling parties, which are those that existed for more than ten years when a leader is elected. Among young ruling parties, 1.9 per cent of those where the leader did *not* create the party collapse; but when the leader has created the party, this figure nearly doubles to 3.7 per cent. We find a similar pattern among older ruling parties: 0.6 of those not created by the leader collapse; but 1.8 per cent of those where the leader created the party collapse. While democratic collapse is more likely when the ruling party is younger—in large part because newer democracies are more fragile and tend to have younger parties—the pattern for party creation holds consistently among both young and old ruling parties. The bottom panel of Figure 4.2 divides democracies in low and high party system institutionalization groups. Recall that this measure encompasses all parties in the democracy, not just the ruling party. This *system* characteristic thus considers all political parties—both ruling and

---

[13] We divide the sample at the median value of ruling party populism.

116 THE ORIGINS OF ELECTED STRONGMEN

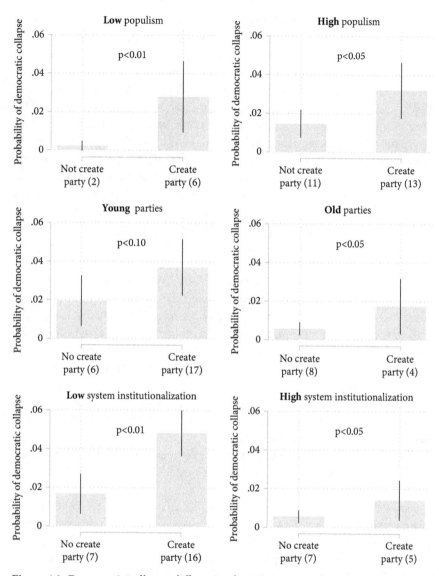

Figure 4.2 Democratic collapse, difference of means tests

opposition parties. Among, democracies with low party system institutionalization, the chances of democratic collapse are 1.7 when the leader does *not* create the ruling party, rising 4.8 per cent when the leader creates their own party. Finally, in democracies with highly institutionalized systems the probability of collapse is 0.5 per cent when the party picks the leader, but increases to 1.4 per cent when the leader creates the ruling party.

THE EVIDENCE   117

These descriptive patterns show that a simple and easily observable indicator of whether the leader created the ruling party is highly correlated with democratic collapse in ways that go beyond extant explanations for backsliding that focus on new parties, populism, or party system institutionalization. We thus identify a feature of parties that is both conceptually distinct from party age, populism, and system institutionalization and explains variation in democratic collapse while holding these other features of parties constant.

Econometric Tests. Next we conducted econometric tests of the relationship between the party personalism index introduced in Chapter 2 and the three ways of measuring democratic backsliding: slow *decay* (using a continuous democracy index), steep declines—or what we call *erosion*—and, ultimately, full democratic *collapse* and transition to dictatorship.

First, we tested a series of models that account for country-specific confounders and time trends in the outcome while adjusting for the initial level of democracy when the leader is selected into power and age of the democracy. This approach rules out the possibility that countries with lower levels of democracy or unconsolidated democracies are more likely to select leaders backed by personalist parties.[14] Further, our approach accounts for country-specific factors that vary mostly between countries—such as geographic region, economic development, inequality, electoral rules, historical legacies of autocratic rule, and colonial histories—and that might influence both selection into personalist parties and democratic stability. This means we are comparing parties with more or less personalism within the same country.[15]

Table 4.1 reports the results. The first column shows estimates for the democracy index.[16] The estimate of −0.036 is negative and significant. This estimate reflects an annual change in the democracy score; thus cumulatively, the marginal effect of party personalism over four years is to reduce the democracy score by roughly 14 per cent. To put that estimate in context, we note that the democracy score fell by 15 per cent during Rafael Correa's presidency in Ecuador and by 14 per cent in Bangladesh during Sheikh Hasina Wazed's most recent stint in power. By contrast,

---

[14] We report standard errors clustered on leader spells because the party personalism variable has identical values for each leader spell. The democracy index has serial correlation; we adjust for two lags of the democracy index to purge the model of serial correlation. This approach, sometimes referred to as a dynamic panel model, produces much smaller standard error estimates than those reported in Table 4.1.

[15] Once we account for democracy age and the initial level of democracy in the year each ruler was selected leader, there is still substantial variation in party personalism over time within countries: 53 per cent of the variation is within—and not between—countries. In contrast, structural factors that might explain democratic survival, such as prior military rule (18 per cent), presidentialism (17 per cent), or level of development (25 per cent) have much less variation over time. Even potential confounders, such as party system institutionalization (28 per cent) or polarization (33 per cent) have substantially less within-country variation than party personalism.

[16] We estimate a linear two-way fixed effects model. Similar results hold with an interactive fixed effects model, a dynamic panel model that adjusts for the lagged outcome, and when the treatment variable is a binary indicator of party creation.

118 THE ORIGINS OF ELECTED STRONGMEN

Table 4.1 Party personalism and democratic backsliding

	Outcome variable:		
	Decay (1)	Erosion (2)	Collapse (3)
Party personalism	−0.036*	1.303*	1.199*
	(0.011)	(0.484)	(0.549)
Democracy age	−0.010	0.340	
	(0.006)	(0.261)	
Initial democracy level	0.075*	−0.179	−0.755*
	(0.006)	(0.164)	(0.138)
Marginal effect of **Party personalism**	−0.036	0.038	0.027
Country effects	✓	✓	✓
Year effects	✓		
Time trend		✓	✓
Democracy age polynomials			✓

* Indicates statistical significance at the 0.05 level.

democracy declined in the US by 8 per cent from 2016 to 2020 but decreased by 25 per cent during Law and Justice Party (PiS) rule in Poland under President Andrjez Duda. The military coup in Thailand that deposed the Shinawatas from power lowered Thailand's democracy score by over 30 per cent.

The second column of Table 4.1 shows the results for the test of steep democratic declines, what we call democratic erosion.[17] Again, the reported specification adjusts for initial democracy level and the age of the democracy, as well as unit effects and a common time trend. The estimate for party personalism is positive and statistically significant, which indicates that party personalism increases the risk of democratic decline by 3.8 per cent for each year a leader is in power.[18] To ensure that the reported result for this measure of democratic erosion is not sensitive to the cut point of 10 per cent decline in the democracy, we tested outcome measures corresponding to cut points using 8 to 15 per cent declines and find similar, significant results for each, again reported in the reproduction files.

Our final measure of democracy is full democratic collapse and subsequent transition to authoritarian rule.[19] Again, the estimate for party personalism is

[17] Because the outcome is a binary variable, we test a correlated random effects (CRE) model that accounts for country fixed effects by adjusting for unit means of all explanatory variables.

[18] The estimate from a two-way fixed effects linear probability model is 4.4 per cent. Results remain when estimating an interactive fixed effects linear probability model or dynamic panel model that adjusts for lagged levels of the democracy index, as shown in the reproduction files.

[19] We tested a CRE model that accounts for country fixed effects by adjusting for unit means of all explanatory variables. Instead of the natural log of democracy age, we adjusted for the cubic polynomial, which mimics modelling duration dependence in a survival model (Carter and Signorino, 2010). We adjust for a time trend and the initial level of democracy.

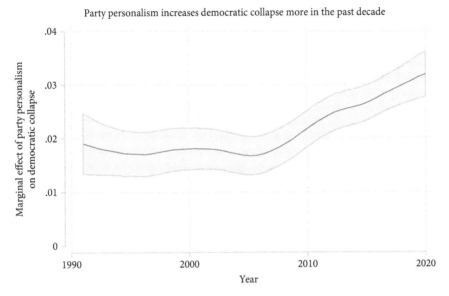

Figure 4.3 Personalist parties increase the risk of democratic collapse

positive and significant, suggesting that personalism increases the risk of democratic collapse. The coefficient estimate corresponds to a 2.7 per cent increase in the risk of democratic collapse, per year.[20] This is a large substantive effect, particularly given the fact that the sample average risk of collapse is 1.4 per year.

To probe how this average marginal effect changes over time, we plot the effect of moving from a low personalism ruling party (tenth percentile of the personalist party index) to a high personalism party (ninetieth percentile) on the risk of democratic collapse over three years.[21] We chose three years for this analysis because the average democratic leader during the past three decades has lasted roughly three years in power. Figure 4.3 shows that party personalism increases the risk of democratic collapse by just under 2 per cent during the 1990s and early 2000s. But in the past fifteen years, party personalism has boosted the risk of collapse even more—by as much as 3 per cent over three years.

This estimator allows us to calculate a point-wise marginal effect for party personalism. We multiply this effect by 0.6, which is the difference between the tenth and ninetieth percentiles of the party personalism score. We then multiply these marginal effects by 3 to obtain the cumulative risk of collapse over three years.

---

[20] The estimated average marginal effect from a two-way fixed effects linear probability model is roughly 4 per cent.
[21] We estimated a kernel least squares model with unit means for all explanatory variables to proxy for fixed effects.

120 THE ORIGINS OF ELECTED STRONGMEN

One concern with the empirical tests we have conducted so far is that there is some other underlying factor that causes personalist parties to win elections and that is also harming democracy. For example, voters in a more politically polarized democracy may be more likely to bet on a personalist party, making it more likely that we will observe these parties winning elections and becoming the ruling party. And if polarization also explains why we observe democratic backsliding, then our observation that personalist parties increase the risk of democratic backsliding might simply be the result of a trend in polarization prior to personalist parties winning elections.

In Chapter 2, we showed that trends over time in two obvious factors that come to mind—polarization and public support for democracy—are not associated with ruling party personalism. However, we also want to be sure that other factors like these are not accounting for our main empirical findings in this chapter. The most direct way to address this issue is to account for these factors in the empirical specification. In the online appendix, we demonstrate that these three empirical findings in Table 4.1—for democratic decay, erosion, and collapse—remain robust in adjusting for any one of fifteen additional factors—including polarization and the alternative dimensions of parties we discussed at length earlier in this chapter—that might influence selection into ruling personalist parties and democratic backsliding.[22]

4.2.3 How Do Democracies Collapse?

Our theory predicts that democracies with highly personalist ruling parties are at risk of democratic backsliding (and, in some instances, collapse). The prior sections provided both descriptive evidence consistent with this theory and evidence from econometric tests. However, not all democracies that collapse do so when the incumbent grabs power for themselves. Indeed while the contemporary focus on democratic backsliding results from the rising trend in incumbent power grabs over the past decades, as we illustrated in the first chapter (see Figure 4.2), an earlier literature on democratic survival often focused on coups—simply because coups, especially those perpetrated at the hands of the military, were so prevalent in the post-colonial period and subsequent decades (e.g., Londregan and Poole, 1990). In fact, one early theory for democratic collapse pointed to presidential systems as the main culprit (Linz, 1990), but it turned out that prior military rule could explain why presidential systems appeared to collapse more often than parliamentary ones (Cheibub, 2007).

---

[22] Covariate adjustment includes: initial level of party system institutionalization, party populism, electoral rules, presidentialism, ruling party seat share, ruling party vote share, initial level of polarization of society in the executive selection year, prior military rule, economic crisis, GDP per capita, population size, and oil and gas resource rents.

THE EVIDENCE   121

Many democracies collapsed at the hands of the military in coups; and this was more likely to happen in regions dominated by presidential systems. However, the key reason these democracies collapsed was not excessive concentration of power in the hands of the president but rather the ease with which militaries that had previously intervened in politics could do so again. In this section, we examine how ruling party personalism shapes different forms of democratic collapse, focusing on incumbent power grabs and coups.

Since 1991, we identify thirty-five cases of democratic collapse. Of these, the majority (eighteen) are clearly instances in which the leader at the time undermined democracy to such an extent that it became nearly impossible for political opponents to win an election. There are also twelve cases in which a coup ousted the incumbent leader.[23] Since our theory points to personalist ruling parties as a prime suspect in the demise of democracy, it is instructive to unpack the *mode* of democratic collapse for two reasons.

First, we want to ensure that our main empirical finding pertains to incumbent power grabs—and is not simply the result of including coups or other exit modes in the outcome. Second, understanding the relationship between democratic backsliding and *how* democracies collapse will shed light on the causal processes we identify. To do this, we examine the data in two ways.

To begin, we look at what happens to democracy under leaders who go on to see democracy collapse under their watch and what happens under those leaders where this does not occur. Importantly, some of the leaders in the latter category—such as Donald Trump and Narendra Modi—ruled democracies where the level of democracy declined on their watch but where democracy did not collapse. For each group of leaders, we examine how the (continuous) democracy score changed during their tenure—up to but *not* including their final year in power. For example, Victor Orban (2018), Daniel Ortega (2016), and Thaksin Shinawatra (2006) all led democracies that collapsed on their watch. We calculate how democracy changed under their rule up to the year prior to the democracy collapsing (i.e., 2017 for Orban). We then compare this change to other leaders who did not rule over democratic collapses, such as Rafael Correa in Ecuador, Ellen Johnson Sirleaf in Liberia, and Benjamin Netanyahu in Israel (up to 2020). These other leaders, under whom democracy did not collapse, are the comparison group.

This test helps us understand whether *prior* to a democratic collapse event, the democracy in a particular country was decaying. For example, did the democracy score decline prior to a military coup that deposed a democratically elected leader? Or did the democracy score decline prior to an unfree and unfair election where the incumbent won and which marked the collapse of the democracy?

---

[23] The remaining five cases are those in which a rebel group displaced a democratically elected leader in the capital city and establishes rule by an unelected government.

122 THE ORIGINS OF ELECTED STRONGMEN

Table 4.2 Declining democracy prior to democratic collapse

	How democracy collapsed		
	Incumbent power grab	Coup d'état	Rebellion
Collapse, change in democracy score	−7.3	−2.9	−1.2
	(2.7)	(1.4)	(0.6)
Comparison, change in democracy score	−0.5	−0.5	−0.5
	(0.2)	(0.2)	(0.2)
Difference	−6.8*	−2.4*	−0.8
	(1.0)	(1.1)	(1.7)
# of collapses	18	12	5

* Indicates statistical significance at the 0.05 level.

Table 4.2 reports the results. In the first column we show the average change in the democracy score up to but not including the leader's last year in power—for leaders who oversaw an incumbent power grab and for the comparison group. For leaders who eventually eroded democracy so much that we code it as a democratic collapse, the democracy score declined on average by 7 per cent prior to the year of collapse. For the comparison group, there is only a very small negative average decline. This difference of −6.8 suggests that even before we code a democracy as collapsing, the level of democracy has been declining in these countries. This should not be surprising because we generally understand incumbent power grabs as the culmination of a gradual erosion of democracy.

The second column shows the result for leaders who were ousted in a coup. Even prior to their being ousted, these leaders were eroding democracy—with an average decline of nearly 3 per cent. The difference (−2.4) between these leaders and the comparison group is significant, which suggests that prior to a coup, incumbent democratic leaders are eroding their democracy—though not to the same extent as the leaders who eventually end the democracy in a power grab. The final column shows that democracy also declines prior to a rebellion that ends the democracy, but this decline is small and not statistically different from the change in the democracy score for the comparison group.

This evidence suggests that democratic leaders whose democracies eventually collapse are eroding democracy prior to the democratic collapse event. We typically understand incumbent power grabs as an incremental process that occurs over many years. So it is unsurprising that democracy declines prior to these incumbent power grabs that we code as democratic collapse.

But we also find that coups which oust a democratic leader may be in response to that leader eroding democracy. For example, Bolivian President Evo Morales' attempt to secure a fourth term in office in 2019 led to a disputed election and protests across the country. These events triggered a military threat to oust

Morales, at which he resigned and fled the country. An unelected opponent then assumed the presidency and gave immunity to the military for committing human rights abuses. The military threat to oust Morales did not occur in a vacuum; instead it was a direct reaction to Morales' attempt to circumvent term limits and stand for re-election.

Even failed coup attempts are often preceded by personalist parties eroding democracy. Indeed, the coup attempt that ultimately failed in Turkey in the summer of 2016 was caused, in part, by President Erdoğan's gradual degradation of democracy. The democracy score in Turkey fell from a peak of 0.69 in 2004, shortly after Erdoğan was elected prime minister, to 0.32 in 2015, the year before the coup attempt. And, of course, the failed coup attempt led to mass government repression targeting political opponents inside the state and government bureaucracy, which we code as marking the end of democracy in Turkey and the transition to fully authoritarian rule.

Because incumbent power grabs and coups are the two primary ways democracies have collapsed in the past three decades, we want to ensure that our evidence for democratic collapse remains consistent across both modes of collapse. Here we present some descriptive evidence to test whether ruling party personalism is associated with both coups and incumbent power grabs. To do this, we divide ruling parties into two groups, showing the baseline risk of different modes of collapse for ruling parties with low and high personalism.

The left plot of Figure 4.4 shows the risk of all modes of democratic collapse, by ruling party personalism. When personalism is low, the risk is less than 0.5 per cent but when ruling party personalism is high this risk rises to over 2.5 per cent. This pattern parallels the patterns in Figures 4.1 and 4.2, where we show that party creation, one indicator of party personalism, is associated with an increased risk of democratic collapse. The middle plot of Figure 4.4 conducts the same exercise but only examines the risk of collapse by coup. This risk is nearly zero when the ruling party has a low personalism score but rises to nearly 1 per cent for personalist ruling parties. Finally, the right plot shows the relative risk of democratic collapse via an incumbent power grab, again illustrating a familiar pattern: low risk when party personalism is low but a high risk for personalist ruling parties.[24]

The descriptive patterns in Table 4.2 indicate that democratic leaders whose democracies collapse—irrespective of the mode of that collapse—have degraded democracy beforehand, while the evidence in Figure 4.4 suggests that party personalism is correlated with the predominant modes of collapse: coups and incumbent power grabs. That party personalism raises the risk of coups in democracies

---

[24] In the online appendix, we report econometric tests where the outcome is either an incumbent power grab (18 cases) or a successful coup that upends democracy (12 cases). We find that ruling party personalism increases the risk of both by about 2 percent per year.

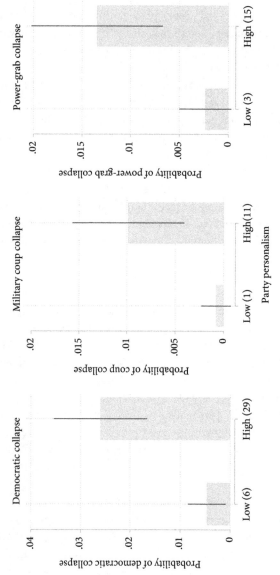

Figure 4.4 Ruling party personalism and modes of democratic collapse

should not be surprising once we understand that leaders backed by personalist parties harm democracy, which may, in turn, trigger coup attempts. In short, even though some democracies do not directly collapse at the hands of incumbent rulers—but rather end when militaries oust elected leaders—party personalism may still be a root cause of such events.

4.2.4 Personalism Matters Most When Ruling Parties Dominate

As the cases above of El Salvador and Hungary have illustrated, when leaders backed by personalist parties secure a majority in the legislature, trouble awaits. This was true in Senegal, too. For a decade, from 2012 to 2022, Macky Sall's coalition (of which his party was the largest) held more than three-quarters of the legislative seats in the Senegalese National Assembly. While ruling party personalism is harmful to democracy even absent legislative dominance, as indicative early on in Bukele's tenure, once ruling parties obtain legislative majorities, we often see leaders supported by personalist parties dismantling democracy.

These cases suggest a potential scope condition for our theory, one based on legislative-executive bargaining. Democratically elected leaders, no matter the nature of the political party that supports them, face possible constraints from the legislature. Indeed, legislatures are the most proximate institutional vehicles for both horizontal and vertical accountability: horizontally, the legislature passes policy legislation; and vertically, voters in all democratic political systems directly elect legislators, even if they do not directly vote for the person taking the chief executive position, as in many parliamentary systems. Further, legislatures typically have some form of agenda-setting, veto, and investigative powers that alter leaders' behaviour once in office. Legislators thus present a primary governing constraint on democratic leaders.

If leaders have an incentive to undermine democracy and personalist parties pave this path for them, we should expect—as an equilibrium outcome of executive-legislative bargaining—that they may not be able to do so where their party lacks control of the legislature. When ruling parties control the legislature, however, opposition parties no longer have the legislative power to check leaders' behaviour, leaving the leader's party as the main vehicle for executive constraint.[25] This logic suggests that party personalism may most strongly shape democratic outcomes when leaders do *not* face legislative opposition, namely when the leader's party holds a legislative majority. Democratic leaders may only have the opportunity to undermine democracy when their party controls the legislature.

---

[25] Courts, by enforcing the rule of law, and the media, by exposing corruption or policy failures, may still serve to constrain leaders' behaviour.

126   THE ORIGINS OF ELECTED STRONGMEN

To test this implication of the argument, we re-examine the evidence for the continuous democracy measure discussed earlier in the chapter.[26] We pair these data with data measuring the lower house legislative seat share from the Varieties of Party data set. Importantly, the latter data measure pre-electoral coalitions led by the ruling party so that we capture pre-election allied party support that can be expected to back the ruling party after the election. For example, in Senegal the United for Hope (Benno Bokk Yaakaar; or BBY) coalition was the pre-electoral coalition that gave Sall and his APR a legislative majority in 2012 and 2017. The pre-electoral coalition contained four parties and the allied parties served as Sall's legislative supporters during his two terms as president.

To ease interpretation we test models that divide the sample into three categories pertaining to low, medium, and high levels of ruling party legislative seat share.[27] Because the specifications include a measure of democracy in each country for the year in which each leader is first selected as executive, we can interpret the marginal effects as the average annual change in the level of democracy during each leader's tenure in power.

The results in Figure 4.5 show the marginal effect of party personalism for low (<40 per cent), medium (40 per cent to 50 per cent), and high (50 per cent or more) ruling party legislative seat share. The estimate on the far left suggests that when ruling parties have less than 40 per cent of the lower house seats, party personalism has little effect on democracy. The middle estimate—for periods when the ruling party has between 40 and 50 per cent of the legislative seats—shows that party personalism is associated with a 3.2 per cent decrease in the level of democracy. Finally, the estimate on the right, for cases where the ruling party has a majority of seats, indicates party personalism is associated with a 5.2 per cent decrease in democracy from the level when the leader was first elected into power.

The evidence in Figure 4.5 is consistent with the argument that party personalism most strongly shapes democratic outcomes when leaders face a weak legislative opposition. This suggests that in democracies, a partisan opposition with substantial power within the legislature can keep leaders in check even when the leader is backed by a highly personalist party. However, when ruling parties control legislatures and legislative opposition is weak, party personalism matters significantly—putting democracies at risk of backsliding.

This point can be interpreted as an important, theoretically informed, and empirically consistent scope condition for our argument: ruling party personalism is most likely to undermine democracy when the ruling party has legislative control. To state the converse, personalist ruling parties backed by strong legislative majorities are the main threat to democracy in the past three decades.

---

[26] The online appendix shows similar results for democratic decline and collapse outcomes.

[27] We estimate a two-way fixed effects linear model and adjust for democracy age and the initial level of democracy in the year the leader is selected; we report cluster-robust error estimates.

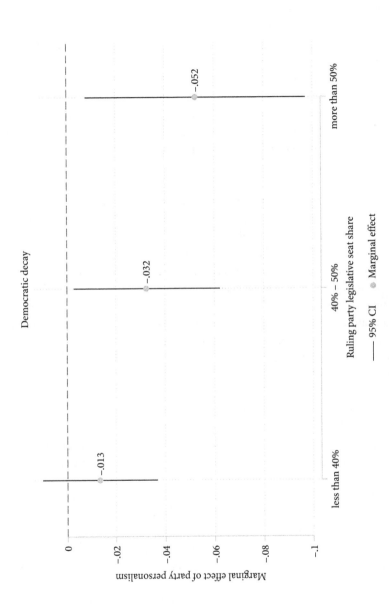

Figure 4.5 Ruling party personalism and legislative majorities

Does the Leader's Popularity Play a Role? A leader's popularity, however, can be an important factor driving whether their party is able to secure a legislative majority in the first place. For example, Bukele's approval rating in El Salvador remained consistently above 80 per cent during his first three years in office (Segura, 2020, 2021, 2022). His popularity paved the way for New Ideas to win big in the 2021 legislative elections (in turn giving a green light to his subsequent attacks on the judiciary).

To be clear, in many instances ruling parties win legislative majorities even when the leader does not have substantial popular support, given the ways in which electoral rules translate votes into seats. Examples abound where personalist ruling parties have won legislative majorities with less than half the legislative vote, as with Georgian Dream in Georgia (28 per cent), Chavez's Fifth Republic Movement (MVR) in Venezuela (11 per cent), the Justice and Development Party (AKP) in Turkey (as much as 34 per cent), and Fujimori's Cambio 90 (18 per cent).

That said, here we consider whether high leadership approval ratings are influencing the relationships we uncover between ruling party personalism, legislative dominance, and democratic backsliding.

To do so, we conduct a similar test to that reported in Figure 4.5, but instead we look at executive approval ratings as a moderating factor. We use data on executive approval from the Executive Approval Project.[28] While this project collects the most comprehensive data on incumbent approval data globally, there is nonetheless a substantial amount missing in the data set. We have executive approval data on less than half of the democratic countries (thirty-nine of ninety-eight) and leaders (214 of 518) in the past three decades. More importantly, the data are not missing at random. We are more likely to lack approval data in countries that are young democracies, have lower democracy scores, and where personalist ruling parties are more common. Thus, any effects we might find are likely to be muted, or relatively conservative, estimates.

We add two covariates to the estimator when examining incumbent approval data, one measuring the electoral cycle and the other capturing how long the leader has been the chief executive (Carlin et al., 2018). When first elected, new leaders may experience a brief moment of popular support, or a 'honeymoon' period; equally, voters may tire of leaders who have remained in power for a long time.

Table 4.3 reports the results. In the first column, we re-examine the result reported in the Figure 4.5, where ruling party seat share is the moderating variable. This test helps ensure that this result remains when we add leader time in power and the election cycle to the specification. We find a now-familiar pattern: ruling party personalism has little effect on democracy when the party has a relatively small legislative seat share but grows stronger as this seat share increases.

---

[28] See http://www.executiveapproval.org/.

THE EVIDENCE   129

Table 4.3 Personalist parties, incumbent approval, and democratic backsliding

	Outcome variable: Democracy level		
	Marginal effect of *Party personalism* reported in each cell		
	(1)	(2)	(3)
Moderator	Ruling party	Legislative seat share	Incumbent approval
Sample	Full sample	Partial sample	Partial sample
Low seats/approval	−0.011	0.007	−0.012
(less than 40%)	(0.012)	(0.015)	(0.017)
Medium seats/approval	−0.029	−0.040	−0.039*
(40% to 50%)	(0.015)	(0.024)	(0.019)
High seats/approval	−0.058*	−0.060*	−0.015
(50% or more)	(0.022)	(0.023)	(0.020)
Countries	98	39	39
Leaders	518	214	214
N × T	2,171	907	907
Country effects	✓	✓	✓
Year effects	✓	✓	✓
Covariates**	✓	✓	✓

* Indicates statistical significance at the 0.05 level. **Covariates: Democracy age, initial level of democracy when leader is selected chief executive, election cycle, and leader time in power.

When the ruling party has at least 50 per cent of legislative seats (reported in the bottom row), party personalism decreases democracy levels by 5.8 per cent.

Next, in column (2), we re-estimate the same model as in (1) but restrict the sample to the leaders for whom there are available approval data. The results for party personalism are again similar. When the ruling party controls at least 50 per cent of the legislative seats (reported in the bottom row), party personalism decreases democracy levels by about 6 per cent. This pattern indicates that ruling party legislative seat share moderates the effect of party personalism even in the smaller, potentially biased sample (214 leaders in thirty-nine countries).

Finally, in column (3), we examine whether executive approval moderates ruling party personalism in the same way. When incumbents have low approval (reported in the top row), the marginal effect of ruling party personalism is modest (−0.012) and not statistically different from zero. We find a similar result (−0.015) when incumbent approval is high (reported in the bottom row). However, when incumbent approval is at medium levels, between 40 and 50 per cent, the marginal effect of party personalism is strongest (−0.039). This indicates that, among these 200-odd leaders with available data on incumbent approval, party personalism is most harmful to democracy when leaders have neither high nor very low approval. This pattern is therefore *inconsistent* with the conjecture that the leader's popularity is what is driving the relationship we see between ruling party legislative

130 THE ORIGINS OF ELECTED STRONGMEN

majorities, party personalism, and democratic decline. Instead, we continue to find that ruling party legislative majorities provide the permissive conditions for leaders backed by personalist parties to degrade democracy.

While it is beyond the scope of our argument to theorize why ruling parties win large legislative majorities even when their leader is not particularly popular, we note that the moderating pattern—which indicates a stronger effect of party personalism when the ruling party has a legislative majority—holds across presidential and parliamentary systems, as well as across different types of electoral systems (majoritarian, mixed, and proportional). Thus, we find strong evidence among different types of democracies that ruling party legislative control is a key scope condition for our argument and findings.

The central point to emerge from these analyses is that when ruling parties have legislative control, they are often the last check on a leader's anti-democratic behaviours. With majority representation, ruling parties can stop leaders from passing legislation that undermines the fairness of elections, for example, and prevent them from subverting other institutional channels of executive constraint, such as the judiciary and the bureaucracy. We take up these themes in more detail in the following chapter, but for now we conclude that ruling party personalism is most likely to undermine democracy when these parties have legislative majorities.

4.3 Conclusion

The core expectation of our argument is that ruling party personalism is harmful to democracy. This chapter provides direct evidence of this relationship. We began by offering anecdotal support of our argument, in the form of case studies from El Salvador under Nayib Bukele and Hungary under Viktor Orban. In each case, leaders backed by personalist parties—in these instances parties they themselves had founded—went on to undermine their country's democracy. Whereas in El Salvador, democracy is hanging on by a thread (at the time of writing), in Hungary it is no more.

We then offered a battery of empirical tests illustrating that the link between ruling party personalism and democratic backsliding documented in those cases is not coincidental. Where leaders supported by personalist parties win power in democracies, the chance of democratic backsliding—regardless of how it is measured—increases. First, we showed that ruling party personalism is associated with an elevated chance of repression of political civil liberties—critical to the health of any democracy. We then went on to show that it increases the chance of broader measures of democratic backsliding as well. This is true regardless of whether we conceptualize democratic backsliding in subtle terms (a simple decline in the quality of democracy) or stark terms (a full transition from democracy to dictatorship). In this way, the election of leaders aligned with personalist parties serves as a red flag that democracy may be threatened in the years to come.

This chapter revealed that personalist parties are fundamentally different from non-personalist parties in ways that are ultimately harmful to democracies. In the chapter that follows, we lay out how this occurs. Specifically, we show that the election of leaders backed by personalist parties in democracies sets in motion political changes that reduce constraints on the executive, thus paving the way for elected strongmen to dismantle democracy from within.

4.4 Appendix A: Regression Results

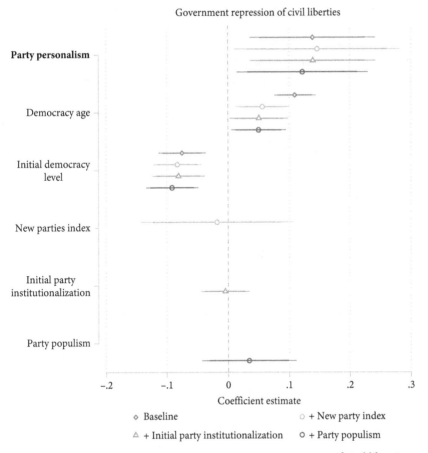

Figure 4.A-1 Personalist parties increase government repression of civil liberties

5

Institutional Pathways

In the *Federalist Papers*, James Madison argued that the separation of powers within government would be 'essential to the preservation of liberty' (1788, 66). Devising a system of 'checks and balances' would keep each 'constituent part' of government—including the executive—'in their proper place' (66). Indeed, executive constraints shape many important outcomes, including the protection of property rights that provide the building blocks of long-term economic development and prosperity; the promotion of human rights; ensuring rule by law; and guaranteeing individual and group security now and in the future. Importantly, executive constraints can protect democracy from incumbent efforts to subvert it.

Standard theories emphasize that leaders establish and ultimately accede to institutionalized executive constraints, such as a council of elites or a representative legislature, because they need to generate revenue to fight a war or keep decentralized subjects from leaving for greener pastures (e.g., Levi, 1989; North and Weingast, 1989; Stasavage, 2020). Similarly, fragmented political power and the expectation of losing power in the future to a competitor may spur incumbent rulers to accede to judicial autonomy that preserves the impartial administration of justice once they leave power (e.g., Ginsburg, 2003, 18; Ríos-Figueroa, 2007).

Our concern is not the origin of executive constraints but rather how societies—and political parties in particular—erode them. Executive constraint, once established, requires institutional actors to preserve it, by both perpetuating norms of appropriate behaviour and exercising the power to block or credibly threaten to block encroachment on it. Political parties play a key role in upholding executive constraint. Parties are filled with people and these people, especially partisan elites, are those who occupy positions within the state institutions with the power to constrain executives. Beyond their role in formal state institutions, party members can also constrain the leadership through the party organization itself. This is particularly the case when leaders care about staying in the party's good favour, given that the party is valuable for their ability to mobilize, strategize, and fundraise. For these reasons, we look to incumbent support parties as critical for upholding executive constraints in democratic systems.

Examples help illustrate this. When Malawian President Bakili Muluzi attempted to overturn executive term limits in 2002, he failed to gain the support of all his party's members in the legislature (VonDoepp, 2019, 298). And when he attempted to remove from the legislature those who had opposed him, the courts

---

The Origins of Elected Strongmen. Erica Frantz, Andrea Kendall-Taylor, and Joseph Wright, Oxford University Press.
© Erica Frantz, Andrea Kendall-Taylor, and Joseph Wright (2024). DOI: 10.1093/oso/9780198888079.003.0005

blocked his move (Dulani and van Donge, 2005, 216; Nowack, 2021, 307). Thus, both some of his own court appointees and his own party's legislators helped derail his attempt to abrogate term limits (Nowack, 2021, 300–8).[1]

Similarly, in 2020, US President Donald Trump attempted to persuade key local officials in his own party to fraudulently manufacture votes to tip the balance sheet in his favour in presidential elections that year (Kumar and Orr, 2020). These officials refused to do so, and Trump was unable to hold on to the presidency (Niesse, 2021).[2]

Finally, when Paraguay's President Nicolanor Duarte, sought to change the constitution in 2006 to allow him to sidestep the country's one-term presidential limit, heavyweights in his party, Colorado, pushed back. The vice president and leader of a rival party faction, Luis Castiglioni, immediately criticized Duarte and 'announced plans to seek the party's presidential nomination himself' (Muller et al., 2012, 1124). Castiglioni's move forced Duarte to back down and the latter threw his weight behind a third Colorado candidate.[3] And while Castiglioni did not win the party's nomination that year, he would resurface a decade later as a Colorado government minister, demonstrating that standing up to the leader's bid to overturn term limits had not sunk Castiglioni's career.

In democracies as different as Malawi, Paraguay, and the United States, we therefore observe institutional actors in the incumbent leader's party blocking an executive power grab. We argue that such actions are much less likely as personalism in the ruling party increases.

We note that executive constraints do not guarantee democracy, as mentioned in Chapter 1. Incumbent-led democratic subversion is still possible in the presence of checks and balances, if sufficient institutional actors have preferences that align with those of the executive. Even in autocratic rule there can be executive constraints, as is common where military juntas or party politburos wield considerable influence. At the same time, the absence of executive constraints in democracy means that leadership efforts to subvert democracy are likely to succeed, regardless of other actors' preferences. Actions to undermine political opponents and give the leadership an unfair electoral advantage—as in the types of developments that undermine democracy—are substantially more probable when leaders face few checks on their power. In this way, while the dismantling of executive constraints is not a *sine qua non* indicator of democratic breakdown, as we conceptualize it in this study, it does boost the odds. For this reason, we see

---

[1] Opposition party legislators as well as many civil society groups also opposed Muluzi's move; and without these groups opposing the term limit change, Muluzi would likely have succeeded.

[2] Party personalism increased under President Trump. The movement towards greater personalism under his tenure helps explain some of the degradation in democratic quality that occurred during it. That said, the Republican Party under Trump is still not on the high end of the party personalism distribution, such that we do occasionally see some of its members attempt to constrain him.

[3] The Colorado Party lost the 2008 election, with Duarte's preferred candidate placing second to Fernando Lugo.

134 THE ORIGINS OF ELECTED STRONGMEN

consolidation of power in the leadership in democracies as opening the door for democratic decline.

Importantly, our argument linking personalist parties to the demise of democracy emphasizes the inability of these parties to effectively push back against incumbent efforts to strengthen control. If this is indeed the pathway connecting personalist parties to democratic backsliding, then we would expect ruling party personalism to bring with it a weakening of constraints on the executive.

In this chapter, we explore these relationships. We first discuss the factors that help explain the maintenance of executive constraints in democracies and how these factors diminish with ruling party personalism, focusing on the hypothesized mechanisms, namely ruling party incentive and capacity. We then turn to a discussion of our empirical strategy for measuring whether institutional actors constrain the executive, paying close attention to the fact that when constraints are strong, we should be less likely to observe efforts to breach them. Next, we offer empirical tests that evaluate whether ruling party personalism influences a variety of indicators of leadership control.

We find that ruling party personalism decreases the chance leaders will face constraints in the state's legislative, judicial, and bureaucratic institutions. Importantly, we find that the whittling away of executive constraints brought on by ruling party personalism is even more severe when the party has a legislative majority. This suggests that personalist parties do little to stand in the way of a personalist leader's agenda. Finally, we find that ruling party personalism increases the likelihood that we will observe direct actions on the part of leaders to expand their power, as reflected in attempts to change term limits.

This chapter thus provides strong evidence that ruling party personalism reduces constraints on the executive in democracies. Leaders are more likely to consolidate control when such parties back them, resulting in the hollowing out of horizontal processes of accountability. This is consistent with our argument that personalist parties lack the incentive and capacity to keep their leaders in check, which ultimately paves the way for the undermining of democracy.

5.1 Executive Constraints in Democracies

Pushback against leadership attempts to weaken executive constraints often occurs through formal institutional pathways—such as court rulings, investigations into incumbent behaviours, or blocking legislation—but it can also transpire outside of these arenas. Individual political actors may openly speak out against a leader's actions and try to build momentum for a movement to oppose them, for example. The threat of such public retribution may even deter leaders from seeking to expand their control in the first place. That said, once a leader has attempted to consolidate power, they can typically only be stopped through accountability mechanisms (Laebens and Lührmann, 2021; Lührmann, 2021), namely formal state institutions (horizontal channels) or at the polls come election time (vertical channels).[4] We discuss the latter avenue in the next chapter; this chapter focuses on the former.

As Madison noted in the *Federalist Papers*, in democracies, institutional actors should have the 'constitutional means and the personal motives to resist the encroachment of others' (66). Executive constraint therefore entails a set of legal rules that empower actors to weigh in on policy or personnel choices, but also informal norms and expectations about adherence to these rules. On the one hand, executive constraint requires that actors have enforcement power bestowed by state institutions themselves—including formal rules, such as law and constitutions, and resources, such as money and personnel—to pursue action and information about the executive's behaviour. On the other hand, such power is meaningless should actors choose not to utilize it in the face of executive abuses or overreach.

Formal powers are part of the story, in other words, but incentive is also important to understanding the maintenance of executive constraints. While we would like to assume that all political actors will prioritize preservation of checks and balances and see them as a valuable part of consensus government, such normative concerns are often secondary to actors' desire for power and influence. The existence of executive constraints—or actions taken to prevent expansion of executive control—do not necessarily mean key political actors intrinsically value these things, but rather that they see them as being in their interest.

Importantly, even with sufficient motivation, some forms of executive restraint require coordination. A lone judge can in some instances block an executive's attempt to expand control, for example, but a lone legislator cannot. Efforts to keep the leader in check often necessitate that political actors join forces to mobilize an effective response.

Our discussion of state institutions and executive constraints centres on three key domains: the legislature, judiciary, and bureaucracy. In most democracies, each of these domains has formal powers granting the ability to check the leader, such that they are a good focal point for understanding executive constraint. For example, legislatures can block policy, the courts can deem actions unconstitutional, and bureaucracies can refuse to implement executive orders that break their rules. We elaborate, below, on the ways in which these state institutions can challenge the executive, as well as how the nature of the leader's support party can influence whether they will.

---

[4] The party itself could sanction the leader, perhaps through passing the leader over for the party's nomination or withholding party resources for campaigns. Such actions, however, would primarily be relevant during the election season. We would expect personalist parties to be far less likely to pursue these sorts of strategies, for all the reasons mentioned in Chapter 3.

136 THE ORIGINS OF ELECTED STRONGMEN

5.1.1 Legislatures

Legislatures have a variety of methods for constraining the executive, perhaps the most noteworthy being their ability to pass or block legislation. Related to this, legislatures can investigate the incumbent's behaviour, propose divergent policy legislation, block personnel appointments, and simply question (in public and private) incumbent actions.

In democracies where leaders have partisan dominance in the legislature, the ruling party plays a crucial role in setting policy and making personnel choices in government. When ruling parties retain partisan legislative control, they become one of the last institutional actors to stand in the way of efforts to undermine constraints placed on the executive. The partisan composition of legislative bodies, however, is important for anticipating whether they will serve to constrain the leader.

Not surprisingly, legislators affiliated with opposition parties are likely to broadly support upholding executive constraints. Representatives of such parties may not only disagree with the incumbent leader on policy but they may also stand to gain politically if the incumbent leader fails to pursue their agenda and is punished by voters—all this would be to the opposition legislators' gain. Opposition parties have a natural motivation, to gain political advantage relative to the leader's party, to investigate executive abuses of power, or even thwart the policy agenda of the leader's party in the legislature—especially if that policy agenda entails stacking the political deck in favour of the incumbent.

Anticipating whether legislators from the leader's support party will check the executive is more complex and dependent on the nature of the party. In parties with low personalism, legislators are more likely to see upholding executive constraint as being in their interest. Though the policy preferences of such actors often align with those of the executive—such that empowering the executive offers the potential to fulfil the party's agenda—doing so is a risky strategy in the long term. Should the party find itself in opposition further down the road, expanded executive powers could render it politically impotent. Moreover, relaxing executive constraint could hurt the party's electoral chances come election time, if doing so would damage the party's reputation. Importantly, when legislators in non-personalist parties seek to push back against the leader, it is easier for them to work as a collective to generate sufficient support for doing so. For these reasons, we often see executive constraints respected even when the leader's support party has the majority, if the party features low personalism.

The conditions are quite different, however, when the leader's support party is personalist; these legislators are more likely to have an incentive to stand with the leader and—even if they would prefer to push back—they often lack the capacity to do so. As discussed in Chapter 3, legislators affiliated with personalist parties have much to lose and little to gain in challenging the leader. Personalist parties may not outlive the leader's tenure, hindering the future political careers of elites should the party lose power. And even if a highly personalist party survives a period out of power, the best path to future political success for elites may still remain with the party—given that the former leader is likely to continue to control funding and nominations necessary for advancement.

Partisan elites in a personalist party also lack the collective action skills and resources required to check the leader. These limitations are particularly apparent in the legislative arena, where coordination is required to generate sufficient support for or against policies. Because personalist parties so often serve as rubber stamps for their leaders' agenda, when these parties comprise a majority of the legislature, the power (and impunity) of the leadership is likely to expand even more.

For these reasons, we expect that when leaders are supported by personalist parties, we will see a decline in legislative constraints on the executive. This relationship is likely to be most pronounced when the leader's party has a legislative majority.

5.1.2 Judiciaries and Bureaucracies

Judicial and bureaucratic state institutions also have various methods with which they can constrain the executive. As with legislatures, judicial institutions represent a quintessential element of checks and balances on executive power (e.g., North and Weingast, 1989). Tasked with the responsibility of interpreting constitutions and laws, the courts can issue rulings that place limits on executive behaviours. Likewise, though we do not often see the state's bureaucracy as part of a system of checks and balances, such groups do in practice play a role in curbing the executive, particularly in terms of overseeing executive activities and limiting abuses of power.

An example from the United States is illustrative here. In November 2020, the Trump administration sought to improve legislative representation of the Republican Party by removing unauthorized immigrants from the census count. The Census Bureau pushed back against this request, however, stating that they could not execute it with accuracy before Trump left office in January 2021. Census experts deemed it unlikely that the bureau would carry out the order, given that it was full of 'data scientists and other experts who have devoted their careers to an accurate head count' (Wines and Bazelon, 2020). As this example demonstrates, organizations within the state's bureaucracy, operating with their own set of rules and requirements, can push back against implementing executive directives should these conflict with their own rules.

Judicial and bureaucratic institutions differ from legislatures in that individuals in these positions are often unelected, such that we are unlikely to see large swings in their partisan composition from one election to the next. That said, many positions within both bodies are appointed by the executive, and a partisan changing of the guard is common when a new leader assumes power, particularly with respect to the most influential positions within them.

While legislative majorities are not nearly as influential in determining the ease with which judicial and bureaucratic institutions can constrain the executive as they are with legislative institutions, they do still matter. Legislatures often must approve a leader's selection of appointees to key posts in the judiciary and bureaucracy. Partisan legislative control therefore enables leaders to handpick the individuals who will fill important positions absent much legislative resistance. For this reason, partisan legislative control typically increases the chance that judicial and bureaucratic appointed positions will be filled by allies in the leader's party.

There is good reason to anticipate that institutional actors operating within the judiciary and bureaucracy will seek to preserve executive constraints. Such individuals usually have career incentives to maintain the autonomy and independent reputation of the institution in which they serve. For example, judicial appointees or civil servants in the bureaucracy and state administration may place value on checks and balances if their career depends on the institution persisting independently in the future. A judge who green-lights an incumbent purge of perceived opposition in the judiciary may come to regret not standing up to the executive should their retaining the job after the incumbent loses power depend on the judiciary's autonomy. Once an institutional actor condones or acquiesces to a purge or encroachment on an institution's independence, this may encourage future executives—including the current leader—to do the same to that very institutional actor.[5] Even if judges and court administrators are apolitical or institutionally isolated from day-to-day partisan political pressures and thus lack a partisan incentive to check executive behaviour, it is likely they still see preserving the institutional autonomy of their organizations as important to their careers.

A different situation emerges, however, when these institutional actors are affiliated with a personalist party. As discussed in Chapter 3, party personalism changes the incentive structure in meaningful ways, discouraging those in positions of influence in the party to challenge the leader. This is particularly true for judicial and bureaucratic appointees, who are apt to tightly link their own political fortunes with staying in the leader's good favour. This should make them reluctant to push back against the leader's agenda, no matter its constitutionality. Importantly, should constraining the leader require coordination across or within the

---

[5] A key component of Recip Tayyip Erdoğan's takeover of the state administration in Turkey entailed appointing Gulenist supporters to key administrative posts, including in the judiciary (Sharon-Krespin, 2009). After the failed coup attempt in 2016, Erdoğan systematically purged Gulenist supporters from the state bureaucracy (Hansen, 2017).

state's judicial or bureaucratic institutions, institutional actors linked to personalist parties will be disadvantaged in mobilizing such an effort.

For these reasons, we expect that when leaders are supported by personalist parties, we will see a decline in both judicial and bureaucratic constraints on the executive. This relationship should be most pronounced when the leader's party has a legislative majority.

To summarize, executive constraint requires formal legal rules that empower state institutions to check the leadership, but institutional actors' incentive to use these rules to do so is critical, as is their ability to act collectively, where necessary. We assume that while all democratically elected leaders will seek to expand their power and influence, some would like to do this by dismantling institutional constraints. Leaders' ability to do so, however, will be contingent on the nature of their support party. Where such parties are personalist, we are likely to see constraints on the executive weaken. Key actors in personalist parties lack the incentive and capacity to restrain the leadership, resulting in the executive's consolidation of control. Our central expectation, therefore, is that ruling party personalism will lead to the relaxation of executive constraints. We expect this relationship to be most pronounced when the leader has majority support in the legislature.

5.1.3 How Do We Know When Institutional Actors Constrain?

A leader may seek to purge an uncooperative court and appoint new (more pliable) judges, nominate officials who will line their pockets at public expense, or overturn a constitutional procedure for selecting new leaders by, for example, extending executive term limits or disrupting the peaceful transfer of power. In 2003, Malawian President Bakili Muluzi attempted (but failed) to change the constitution to allow himself a third term as president. In another example, US President Donald Trump and allied legislators from his party attempted to overturn an election in 2021 by urging loyal voters and aligned militias to violently seize the legislature and block the certification of an election he had lost.

Each of these incumbent behaviours met resistance from institutional actors, and the incumbent was forced to back down. In the end, Muluzi failed to persuade enough legislators, including members of his own party, to pass a constitutional amendment; and Trump's supporters were defeated by internal security agents and armed forces loyal to the legislature. As importantly, perhaps the most powerful institutional actor in Trump's party, the vice president, refused to go along with the president's plan to steal the election. Both Muluzi and Trump left power shortly after their attempts to remain there were defeated. Institutional actors exercised constraint in response to an executive power grab and won the day; and in these instances, we observe executive constraint in practice.

140 THE ORIGINS OF ELECTED STRONGMEN

However, most of the time, we do not see leaders seeking to expand their control. This is not because they do not wish to stay in power; indeed, most leaders remain in office to the end of their terms rather than resigning early. Rather, it is often the case that leaders—anticipating that institutional actors will constrain them—do not even attempt these behaviours. For this reason, executive constraint most often works in a *negative* fashion: when constraints exist and have teeth, leaders expect these constraints to be exercised and so we do not see leaders attempting to transgress the system or consequently institutional actors defending it. In the language of social scientists, when strong executive constraints are in place, we should observe the following equilibrium behaviour: the executives choose *not* to break the boundaries of their remit and so institutional actors never have to block leaders' moves to break those boundaries.

This has implications for how we test whether personalist parties can enable leaders to dismantle executive constraints. To take the term limit example further, when strong executive constraints operate, we should not necessarily observe the absence of term limit changes but rather the absence of *attempts* to change term limits. Leaders should only attempt to extend their terms when they think there is a reasonable chance that they will succeed. When an attempt fails, it suggests that executive constraints are higher than the leader anticipated, albeit still lower than in environments where we do not see attempts in the first place. For this reason, we must carefully consider how we measure the executive constraint outcomes we analyse in this chapter.

In the empirical section that follows, we first examine *constraint* leveraged by three government institutions in democracies outside the executive office: the legislature, judiciary, and bureaucracy. We use measures of constraint that reflect both deliberate and observable moves by institutional actors to challenge the leaders' behaviour as well as their institutional resources to do so. For example, the expert-coded question about executive oversight we explain shortly taps into whether institutional actors '*would* question or investigate [the executive] and issue an unfavorable decision or report' (Coppedge, 2021, 147). This hypothetical question wording implies the capacity to exercise constraint in the event of a leader transgressing. However, the question does not require the expert coder to observe a leader's transgression followed by an institutional actor exercising constraint (though the measure does not preclude this). Thus, even when a leader chooses not to transgress—precisely because they anticipate an institutional actor blocking their attempted transgression—we can still assess institutional constraint.

5.2 Empirical Tests

In this section, we examine the relationship between ruling party personalism and constraints on the executive. We begin by analysing these dynamics in three institutional domains: the legislature, judiciary, and bureaucracy. Our central expectation is that ruling party personalism will decrease executive constraints in each of these domains, a relationship that will be more pronounced when the party has a legislative majority.

We measure legislative, judicial, and bureaucratic constraint on the executive with global data coded by country experts from the Varieties of Democracy project. The benefits of these measures lie in their global and temporal coverage as well as the fact that they are intended to capture equilibrium concepts. The downside to these measures is that even expert coders may use assessments about the present state of affairs in a country to infer conditions in that country in the past. We mitigate this concern by always including lags of the outcome variable in the specification, allowing the tests to make inferences from changes over time in trends within countries.

After presenting these tests, we then turn to an additional indicator of executive constraint (or its absence): presidential attempts to overturn term limit rules. This test has less geographic coverage because it is only applicable in presidential systems, but it nonetheless examines an objective, real-world behaviour that still reflects an equilibrium outcome. We discuss how this indicator relates to executive constraints in more detail below.

5.2.1 Legislative Constraints on the Executive

We begin by looking at legislative constraints on the executive. To test our expectations, we use the Varieties of Democracy measure of legislative constraints on the executive (v2xlg legcon), which seeks to capture the extent to which the legislature is 'capable of questioning, investigating, and exercising oversight over the executive' (Coppedge, 2021, 50). This variable is a composite index that combines information on the following items: whether the legislature questions officials in practice; legislative oversight of the executive; legislative investigations; and whether opposition parties exercise oversight of the executive.

There is substantial variation in legislative constraint within countries, in part due the wide variation in legislative seat shares for the leader's party. Indeed, when the leader's party has a majority in the legislature, constraint is over half of one standard deviation lower than when the leader lacks a legislative majority. In Poland, for example, legislative constraint was relatively high during the first four post-Communist presidencies, including Lech Kaczynski's; and each of these leaders lacked a legislative majority. In contrast, during the first five years of Andrzej Duda's tenure, during which the ruling Law and Justice Party (PiS) has held a small legislative majority, legislative constraint has deteriorated substantially.

As a first assessment of the data, we compare legislative constraint for leaders who have created their own party and those who have not; reported in Table 5.1.

142 THE ORIGINS OF ELECTED STRONGMEN

Table 5.1 Party creation and legislative constraint

	Party creation estimate
Pooled comparison	−0.41* (0.11)
Within-country comparison	−0.14* (0.06)
Adjustment for legislative majority	
Within-country comparison Legislative **majority**	−0.52* (0.17)
Within-country comparison Legislative **minority**	−0.04 (0.04)

We find that, on average, those who create their own parties encounter 41 per cent less legislative constraint. Looking only at comparisons of leaders to other leaders in the same country, the pattern persists but is weaker: leaders who create their own parties face 14 per cent less legislative constraint than those who do not. A similar difference remains when we account for whether the leader's party holds a majority of seats.

Next, we look at the data from a slightly different angle: whether legislative constraint varies by party creation when leaders hold a legislative majority as compared to when they do not. The last two rows of Table 5.1 show that when the leader has a majority in the legislature and created the party, legislative constraint is 52 per cent lower than when the leader has a majority but did not create the party. For leaders who do not have a legislative majority, party creation makes little difference in the level of legislative constraint. Legislative constraint is thus lowest when the leader creates their own party and holds a legislative majority.

We now look at the relationship between ruling party personalism and legislative constraint using the measure of ruling party personalism that we introduced in Chapter 2. We test an empirical model that accounts for all differences between countries and adjusts for the age of democracy and the initial level of democracy when the leader first wins power.[6] The first estimate in the left panel of Figure 5.1 reports the result of this test: we find that, on average, ruling party personalism reduces legislative constraint by about 16 per cent of one standard deviation. We note that the size of this estimated effect captures the year-to-year changes in the level of legislative constraint. So if we compare leaders in power for four years, the cumulative difference in legislative constraint is over 60 per cent of one standard deviation. This is consistent with the analysis of party creation discussed above.

---

[6] We test a country fixed effects model with two lags of the outcome variable to account for serial correlations. Covariates include democracy age, initial democracy level, ruling party legislative seat share, and a calendar time trend. Cluster robust errors estimated.

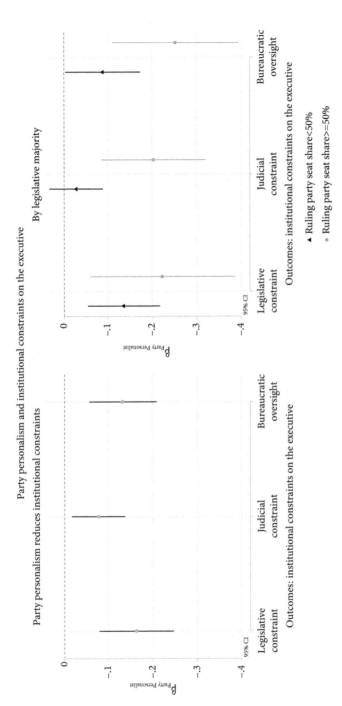

Figure 5.1 Personalist ruling parties decrease executive constraint

144 THE ORIGINS OF ELECTED STRONGMEN

Next, we look at how party personalism shapes legislative constraint when leaders have a legislative majority as compared to when they do not. The first two estimates in the right plot of Figure 5.1 show the following results. When leaders lack a majority, the decline is 13 per cent; when they have a majority, it is about 22 per cent. Substantively a decline of 22 per cent is roughly the change in legislative constraint faced by Polish President Duda from his first full year as president in 2016 to what he encountered in 2020. Thus, the effect of party personalism on legislative constraint is much stronger when the leader holds a majority, as we expected.

It is important to note here that although presidential and parliamentary systems differ substantially from each other in terms of the powers they bestow on the executive and the likelihood of the executive facing majority legislative support, we find similar patterns for how party personalism shapes legislative constraint in both types of systems. Splitting the sample between presidential and non-presidential systems, we find the estimate is roughly the same and statistically significant among both groups.

In short, personalism in the ruling party—regardless of whether it is captured in basic terms by looking at party creation or more broadly with our party personalism index—leads to less legislative constraint on the executive. This relationship is particularly pronounced when the leader's party has a legislative majority. Indeed, it is precisely when the legislature is filled with partisan backers of the executive that the constraint by the ruling party matters most.

5.2.2 Judicial Constraints on the Executive

We now turn to the role of judicial institutions in constraining the executive. To test our expectations, we look at judicial constraints on the executive using data from Varieties of Democracy (v2x jucon), which measures the extent to which the executive complies with court rulings and the extent to which the judiciary can act independently of the executive (Coppedge, 2021, 50). Again, judicial constraint on the executive varies widely across democracies. For example, the judicial constraint score in Malawi during President Muluzi's attempt to extend term limits—which the high court helped thwart—is among the highest for all new democracies.[7] In contrast, judicial constraint in El Salvador plummeted in the first year of Nayib Bukele's presidency, dropping more than one standard deviation from the score during his predecessor's presidency.

For this analysis, we once again make comparisons between leaders in the same country while accounting for democratic consolidation.[8] The second estimate in

---

[7] Malawi's score for judicial constraint in 2002 is in the sixty-ninth percentile for all democracies less than ten years old.

[8] We estimate a dynamic panel model, with country fixed effects and two lags of the outcome variable to account for serial correlation and cluster robust standard errors. We adjust for age of democracy, initial level of democracy, and a time trend.

the left plot of Figure 5.1 shows the result: ruling party personalism reduces judicial constraint by roughly 7 per cent (of one standard deviation) per year. Thus, for a leader in power for four years, the substantive effect of party personalism, on average, is just under 30 per cent.

Again, we break down this finding to examine whether party personalism shapes judicial constraint on the executive differently when the ruling party has a legislative majority. Executive power backed by legislative controls often allows leaders to purge or pack courts, especially when the legislature has veto power over judicial appointments. Further, a legislative majority may give the leader room to change the laws governing judicial appointments and pay. Thus, if ruling party personalism undermines judicial constraint, we should expect this to be stronger when the ruling party has legislative control.

The second set of estimates in the right plot in Figure 5.1 shows how party personalism shapes constraint under different legislative configurations. When the leader's party lacks a legislative majority, party personalism has almost no effect on judicial constraint. However, when the leader has legislative control, party personalism lowers judicial constraint considerably, with the estimate of the yearly drop in constraint roughly 20 per cent of one standard deviation. Indeed, the size of this effect mirrors the decrease in judicial constraint in Poland during the first four years of rule by PiS.[9] This result suggests that party personalism substantially undermines judicial constraint on the executive—but only when the ruling party has legislative control.

5.2.3 Bureaucratic Constraints on the Executive

Next, we examine bureaucratic constraints on the executive. We measure bureaucratic constraints on the executive by looking at executive oversight, as measured by Varieties of Democracy (v2lgotovst). This measure assesses the following hypothetical question, 'if executive branch officials were engaged in unconstitutional, illegal, or unethical activity, how likely is it that a body other than the legislature ... would question or investigate them and issue an unfavourable decision or report?' (Coppedge, 2021, 147). This concept and measure of bureaucratic oversight differs from legislative oversight insofar as the latter focuses on legislative bodies while the former points to government officials embedded within the state bureaucracy who have the institutional power, in principle, to conduct an oversight of the executive.

These non-legislative oversight personnel have a variety of titles—including comptroller general, general prosecutor, inspector general, auditor, or ombudsman—and are embedded throughout various parts of governments.

---

[9] From 2016 to 2019, the judicial constraint score in Poland drops by 0.75 standard deviations; the cumulative effect of the estimate over four years is 0.81 standard deviations.

Bureaucrats monitor budgets, the implementation of government rules, and even the procedures for personnel appointments to ensure executive actions in these areas comply with the rule of law governing the operation of the state. In contrast to judicial and legislative oversight, bureaucratic oversight occurs on a daily basis and rarely makes the news in the way that crucial judicial decisions or legislative proposals garner attention. Thus, bureaucratic constraint, while mostly observed in the negative, is more hidden than other forms of horizontal checks, even in the rare moments when bureaucrats publicly push back against executive behaviours.

That said, perhaps the most brazen form of circumventing bureaucratic constraint is to create a new, parallel state when the existing state apparatus appears to pose too great a constraint on the leader. Patrice Talon, the president of Benin since 2016, has done precisely this. Soon after winning the 2016 election, he 'created in all the most important domains a certain number of agencies, located at the Presidency, and whose prerogatives are the same, if not more, with those of traditional ministries' (Ologou, 2021, 46). These new 'agencies'—with names such as Agency for the Construction of Infrastructures in the Education Sector, the National Agency for Primary Health Care, and the National Agency for the Provision of Potable Water in Rural Areas—not only reported directly to the presidential administration, thus circumventing the cabinet ministries, but were quickly provided government resources traditionally allocated to the ministries they effectively replaced. During Talon's first four years as president, the measure of bureaucratic constraint dropped by roughly one standard deviation—one of the largest decreases in oversight during any democratic leader's tenure in the past three decades.

To examine how party personalism shapes bureaucratic constraint, we follow a similar strategy as before: we compare leaders to each other within countries and thus account for differences between state bureaucracies in different countries.[10] The third estimate in the left plot in Figure 5.1 indicates that ruling party personalism decreases bureaucratic constraint by about 13 per cent of one standard deviation per year. Next, we examine party personalism and bureaucratic oversight when the leader controls the legislature relative to when the ruling party does not have a majority. The last set of estimates in the right plot in Figure 5.1 shows that party personalism reduces bureaucratic constraint by 9 per cent when the leader lacks a legislative majority but decreases by over 25 per cent (of one standard deviation per year) when the leader controls parliament.

Similar to the results for legislative and judicial constraint, we find evidence that ruling party personalism is associated with steep declines in bureaucratic constraint, especially when the ruling party has a legislative majority.

---

[10] We estimate the dynamic panel model, with country fixed effects and two lags of the outcome variable to account for serial correlation, reporting cluster robust standard errors. We adjust for age of democracy, initial level of democracy, and a time trend.

5.2.4 Term Limit Extension Attempts

The evidence we have presented thus far supports our argument that ruling party personalism reduces constraints on the executive, as seen in the legislative, judicial, and bureaucratic arenas. We now turn to an additional indicator related to executive constraints: term limit extension attempts. In contrast to the outcomes we have analysed so far, which are measured using country-expert assessments of institutional sources of executive constraint, the next analysis captures a real-world behavioural manifestation of declining executive constraint: term limit rules constrain leaders by forcing leaders from the chief executive position.

Term limit extensions are perhaps one of the more obvious indicators of an executive effort to expand control. Term limits are a hallmark of many democratic systems, given their role in ensuring regular, institutionalized rotation of power. As one observer writes, '[r]epeated transfers of power demonstrate that change through elections is possible, discouraging coups and other unconstitutional efforts to seize power' (Temin, 2020). In this way, the existence of term limits that prevent leaders from ruling indefinitely is a sign of a healthy democracy. Indeed, they not only enhance the chances of leadership change, but also 'foster horizontal accountability between government branches' (McKie, 2019, 1501). Efforts to extend or dismantle term limits, in contrast, often signals the opposite.

While dictators frequently change the rules of the game to prolong their tenure in power, including by extending term limits, democratic leaders have, at times, also attempted to alter term limit rules to keep themselves in power. The process of dismantling these democratic checks on the power of the leader may entail abolishing term limits altogether or altering the number of terms a leader may serve. Sometimes this takes the form of proposed legislation or changes to the constitution. Or it may be the leader's supporters who demand the change. Philippine President Fidel Ramos' supporters pushed for a constitutional change in 1997 to abolish presidential terms and allow Ramos to run for re-election, for example, though this bid failed when the high court stopped a voter-initiated referendum on the matter (Linden, 1997).

Importantly, we should only observe leaders *attempt* to extend their term when they assess that they have a reasonable chance of getting away with it. An observed attempt is therefore the result of both leader-specific preferences or incentives to alter the rules and the leader's perception that such an attempt will succeed. When leaders believe they may succeed in altering term limits because horizontal checks on their power (including from within their own party) are weak, they will be more likely to try it. By contrast, when leaders view domestic institutional checks on their power—including term limit rules—as credible constraints, they will not attempt to alter the rules. In this way, the failure of an attempt suggests that executive constraints are higher than the leader anticipated, albeit still lower than in environments where no extension is attempted in the first place.

148 THE ORIGINS OF ELECTED STRONGMEN

For these reasons, we focus on term limit extension *attempts*, not just successes, so that we can capture the *negative* effect of executive constraints. Most leaders, most of the time, do not consider altering these rules precisely because they know they will fail. Thus most of the time, these rules constrain leaders, and we do not observe attempts to alter term limits very often.

To evaluate the influence of ruling party personalism on term limit extension attempts, we use data from McKie (2019), which cover the period from 1993 to 2018. Because term limit rules apply to presidential systems with a directly elected chief executive, we limit our analysis to presidential systems. Thus the geographic coverage encompasses regions with presidential governments, with most cases coming from the Americas (46 per cent) and Africa (26 per cent), and fewer from Asia (17 per cent) and Europe (11 per cent). Among presidential democracies during this twenty-five year period, there are only twenty-nine attempts to change term limit rules.

The data on leaders' attempts to alter term limit rules include attempts to abolish limits as well as to extend them. These attempts must have concrete, observed manifestations, such as proposed legislation or a referendum on a constitutional change. The data do not capture leaders' 'floating' the idea. For example, US President Ronald Reagan once backed abolishing presidential term limits, albeit only once he had left office (Molotsky, 1987). And, prior to his election defeat in 2020, Donald Trump teased reporters about seeking a third presidential term (Cilliza, 2019). These types of remarks, which never resulted in concrete proposals to alter term limits, are not recorded in the data as attempts to change term limit rules.

To examine whether ruling party personalism influences the likelihood that a leader will attempt to change term limit rules, we first look at the descriptive patterns. Splitting the sample at the median value of ruling party personalism, we find that when party personalism is high the chances of a term limit attempt (3.5 per cent) is almost twice as high as when party personalism is low (1.8 per cent)—a difference that is statistically significant. Next we test a series of econometric models that allow us to compare the incidence of term limit attempts across different levels of ruling party personalism within the same country, thus accounting for all difference between countries.[11]

Figure 5.A-1 in the Appendix to this chapter reports the results of these tests. A first specification adjusts for the age of the democracy while a second also adjusts for initial level of democracy and the election cycle. This latter variable accounts for the fact that leaders are more likely to attempt term limit changes in election years or the year just prior to a scheduled election. Next we account for the popularity of the leader as well as institutional sources of executive constraint.[12]

---

[11] We test a linear probability model with country and year effects, with clustered robust errors.

[12] The popularity of the leader is a combined measure of the ruling party vote share, ruling party seat share, and most recent presidential vote share. More popular leaders with more partisan legislative support may be more likely to attempt to alter term limits.

A final specification adds the initial level of party populism—using the Varieties of Party data on this concept—to ensure party personalism is not picking up populism. In all specifications, party personalism is associated with a nearly 2 per cent (annual) increase in the likelihood of the incumbent leader attempting to change term limit rules.

Finally, we tested whether the evidence linking party personal to presidential attempts to alter term limits is stronger when the ruling party holds a legislative majority. In tests reported in the online appendix, we find a familiar pattern. When the ruling party has a legislative majority, party personalism boosts attempts by about 6 per cent per year; but when the ruling party does not hold the legislature, party personalism has a negligible effect on term limit attempts.

The results indicate that ruling party personalism increases the likelihood that democratic rulers will attempt to change term limit rules. Whether we interpret this finding as a sign that leaders backed by personalist parties believe they have already accumulated sufficient power to break through institutional constraints on their rule or whether these attempts are simply among many possible steps in the process of leaders dismantling horizontal constraints, the finding indicates that ruling party personalism is harmful to an important institutional check on executive power in presidential systems.

5.3 Conclusion

In this book, we argue that the institutional pathway through which ruling party personalism undermines democracy is via its weakening of executive constraints. This chapter provided strong empirical support consistent with this assertion. In it, we showed that where leaders are backed by personalist parties, executive constraints deteriorate in a variety of domains. Specifically, ruling party personalism lessens the likelihood that leaders will face constraints in the state's legislative, judicial, and bureaucratic institutions. The deterioration of executive constraints brought on by ruling party personalism is even steeper when the party has a legislative majority. This is because personalist parties do little to block their leader's attempts to consolidate power. In essence, they serve to rubber stamp the leader's agenda.

We also find that ruling party personalism elevates the chance that we will observe direct actions on behalf of the leader to expand power, specifically in the form of attempts to change term limits. Efforts to alter term limits, while infrequent in democracies in general, are substantially more likely to occur when the leader is backed by a personalist party.

Taken together, this chapter provides strong evidence that when leaders come to power backed by personalist parties, constraints on the executive are likely to erode. This dismantling of mechanisms of horizontal accountability that occurs—while not indicative of democracy's demise in and of itself—opens the door for leaders to subvert democracy. In this way, this chapter explained the institutional pathway through which ruling party personalism contributes to the undermining of democracy.

5.4 Appendix A: Regression Results

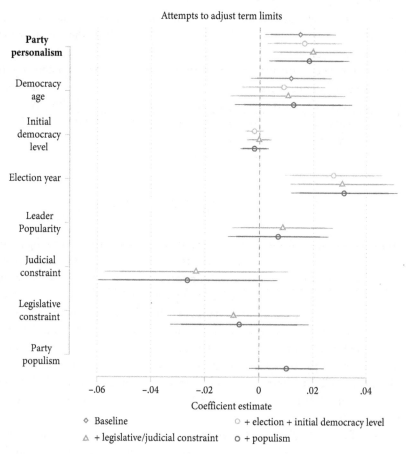

Figure 5.A-1 Ruling party personalism boosts presidential attempts to extend term limits

6

Societal Pathways

This chapter begins where we left off in the last one: ruling party personalism facilitates a leader's efforts to weaken institutional checks on executive powers. As state institutions grow impotent and defanged, a leader's attempts to undermine democracy are more likely to succeed. Yet the effects of ruling party personalism do not stop there. As we show in this chapter, the leadership's anti-democratic actions have far-reaching societal consequences. Importantly, they lessen the chance that leaders of personalist parties will face checks on their rule from below. In this way, ruling party personalism erodes both horizontal and vertical constraints on the leader's power.

In this chapter, we explore the societal pathways through which ruling party personalism facilitates democratic decay. Democracies are exceptional because they provide their citizens with the opportunity to hold their leaders accountable at the ballot box. This bottom-up check provides a critical safeguard against leaders intent on dismantling democracy. When presented with evidence of a leader's anti-democratic actions, citizens have the opportunity to 'throw the bums out'. Yet, as recent history has shown, voters do not always punish such aspiring autocrats. In cases as wide ranging Mackey Sall, Viktor Orban, and Nayib Bukele, voters have re-elected leaders who exhibited anti-democratic behaviours in office. The critical question is: why?

We argue that ruling party personalism creates dynamics that weaken vertical accountability. The actions of personalist leaders make voters more willing to tolerate and accept anti-democratic behaviour, thereby reducing bottom-up resistance to the leader's agenda. First, leaders backed by personalist parties increase polarization. Their rhetoric, but especially their weakening of executive constraints—which we refer to as *attacks on state institutions*—amplifies divisions in the societies they govern. Party supporters, in turn, become more willing to tolerate abuses of power to keep the other side out. Concurrently, the behaviour of these leaders, along with the partisan elite's acceptance and even endorsement of it, shifts supporters' perspective of what is acceptable in a democracy. Seeing little wrong with the leader's conduct, they have little reason to withdraw their support. Notably, the personalist party elite play an important role in facilitating both polarization and norm changes. Because their careers are tightly linked to that of the leader, the elite in personalist parties have a strong incentive to tolerate (and in some instances provide explicit support for) the leader's anti-democratic behaviour, thereby providing critical elite cues to supporters to do the same.

The Origins of Elected Strongmen. Erica Frantz, Andrea Kendall-Taylor, and Joseph Wright, Oxford University Press.
© Erica Frantz, Andrea Kendall-Taylor, and Joseph Wright (2024). DOI: 10.1093/oso/9780198888079.003.0006

152 THE ORIGINS OF ELECTED STRONGMEN

These dynamics were indeed present in the United States during the tenure of President Donald Trump (2016–20). While Trump governed with the support of an established party (the Republican Party), levels of party personalism increased under his leadership, largely given his lack of a prior relationship with or experience in the party. The loyalty of many of Trump's backers (including those in his inner circle) was to Trump rather than the Republican Party, which many of his strongest supporters viewed as weak and corrupt. As Robert Kagan aptly noted in September 2021, 'the movement's passion was for Trump, not the party' (Kagan, 2021).

Although polarization was already high and contributed to Trump's victory in 2016, he undoubtedly generated more of it (Abramowitz and McCoy, 2019). Trump created a new division within society around his own persona, such that personal views of Trump became one of the most divisive issues in the country. Gallup polling on approval ratings for a president by party provides insight into levels of polarization. According to this measure, polarization under Trump increased to such an extent that 2020 was a historically polarized year: the gap in approval of Trump's presidency between Republicans and Democrats was 85 points, greater than at any time previously recorded (Bump, 2021). In other words, Trump, as the leader of an increasingly personalized party, did not just benefit from polarization—he produced it. As greater polarization raised the stakes of holding power, Republican voters grew more willing to accept Trump's anti-democratic actions, reducing the accountability he faced for them.

Meanwhile, Trump's conduct also weakened his supporters' commitment to democratic norms of behaviour. The Republican elite played a critical role in this process, in that their refusal to denounce, and in many cases their endorsement of, Trump's troubling behaviour provided cues to party supporters that all was well for democracy. Although there are myriad examples, we highlight one. When then-President Trump attacked a federal judge who ruled against one of his executive orders on immigration, Republican Party elites implicitly condoned the attacks: one journalist noted '[n]ot a single member of House GOP leadership, nor House Judiciary Committee Chairman Bob Goodlatte (R-Va.), came to [judge] Robart's defense or rebuked Trump. Many senior House Republicans privately feel Trump's comments are counterproductive, but they aren't willing to criticize Trump publicly' (Everett et al., 2017). The more Trump personalized the party, the less willing the elite were to speak out against Trump's conduct for fear of being marginalized or losing influence within the party.

Even Trump's false claim that he had won the 2020 presidential election did not lead to the sort of response from supporters or Republican elites one would anticipate in a healthy democracy. Rather, it paved the way for the insurrection at the US Capitol in January 2021—levied by Trump's backers—which killed five people and injured dozens of law enforcement officers. While multiple factors converged to catalyse the violence, the fact that ruling party elites had spent much of Trump's presidency condoning their leader's norm breaking behaviour likely contributed to the violence.

This chapter examines the societal pathways that link ruling party personalism with democratic backsliding. We begin by asking whether citizens' changing views of democracy might be responsible for weakening vertical constraints on personalist leaders. It could be the case, after all, that citizens who have grown dissatisfied with democracy might support anti-democratic leaders who promise to restore the country to a better time. We draw on our findings from Chapter 2 and a body of recent research to dispel that connection. We then turn to our explanation for how ruling party personalism weakens vertical constraints on a leader, focusing on the role of polarization and changing citizen views of acceptable democratic behaviour.

We discuss polarization first. We argue that personalist leaders' behaviour while in office is divisive for the societies they govern, particularly their attacks on state institutions. This generates concerns about the future of democracy among opponents while hardening supporters' defence of the leader. Though some scholars argue that pre-existing polarization enables the rise of anti-democratic leaders, the evidence we offer tells a more fulsome story. Polarization is not just something that opportunistic leaders leverage for their political benefit. Rather, we argue that leaders themselves *deepen* polarization. Ruling party personalism amplifies this relationship because elites in personalist parties are more likely to endorse the leader's behaviours, hardening supporters' loyalty to the party and deepening their disdain for the opposition, yielding increased polarization.

We then examine the link between ruling party personalism and voters' views of acceptable democratic norms. We argue that personalist leaders' conduct, and especially elites' justification for it, shifts supporters' understanding of what is tolerable in a democracy. Because observing norm changes is difficult in practice, as we discuss below, we focus on a particularly egregious but observable breach of norms: support for election violence. We expect that ruling party personalism increases the chance that supporters will justify the use of violence in elections that they lose. We focus on electoral losses because they provide a good scenario for observing changes in norms, given that in a healthy democracy citizens should not support violence when their party loses an election.

After discussing the link between ruling party personalism and both polarization and norm changes, we provide case studies from Turkey and Brazil to illustrate the underlying dynamics. We then turn to empirical tests of our claims, which use micro- and macro-level data to demonstrate that ruling party personalism both increases social polarization and shifts citizens' views about political violence—two pathways through which ruling party personalism reduces vertical accountability.

154 THE ORIGINS OF ELECTED STRONGMEN

6.1 Are Citizens to Blame for Decreasing Vertical Constraints?

In all political systems, institutional actors constrain the behaviour of leaders. Democracies are unique, however, in that ordinary citizens can do so too. Elections—the defining feature of democratic governance—offer voters the regular opportunity to weigh in on the leader's behaviour. Leaders who act in ways that run counter to popular opinion will lose electoral contests, providing democracies with a pathway of vertical accountability.

It is therefore perhaps surprising that in some instances leaders in democracies who undermine democracy by attacking state institutions while in power win re-election or see large victories for their supporting party during legislative elections. Yet, in several cases across the globe, such as Orban in Hungary or Chavez in Venezuela, norm breaking incumbents have continued to win electoral contests—even elections early in their tenures that were considered free and fair. The absence of negative consequences at the polls for their anti-democratic actions while in office is a clear indicator that vertical constraints have eroded.

Of course not all norm breaking personalist leaders win re-election, as the cases of Trump in the US and Jair Bolsonaro in Brazil illustrate. But even when such leaders lose re-election, it is often by very narrow margins. Trump lost his re-election bid in 2020, for example, by four percentage points. Despite losing, Trump still won over seventy-four million votes—more than any other US presidential candidate except Joe Biden. Likewise, Bolsonaro very narrowly lost his re-election bid in 2022, winning 49.1 per cent of the votes to President Luiz Inacio Lula da Silva's 50.9 per cent.

This begs the question of why? While support for the leader's original victory at the polls might be chalked up to a lack of information regarding the leader's intentions, why voters continue to support the leader after observing the leader's harm to democracy is more perplexing. Is it because these voters do not genuinely support democracy and the system of checks and balances that prevents abuses of power?

While it is tempting to look to a voter's distaste for democracy as providing the answer, the electoral success of personalist parties and their leaders is *not* in fact a product of declining public support for democracy, as we showed in Chapter 2. In our tests reported in the appendix to that chapter, we looked at trends over time in citizen support for democracy and found no evidence that a declining public support for democracy was correlated with ruling party personalism.

This null finding is consistent with recent research, which has unearthed little evidence that attitudes towards democracy are responsible for fuelling the contemporary wave of democratic backsliding (Tai et al., 2022).[1] Moreover, additional

---

[1] While initial research into this question suggests declining mass support for democracy is correlated with backsliding (Claassen, 2020), this more recent study shows that, once measurement

studies underscore that about 90 per cent of the world's population sees democracy as the best form of government, a preference that has remained steady over the last twenty-five years or so (Anderson et al., 2021). Although people hold divergent and occasionally inconsistent understandings of what it means, they nonetheless report support for democracy (Kirsch and Welzel, 2019; Kruse et al., 2019). Likewise, regional research using surveys from the Americas finds that the vast majority of citizens oppose anti-democratic actions (Albertus and Grossman, 2021), just as surveys from Africa indicate that citizens strongly support presidential term limits and disapprove of efforts to extend them (Dulani, 2021). While it is certainly possible that some elected strongmen retain office because sizable sectors of the population have become disenchanted with democracy, the evidence does not suggest that this is a widespread trend.

Instead, we argue that today's wave of democratic decline is occurring amid strong voter support for democracy. Put differently, citizens are increasingly finding themselves supporting would-be authoritarians even while holding pro-democracy views. As Chiopris et al. (2021a, 29) write, '[e]ven voters who are opposed to authoritarianism may, unwittingly, promote backsliding'. It is possible, in other words, for voters to support both an incumbent power grab and democracy at the same time (Grossman et al., 2022).

So what accounts for continued voter support for leaders demonstrating anti-democratic actions? There are a variety of reasons that have been suggested in the literature. We focus on two, though others may also be at play: (1) polarization and (2) shifting views of acceptable democratic norms. Both of these factors provide insight into why leaders backed by personalist parties are able to erode vertical constraints on their power, reducing the resistance they face to their efforts to degrade democracy.[2] While we concur with the broader literature that polarization and shifting norms are important, we propose that these factors, by themselves, cannot explain weakening vertical constraint. Instead, we posit, parties explain why some leaders and their elite supporters have incentives to endogenously boost polarization and alter citizens' norms about acceptable democratic behaviour. Thus, the origins of this mass political behaviour lies, in part, in the types of parties that rule.

6.2 Polarization

The first factor that helps explain why party personalism weakens vertical constrains on leaders is *affective* polarization, which we define as individual-level

---

uncertainty is incorporated into the estimate of democratic support, the relationship between public views of democracy and changes in levels of democracy disappears.

[2] Motivated reasoning likely underlies both of these dynamics, such that supporters have an incentive to seek out information and evaluate evidence consistent with their existing beliefs and corresponding to their party's position (Singer, 2023).

distance in relative attitude towards a partisan incumbent and a partisan opponent, or—more simply—the tendency of partisans to like members of their own party and dislike members of the opposing one (Iyengar et al., 2012).[3] When these relative affective attitudes change for many citizens, macro—or mass—polarization results. A wide body of research shows that such polarization often accompanies democratic backsliding (McCoy and Somer, 2019; Svolik, 2019; Chiopris et al., 2021b; Haggard and Kaufman, 2021; Horz, 2021; Miller, 2021; Orhan, 2021). In their study of sixteen cases of democratic backsliding since the onset of the 'third wave' of democratization (1974–2019), for example, Haggard and Kaufman (2021) find that all cases had significant histories of polarization or recent periods when it spiked significantly.

Polarization weakens vertical constraints on leaders because it compels voters to tolerate a leader's abuses of power if it means keeping the other party out of office (Svolik, 2020).[4] Surveys from Latin America, for example, show that individuals are more likely to turn a blind eye to democratic erosion when the party they support is in power (Singer, 2023). Polarization thus changes voters' perceptions of the costs of their party losing office. When polarization is high, the incumbent's supporters understand that punishing the incumbent for undemocratic behaviour by not voting for them amounts to supporting a challenger they detest, increasing tolerance for democratic manipulation. In this way, citizens can continue to support democracy, but their disdain for the 'other' camp grows, making them more willing to accept abuses of power perpetrated by the leader of the party they support.

Ruling party personalism increases levels of polarization in society. For one, the rhetoric of personalist party leaders often inflames societal divisions. For example, Brazil's Bolsonaro—a president who was elected with the support of a small party he joined the year of the election and then ditched shortly afterwards—openly disparaged democracy and extolled the virtues of rule by the military during his 2018 presidential campaign. Such rhetoric ratcheted up polarization and triggered violence (primarily perpetrated by his supporters) even before he assumed power. That said, we posit that we should be most likely to observe polarization when the leader backs their rhetoric with concrete action. For this reason, we focus our discussion on the ways in which polarization intensifies following *attacks on state institutions*.

Put simply, a leader's attacks on state institutions are divisive. First and foremost, they increase the stakes of political office. The opposition sees such attacks as threatening the quality of their democracy. They, therefore, react with shock,

---

[3] For simplicity, throughout this chapter, we use the term polarization to refer to *affective polarization* among voters, specifically.

[4] We note, however, that there are many difficulties involved in accurately capturing public attitudes about democratic transgressions (Ahmed, 2022).

appalled by the leader's actions and fearful for the future of their country's democracy.

Conversely, supporters of the leader get in line with the leader's agenda. They respond to opponents' concerns over democracy defiantly, digging their heels in and hardening their stance. The opposition's criticism may itself even work to help the incumbent, by rallying supporters and increasing their disdain for the opposition.

Further amplifying division, supporters of backsliding leaders may also engage in a form of 'whataboutism' when presented with evidence that their party's leader is undermining democracy, doubling down with counter-accusations.[5] 'Whataboutism' entails motivated reasoning that produces concrete (real or imagined) examples of *other* parties' egregious behaviour, a form of implicit counter-accusation mixed with either 'differential treatment of similar behaviour' by partisans or making the case that one behaviour is the moral equivalent of another. For example, when Hungarian justice minister Judit Varga attempted to defend Orban's attacks on the rule of law, she cited supposedly similar moves by other EU countries, such as the abolition of referenda in the Netherlands, to justify changes to the law that criminalized social media outlets that were critical of the government (Pech and Bard, 2022, 77). By conjuring negative examples of the *other*'s behaviour, the motivated reasoning that underpins 'whataboutism' boosts negative attitudes towards the *other* party. The result is intensified societal divisions.

In short, incumbent behaviours that degrade democracy deepen individual-level polarization by increasing negative affect towards other parties among incumbent opponents and supporters. While it is natural to expect opposition voters to view the incumbent in a more dim light in the face of democratic subversion, incumbent supporters are likely to view the opposing party more negatively at such times too. In this way, personalist attacks on the state increase polarization, widening the relative affect of opponents *and* supporters towards the other group.[6]

---

[5] In popularizing the term 'whataboutism', Lucas (2008) writes, 'Soviet propagandists during the cold war were trained in a tactic that their western interlocutors nicknamed 'whataboutism'. Any criticism of the Soviet Union (Afghanistan, martial law in Poland, imprisonment of dissidents, censorship) was met with a 'What about...' (apartheid South Africa, jailed trade-unionists, the Contras in Nicaragua, and so forth).'

[6] The individual-level behavioural link between incumbent-led democratic subversion and negative affect among partisans, which manifests as polarization, is similar to a 'backlash' effect where partisans—via motivated reasoning—strengthen their pre-existing beliefs when presented with evidence that is contrary to those beliefs (e.g., Taber and Lodge, 2006; Guess and Coppock, 2020): both 'backlash' theories and our argument rely on individuals' motivated reasoning. However, we focus specifically on the issue of incumbent leaders' attacks on state institutions, which—as demonstrated in the previous chapter—are a key mechanism in democratic backsliding. Thus, leaders who attack the state to subvert democracy may produce a 'backlash' insofar as information about this *political behaviour of leaders towards the state* leads to polarization. Further, while some studies posit that voters employ motivated reasoning to accentuate opposition party elites' anti-democratic behaviour but

Ruling party personalism intensifies these dynamics by incentivizing personalist party elites to back the leaders' anti-democratic behaviour. Top-down messaging from personalist leaders and party elites makes the attacks even more polarizing by casting doubt on detractors and providing partisan cues that frame the leader's actions as 'normal' in a healthy democracy. This further hardens the stance of personalist party supporters and deepens the societal divide. Personalist leaders—lacking a party elite that will restrain or temper their actions—justify their behaviours combatively, splitting voters into two camps: those who support them and everyone else.

Elites in personalist parties provide partisan cues that fuel and reinforce this. Partisan cues play a critical role in influencing citizens' view of actions that threaten democracy. When elites in power push back against democratic norms that constrain them, it gives supporters 'a clear partisan cue about whether to support such norms' (Kingzette et al., 2021, 665). In surveys from Indonesia, for example, even when respondents reported strong support for democracy, partisan cues swayed their opinions and moved them towards anti-democratic positions (Fossati et al., 2021). As Clayton et al. (2021, 5) write: 'Just as elites can shape policy views along partisan lines, elite rhetoric can shape normative beliefs in core democratic values such as confidence in elections and support for peaceful transfers of power'. Indeed, this was the case in the US and Brazil ahead of their elections in 2020 and 2022, respectively.

Ruling party personalism increases the chance that elites will propagate such partisan cues. As this book has shown, personalist party elites lack the capacity and incentive to push back against a leader's efforts to get rid of constraints to their rule. The calculus of elites is simple: they have little to gain and much to lose from condemning the leader's actions. To stay in the leader's good books, elites in personalist parties instead are likely to endorse the leader's behaviours and frame them as being compatible with a healthy democracy. For these reasons, when leaders backed by personalist parties attack the state, the resulting polarization is even greater.

To summarize, personalist leaders' behaviour while in office—specifically their attacks on state institutions—divide society into two political camps: those who support the leader and everyone else. When opponents of the leader sound the alarm bell that the leader's actions are putting democracy under threat, supporters of the leader go on the defensive, deepening their commitment to the leader's rule.

Ruling party personalism exacerbates this polarizing effect. Leaders of personalist parties—unencumbered by their elites—do little to bridge the societal divide, and if anything, they go to great pains to intensify it as a means of securing their

---

downplay their own party elites' poor behaviour (e.g., Claassen and Ensley, 2016; Carey et al., 2022), this sort of 'downplaying' of one's party's actions goes hand in hand with increased negative affect towards the other party.

political goals. Elites in personalist parties—lacking the capacity or incentive to push back against the leader and having enabled the behaviour in the first place— usually defend it as 'normal'. In this way, they provide critical messaging to party supporters to dig in their heels.

This perspective differs from that of the bulk of existing literature in linking polarization to democratic backsliding, the latter tending to see polarization as exogenously determined. Instead, we put forward the argument that polarization is driven from above (Nalepa and Cinar, 2021). This insight is consistent with McCoy and Somer (2019), who note that 'enterprising political actors who understand the power of polarizing tactics often build on existing cleavages in a society to simplify and emphasize differences and help to build politically winning coalitions' (237).[7] We likewise see polarization as a strategy and consequence of opportunistic leaders seeking to advance their political ambitions. In Hungary, for example, Korosenyi (2013, 15) observes that 'polarization of citizens' preferences ... is not simply something given (exogenously) to parties, but is the result of the strategies of the parties and their leaders; that is, it is an endogenous factor'. Growing polarization, in turn, decreases the chance that personalist parties and their leaders will face vertical checks for such behaviours.

6.3 Shifting Democratic Norms

The second factor that helps explain why ruling party personalism weakens vertical constraints on a leader is norm changes, or shifts in supporters' views of acceptable democratic behaviours. Democracy requires more than rules on paper to function. As Fossati et al. (2021, 11) write, '[w]hile democratic regimes provide formal checks and balances to constrain the powers of executives, such institutional arrangements ultimately rest on the informal social norms that underpin them, as their survival is contingent on whether such norms are widely shared and valued by both elites and the citizenry'. Key norms critical to a healthy democracy include respecting election outcomes, tolerating dissent, and treating opponents with civility (Levitsky and Ziblatt, 2018).

That said, understandings of what these norms are can vary from one individual to the next, often based on political affiliation (Carey et al., 2019). Importantly, changing political circumstances can lead to changes in these understandings, particularly in response to political messaging (Bergan, 2021). Indeed, partisanship often shapes how citizens perceive real-world conditions (Zaller, 1992; Slothuus

---

[7] Note that our view of polarization as endogenous to incumbents' attacks on the state does not rule out the possibility that elected leaders leverage existing polarization to 'get away' with anti-democratic behaviour.

and Bisgaard, 2021), and this partisan lens often results from elite cues offered to partisan supporters (Bisgaard and Slothuus, 2018).

We argue that supporters' perspectives of what constitutes healthy behaviour in a democracy are often endogenous to the leader's (and the party elites') actions. We draw this insight from research showing that incumbents' anti-democratic behaviour can increase supporters' tolerance for future similar behaviour (Grillo and Prato, 2023). Citizens can have context-dependent preferences, such that their positions on challenges to democratic norms change in response to incumbent conduct. For this reason, even when citizens value democracy and democratic norms of behaviour, incumbents who degrade democracy can remain popular. Grillo and Prato (2023) argue that this is particularly likely when leaders lack a strong ideological and programmatic agenda, which is often the case with party personalism. In slowly chipping away at democracy, leaders gradually lower their supporters' expectations of how they should behave such that anti-democratic behaviours do not disappoint supporters, and backing for their rule remains strong.

According to this perspective, leaders challenge democratic norms through conduct that threatens democracy and then supporters decide whether to continue to back them. The response of supporters, in turn, informs leaders' decisions over whether to escalate their anti-democratic efforts. While most citizens are averse to challenges to democratic norms of behaviour, this research illustrates that their perspective of what is acceptable is endogenous to the behaviour of the leadership.

As such, we see how citizens could support democracy but also continue to back a leader who seeks to undermine it. Even where incumbent supporters value democracy in principle, they may be unlikely to view their party's actions to subvert democracy as sufficiently troubling for them to withdraw their support. This is consistent with work by Grossman et al. (2022), who find that some voters may support democracy but not see a leadership power grab as incompatible with it, given that the leader was popularly elected and had the people's backing. In this way, as discussed earlier, voters who are committed to democratic values can support would-be autocrats (Chiopris et al., 2021b, 2). By shifting their supporters' reference point for the sorts of behaviours acceptable in a democracy, personalist leaders' behaviour weakens vertical accountability in the wake of further actions that threaten democracy.

Importantly, this shift in supporter perspective is often reinforced by top-down messaging from the government and party elite justifying the leader's actions and selling them as being compatible with democracy. As we discussed in the last section, elite cues can be highly influential in shaping citizen perspectives of democratic norms (Clayton et al., 2021; Fossati et al., 2021; Kingzette et al., 2021). When elites fall in line and endorse a leader's anti-democratic conduct, it sends a critical message to supporters that nothing is wrong. Ruling party personalism increases the chance that elites will provide such partisan cues. Reluctant to challenge the leader in any way, personalist party elites instead seek to validate the leader's troubling behaviour and justify it as 'normal'. As such, ruling party personalism should exacerbate the shifts in supporters' views of acceptable democratic behaviours that we see.

Note that in our discussion we focus on the attitudes and beliefs of the leader's partisan supporters, given that they are the portion of the electorate responsible for getting the leader elected in the first place. Defeating the leader (or their party) come re-election time requires that at least some of these individuals defect from the leader's party or otherwise withdraw their support.

6.4 Case Studies

We turn now to two case studies that illustrate how the actions of personalist leaders and the parties that back them lead to changes that erode vertical constraints on their power. In the case of President Erdoğan in Turkey, rising polarization and the resulting weakening of vertical constraints help explain his successful re-election bids since his party first won the election in 2002. Weakening vertical constraints on his power contributed to Erdoğan's successful efforts to dismantle democracy in Turkey. In Brazil, Bolsonaro's leadership also polarized society and changed his supporters' views of acceptable democratic norms. Although he was ultimately held accountable at the ballot box, we use this case study to illustrate how these personalist leaders are able to change norms. Because pinning down norm change is difficult, we focus on an instance where a personalist leader loses an election, since changes in norms should be particularly apparent in such a circumstance. As this case makes clear, even when personalist leaders and their parties lose an election, they can still generate dynamics that are harmful for democracy.

6.4.1 Turkey under Reccep Tayyip Erdoğan

Reccep Tayyip Erdoğan came to power in 2003 as prime minister of Turkey (and subsequently became president in 2014) with the backing of the Justice and Development Party (the AKP)—a party he helped establish a few years previously. The electoral success of this new personalist party was facilitated, in part, by an economic crisis in 2001 that undermined the credibility and attractiveness of many of the more established, centrist parties in Turkey (Aydin-Duzgit, 2019). The AKP also received strong support from segments of Turkish society that had previously been marginalized, particularly political Islamists. In the earliest years of AKP rule, Turkish democracy remained secure. The rise of the AKP was even perceived favourably in the West, where its record of democratic reforms was viewed as providing a possible model for other Muslim-majority countries.

162   THE ORIGINS OF ELECTED STRONGMEN

Over time, however, there were signs that trouble was on the horizon, ranging from the 2010 referendum that amended the constitution to give the executive greater control over judicial appointments to the 2013 crackdown on anti-government protesters at Gezi Park. After a failed coup in 2016, Erdoğan's efforts to consolidate control and undermine democracy grew more overt. The government declared a state of emergency, began to rule by decree, purged the government of those whose loyalty Erdoğan questioned, and pushed through a referendum (under threat of repression) that further changed the constitution to substantially increase Erdoğan's power. That year marked the onset of authoritarianism in Turkey in the eyes of many observers (Freedom House, 2021d).

Erdoğan's behaviours in the years leading up to this point had cultivated his supporters' acquiescence. Rather than leaving the AKP or punishing it at the polls for seeking to consolidate power, supporters stood firm. As one observer wrote in 2016: 'The awkward fact for Erdogan's critics is that his popularity has not been hurt by his authoritarianism' (de Bellaigue, 2016). While there are certainly many underlying reasons for this, Erdoğan's attacks on state institutions (and the messaging used to justify it) were influential in entrenching AKP support. The critical question, then, is why did so many Turkish voters continue to support Erdoğan, despite his increasingly clear, quite brazen efforts to dismantle Turkish democracy?

Polarization of Turkey's political landscape holds part of the answer. Since Erdoğan and the AKP came to power in 2002, polarization in Turkey has increased dramatically. Such polarization and the rising stakes of holding office, in turn, have made AKP party supporters more tolerant (if not supportive) of anti-democratic measures to safeguard the AKP's hold on power. This is not to say that Erdoğan created the polarization in Turkey. The seeds of Turkey's polarization were already present before Erdoğan and the AKP came to power. Reforms in the 1920s that had sought to remove religion from public life, for example, had fomented a political and cultural divide between secularist and Islamist camps. But while this and other fissures predate Erdoğan, they were not politically relevant or decisive prior to his assumption of power. It was Erdoğan and the AKP who brought these divisions to the political fore and amplified them.

Erdoğan and the AKP stoked polarization as a way to strengthen their core base of support. Erdoğan used elections, in particular, as an opportunity to stoke divisions and galvanize votes. As Keyman (2014, 29) notes, 'Since 2002, every election that the AKP party won resulted in increasing polarization in terms of secularism, ethnicity, and religion'. Erdoğan instrumentalized polarization. According to Keyman (2014, 29), 'He [Erdoğan] preferred to act in a way that made polarization beneficial to his campaign'. Observers point to Turkey's 2007 elections as an important marker in Turkey's trajectory towards polarization. In this election, the AKP capitalized on feelings of 'victimhood' among large parts of the population who felt alienated and discriminated against by the secular state establishment. Moreover, resistance from the secularist establishment fuelled the AKP's efforts. Secularists inside the Turkish military and judiciary took action to try and prevent the AKP from winning the presidency. According to Aydin-Duzgit (2019, 23), 'This secular resistance ... provided fertile ground for the AKP's polarizing rhetoric to flourish and resonate in the broader society'. The success that Erdoğan had with such polarizing rhetoric and actions in the 2007 election—the AKP won 47 per cent of the vote, the largest share for a single party since elections in 1957—encouraged him and the AKP to replicate this approach in subsequent elections.

Beyond elections, Erdoğan's attempts to expand control also fuelled polarization. As Aydin-Duzgit (2019, 23) writes, 'starting with the 2010 constitutional referendum, the AKP's efforts to consolidate its power over state institutions and crack down on the opposition have been a primary driver of polarization'. According to the author, 'As the AKP's dominance has grown since the late 2000s, its own authoritarian behavior has largely driven further polarization. The problem of constant electioneering, the rise of majoritarianism, an erosion of democratic institutions, and a polarized and unfree media landscape have further deepened Turkey's divisions' (Aydin-Duzgit, 2019, 18). The failed coup in 2016 provides a particularly poignant example. Erdoğan used this failed coup to foster an 'everyone is against us' mentality. This 'us' versus 'them' frame has been effective in Erdoğan's and the AKP's efforts to galvanize support. Moreover, as Erdoğan has been able to centralize power, polarization in Turkey has taken on a more personalized form. According to Aydin-Duzgit (2019, 25), 'With Erdogan now wielding more formal and informal power than ever, polarization has become increasingly personalized and defined by support for or hatred of the president'. This dynamic—the personalization of polarization—is often observed in personalist settings, as illustrated by the case of Trump and his personally polarizing effect on the American public discussed earlier.

Intensified polarization in Turkey, in turn, made the stakes of holding office for AKP supporters tremendously high, incentivizing them to stick with the Erdoğan government even in the face of anti-democratic behaviour. Polarization 'nurtured rigidly loyal AKP constituencies and new elite supporters who were ... ready to tolerate—or, in the case of the elites, implement—the party's illiberal policies' (McCoy et al., 2018, 32). Turkish scholar Murat Somer agrees. The AKP got away with its anti-democratic moves because, 'polarized and captive constituencies in civil society and politics were willing to overlook and sometimes actively support these policies' (Somer, 2019, 45).

6.4.2 Brazil under Jair Bolsonaro

In January 2023, seven days after the inauguration of Brazilian President Luiz Inacio 'Lula' da Silva, thousands of his supporters stormed the country's federal representative institutions. The events were eerily reminiscent of the attack on the US Capitol two years earlier. The assailants similarly claimed that Brazil's 2022 elections were 'stolen' and 'rigged'—cues manufactured by outgoing President Jair Bolsonaro and propagated by partisan elites.

Even before the election, ex-president Bolsonaro, his son, and Bolsonaro's leading congressional supporters took to social media to craft a persistent message of electronic voting machine fraud. For example, the personal accounts of elite supporters such as Carla Zembelli, Bia Kicis, and Felipe Barros each generated over one million social media interactions pertaining to vote fraud before the 2022 election (Ruediger, 2022). The ruling personalist party leader's attempts to undermine the election, even well before the election itself, were amplified by loyal party elites.

The key question is: how did Brazil—the world's fourth largest democracy— find itself facing such a critical democratic test nearly four decades after replacing its twenty-one-year military dictatorship? We suggest that heightened party personalism in Brazil under Bolsonaro produced changes in Bolsonaro's supporters' views of what behaviours were acceptable in a democracy, culminating in their violent attempt to overthrow their newly elected democratic government.

Bolsonaro entered office in January 2019 essentially as an independent, lacking any meaningful connection to any existing political party. He joined a small party, the Social Liberal Party (PSL), the year of the election and then ditched it shortly afterwards. As Hunter and Power (2019) describe, Bolsonaro joined the 'party for rent' in 2018 'merely to qualify for a place on the presidential ballot' and understanding 'he would have full operational control' within a party 'dominated by inexperienced newcomers elected on his [Bolsonaro's] coattails'. Under Bolsonaro, incumbent party personalism increased considerably in Brazil.

Like Trump, Bolsonaro was a polarizing figure. Even prior to his election, his rhetoric was inflammatory. In 1999, Bolsonaro called for President Fernando Henrique Cardoso to be shot by firing squad as a punishment for privatizations (Meredith, 2018). Bolsonaro regularly proffered praise of the country's former dictatorship and derogatory comments relating to women, race, and human rights.

Beyond the rhetoric, his actions in office were divisive, increasing polarization in an already polarized society. Indeed, there is widespread consensus that levels of polarization grew in Brazil under Bolsonaro's tenure.

Critically, Bolsonaro and the elites around him regularly justified their attacks on state institutions. As with Trump, there are myriad examples. For instance, when Bolsonaro requested the Senate to impeach judges who were investigating fraud among his family members, Bolsonaro accused the judges of 'going beyond constitutional limits with actions' and pointed to a constitutional provision that allows the legislature to sack judges who have been convicted of crimes (Álvares and de Sousa, 2021). In doing so, Bolsonaro sent a message to his supporters that this sort of behaviour—impeaching contrarian judges who had never been indicted much less convicted of crimes—is business as usual in a democracy. Bolsonaro's assault on the country's electoral institutions and the narratives he proffered to undermine their legitimacy also tarnished his supporters' confidence in elections and support for a peaceful transfer of power. Prior to the 2022 election, Bolsonaro recognized the possibility of suspending it if there were 'something abnormal' in the process. He also made accusations about a 'secret room' within the Superior Electoral Court (TSE), suggesting electoral officials could manipulate results. The *New York Times* examined hundreds of hours of Bolsonaro's interviews, speeches, and weekly livestreams and thousands of his social-media posts to map his efforts over eight years to criticize or question Brazil's voting system (Nicas et al., 2022). It concluded that Bolsonaro had 'built a narrative of fraudulent elections based on inaccuracies, out-of-context reports, circumstantial evidence, conspiracy theories and downright falsehoods', noting also how such claims were amplified by the political elite, including members of Brazil's Congress.

These elite cues appear to have had an effect. For example, one supporter, a police sergeant, was quoted as saying, '"exceptional actions" are needed to save the country: "This is the only way to fix the system. One cannot make omelettes without breaking some eggs"' (International Crisis Group, 2022, 15). In the run-up to the election, three-quarters of Bolsonaro's supporters told pollsters they had little to no faith in Brazil's election system (Nicas and Spigariol, 2023). When Bolsonaro lost, it was therefore unsurprising that so many doubted the results. By tarnishing his supporter's faith in the election and altering what they viewed as acceptable in a democracy, Bolsonaro set the stage for Brazil's Capitol Riot.

In January 2023, in the immediate aftermath of the attacks, a Brazilian Supreme Court justice asserted that Bolsonaro's past questioning of Brazil's election system and his attacks on Brazil's institutions, including the Supreme Court, 'may have contributed, in a very relevant way, to the occurrence of criminal and terrorist acts', including the storming of government buildings (Nicas and Spigariol, 2023).

Though many supporters of democracy expressed relief that Bolsonaro had lost the election and actually left office, the violence that erupted on his departure illustrates how supporters' norms had changed under Bolsonaro's tenure. And although Bolsonaro was ultimately held accountable at the ballot box, the dynamics he had set in motion created real uncertainty about the future of Brazilian democracy. Sizable sectors of the Brazilian population continue to see Bolsonaro as the rightful winner. Following the Capitol Riot, for example, surveys showed that 40 per cent of Brazilians thought Bolsonaro had been robbed of victory (Gortazar, 2023).

We consider these relationships empirically in the section that follows.

6.5 Empirics

To summarize our expectations, we anticipate that ruling party personalism will weaken vertical constraints on the leadership, specifically by ratcheting up polarization and shifting supporters' understandings of acceptable democratic norms of behaviour. We test these expectations next, starting with polarization.

6.5.1 Does Ruling Party Personalism Boost Polarization?

Our argument is that personalist parties do not just capitalize on existing polarization, they manufacture it—to the detriment of the societies they govern. Beyond the cases of Turkey and the US discussed earlier, examples of this dynamic abound. In Poland, for example, the Law and Justice Party (PiS)—a highly personalist party dominated by its co-founder Jarosław Kaczyński—entered office in 2005. Since then, the quality of Polish democracy has declined. Some observers of Polish politics view rising polarization as an important factor in facilitating the country's democratic deterioration (Applebaum, 2018). PiS sought to stoke divisions in society to consolidate control and expand its influence. More specifically, the party created a new cleavage in Polish politics—'liberalism vs. solidarism', or the pitting of the beneficiaries of the post-1989 economic and political transformation against those who felt that they had experienced a decline in their economic well-being or their social status. As Tworzecki (2019, 97) explains:

> The lack of strong underlying cleavages [in Poland] indicates the polarization was not bottom up. Instead ... polarization was driven from the top down by a segment of the political class that donned the cloak of radical populist anti-establishmentarianism to gain popular support, win an election, and rewrite the constitutional rules of the game to its own benefit.

To empirically evaluate our expectation that personalist leaders and their parties increase polarization, we use both macro- and micro-level polarization data. The former enable us to look at whether incumbents' anti-democratic actions are associated with increased mass polarization, while the latter allow us to see whether citizens respond to information about such actions by exhibiting increased polarization.

Our measure of macro-level polarization comes from Coppedge (2021) (v2cacamps). It is based on country experts' assessments of the 'extent to which political differences affect social relationships beyond political discussions' (224). Conceptually, 'societies are highly polarized if supporters of opposing political camps are reluctant to engage in friendly interactions, for example, in family functions, civic associations, their free time activities and workplaces' (224). This

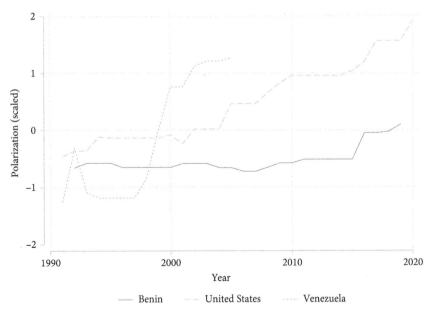

Figure 6.1 Polarization in Benin, United States, and Venezuela

measure captures the key feature of affective polarization, namely the relative distance between citizens' attitudes towards their own party and those in an opposing 'political camp'. The advantage of this measure lies in its geographic and temporal reach. It covers all of the years for which we have original party personalism data (1991–2020) for 107 democracies across the globe.

Figure 6.1 illustrates trends in macro-level polarization using this measure in three countries in different regions of the world: Benin, the United States, and Venezuela. The horizontal axis displays the year while the vertical axis shows the scaled level of polarization in each country for each year.[8] For all three countries, polarization increased over time. Identifying the specific years in which polarization rises, however, is instructive.

In Benin, for example, polarization was slightly below average and stable for the first twenty-five years or so of multi-party democracy. Observers report that during this time, while the party system had a 'low degree of institutionalization and high fragmentation', 'polarization is very low in ideological terms and severe confrontations between parties are rare' (Stiftung, 2018, 12). This changed, however, with Patrice Talon's 2016 election to the presidency. Talon—who had won the contest as an independent—went on to govern with the support of the Progressive Union, a group of twenty parties supportive of Talon that had joined forces in 2019.

---

[8] The trend line for Venezuela stops in 2005, the last year in which the Chavez government is still coded 'democratic' as of 1 January.

Talon was a divisive figure from the start of his presidency, having fallen out with his predecessor Boni Yayi (whose presidential campaigns Talon had once helped finance) in 2012. This is reflected in the jump in polarization that occurred after his election.

In the US, recent presidential election years of 2008, 2016, and 2020 (as well as the 1994 legislative election that marked the ascendancy of the Republican Party in southern states) all boosted polarization. But the largest increases in polarization were actually seen to occur in the first years after an election (in 2005 and in 2017). While the uptick in polarization in 2005 largely reflected divisions over the 'War on Terror' and the US occupations of Afghanistan and Iraq, Trump—the most personalist president in recent US history—undoubtedly stoked further polarization in 2017.

Finally, the Venezuelan trend in polarization shows two big increases—one in 1992 and a second in 1999–2000—both of which mark the rise of Hugo Chavez. In 1992, Chavez unsuccessfully attempted a coup, and that same year—while he was still in prison—his supporters attempted a second coup. Seven years later, Chavez successfully won power in a fair and free election, setting off one of the steepest increases in polarization seen in any country in the past three decades.

In addition to this expert-coded macro-data on polarization, we analyse individual-level survey data from the Comparative Study of Election Systems (CSES), which includes over a hundred surveys from democracies in forty-eight countries over two decades between 1996 and 2016. These surveys contain respondents' affective ratings of different political parties, including the party for which respondents vote. While these responses likely capture voters' feelings towards party elites, the ratings should still be seen as closely related to voters' feelings towards parties' rank-and-file members (Gidron et al., 2020). Following the extant literature, we operationalize affective polarization as the difference between partisans' feelings towards their own party versus its opponents (Iyengar et al., 2012; Reiljan, 2020). This operationalization captures the relative liking for one's own party and dislike for other parties, while incorporating the intensity of feelings towards different parties. Each component of the polarization measure is a ten-point feeling thermometer; thus, calculating the difference yields a twenty-point scale of individual-level affective polarization.[9]

The advantage of the survey data on polarization is two-fold. First, we propose a mechanism that occurs, at least initially, at the micro-level: *individuals* become more polarized and this translates into macro-polarization as more voters increase their relative partisan affect—either liking their own party more or disliking other parties more intensely. Second, because the micro-data allow us to link each respondent to a specific political party we can examine the extent of

---

[9] For econometric tests using this outcome variable, we rescale on (0,1) to allow testing a generalized linear model that accounts for the bounded nature of the outcome.

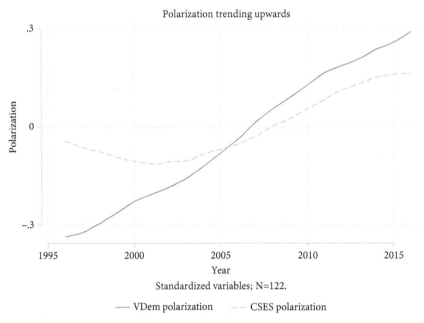

Figure 6.2 Macro- and micro-polarization trends

polarization for voters supporting different parties in the same country, allowing us to analyse whether polarization is higher among personalist party supporters than other voters.

Figure 6.2 shows the temporal trends in the polarization measures for the forty-eight countries in the CSES sample. The plot compares the V-Dem measure of macro-polarization with the average level of polarization for each survey year in CSES data. The polarization trend in the V-Dem data shows an increase almost every year over this two-decade period, and the trend line in the CSES survey data shows an increase from the early 2000s. Both sources therefore indicate growing polarization over time.

The CSES contains multiple waves for each country, allowing us to test whether the two measures are highly correlated over time *within* countries. Again using the survey average (or country-year mean) level of micro-polarization as the CSES measure, we find that, after accounting for fixed country differences, the two measures are positively correlated. In short, while each measure has its strengths and weaknesses, the fact that they correlate with one another over time within countries is reassuring. Moving beyond this descriptive data, we next test some empirical models. We begin with the micro-level data.

Micro-Polarization. Mass polarization stems from partisans in the electorate either liking their party more intensely or, as often as not, *disliking* opposition

170   THE ORIGINS OF ELECTED STRONGMEN

parties and affiliated groups more energetically. We cannot observe mass polarization into competing political camps unless individual partisans become more polarized (Druckman and Levendusky, 2019). In this sense, negative partisanship is simply one component of a larger concept of micro-polarization. If democratically elected leaders backed by personalist parties strategically boost polarization, and at least in part do so by their attacks on state institutions, then we should observe this occurring not only at the macro-level, but also among individual voters. In this section, we examine whether government attacks on the state are related to individual-level polarization.

To test this proposition with the CSES data, we measure affective polarization as the distance between liking one's own party and the average dislike of other parties.[10] We estimate specifications with individual demographic covariates: age, sex, marital status, employment, union membership, income level, urban residency, and education level. We also adjust for self-reported identification as a left-wing or right-wing ideological voter. We do so for two reasons. First, we do not want our measures of party attachments to simply pick up ideology. Second, because ideological voters tend to have strong attachments to parties, they are more likely to be polarized, such that these identities make a useful comparison for understanding the magnitude of the relationship between party attachments and polarization. These individual-level variables are indexed by i, c, y because they vary across respondents (i), country (c), and survey year (y).

The treatment variable is incumbent attacks on the state. To operationalize the concept of 'attacks on the state', we look at incumbent attacks on the judiciary. We focus on the judiciary for a number of reasons. First, the judiciary is a state institutional body that has the potential to constrain executive behaviour, particularly when the leader attempts to undermine democracy. Building on the premise of the previous chapter, we want to investigate whether attacks on institutional (or horizontal) checks on the executive breed polarization. Second, for incumbent attacks on the state to polarize voters, citizens must observe these attacks. That is, individuals must have information that the leader has, in fact, done something. Incumbent attacks on the judiciary tend to be newsworthy and thus highly visible to the public. For example, leaders' attempts to undermine judicial independence in Pakistan (2007), Poland (2017–19), and Israel (2023) have not only been highly visible but have generated mass protests, magnifying the issue in public discourse. And, far from concealing his attack on the court, Salvadoran President Najib Bukele broadcast to his Twitter audience his purge of five incumbent Supreme Court justices in 2021. Further, the behaviour of the leader towards the courts can typically be attributed to the leader—and not to some other actor—making the judiciary a good area to measure incumbent attacks on the state.

---

[10] The outcome variable has a minimum value of −10 and a maximum value of 10, though we rescale this to (0,1) to ease interpretation.

Leader attacks on the judiciary can occur in a variety of ways, including verbal attacks on judges, purging the court of judges who rule against the executive, and packing courts with more loyal judges. In El Salvador and Poland, for example, personalist leaders and their partisan legislators passed laws that forced the retirement of an entire generation of established jurists, allowing these leaders to replace the ousted judges with loyalists. These moves entailed both judicial purges and court packing. And, of course, in the US Trump used Twitter to post a steady stream of verbal attacks against judges who ruled against his executive orders.

To measure judicial attacks, we aggregate information from three variables from Coppedge (2021): public government attacks on the judiciary, judicial purges, and court packing.[11] Some of the highest values on this measure are the usual suspects: court purges by PiS in Poland in 2018; Hugo Chavez's restructuring of Venezuelan courts in 2004 and 2005; and Erdoğan's purge of the judiciary in the aftermath of the failed coup attempt in 2016. On the other end of the scale, Finland, Japan, and the US during G.W. Bush's first term have some of the lowest scores for incumbent attacks on the judiciary.

Recall that this measure only varies by survey (i.e., country year). As a result, we estimate a model with survey-year random effects, to model any systematic differences between countries in their party systems, electoral rules, and prior trends in polarization—all factors that might shape both current polarization and the leaders' incentive to attack the state. Identification of the treatment effect comes from comparing average levels of polarization across surveys when there is a low score on judicial attacks with average levels when there is a high score on judicial attacks.

The CSES sample is drawn from mostly relatively consolidated democracies with high levels of judicial independence. As such, attacks on the judiciary are less common in this group of countries than in the global sample used in the previous chapter and that we will use when examining macro-polarization. But even in this restricted sample of CSES countries, we still find that ruling party personalism is strongly associated judicial attacks: using a standardized measure of incumbent attacks on the judiciary, we find that attacks are one-half of standard deviation larger when ruling party personalism is high compared to when personalism is low.

First, we test whether attacks are associated with more polarization. As the last chapter demonstrated, personalist ruling parties are more likely to attack state institutions than their non-personalist counterparts.[12] This first test thus examines whether these attacks boost voter polarization. We then test whether attacks

---

[11] We use a standardized, linear aggregation of the three continuous variables: v2jupoatck, v2jupack, and v2jupurge. Cronbach's alpha is 0.77. We lag this variable one year to ensure the attacks on the court were conducted by the incumbent ruler prior to the election.

[12] In a restricted sample of countries included in the CSES sample, we also find that: (a) ruling party personalism is strongly associated with attacks on the judiciary; and (b) attacks on the judiciary are strongly associated with the survey mean level of micro-polarization.

172 THE ORIGINS OF ELECTED STRONGMEN

carried out by personalist parties breed more polarization than attacks by less personalist parties. We therefore add both ruling party personalism and judicial attacks to the specification, as well as the interaction of the two. As before, we adjust for the age of democracy and the initial level of democracy whenever we test the impact of the ruling party personalism variable. We also adjust for the initial level of judicial constraint in the year each leader is elected into power to account for the fact that there are fewer attacks on the judiciary where this baseline level of judicial constraint is higher.

The results are reported in Figure 6.A-1 in the Appendix to this chapter. The first estimate yields the *average* effect of judicial attacks across all surveys. The estimate for attacks is positive and statistically significant, indicating that government attacks on the judiciary increase polarization. The second set of estimates is from a specification that includes the interaction between attacks and ruling party personalism. The estimate for the interaction term is positive and statistically significant. This suggests that as ruling party personalism increases, incumbent attacks on the judiciary increase polarization to a greater extent. In a third specification we exclude all survey respondents who are either new voters or who switched parties before the most recent election. This leaves us with a sample of voters who have longer lasting ties to the party they supported in the previous election. We find slightly larger estimates for the main interaction term of interest.

This figure also reports estimates for voters' ideological orientation, along a right-left cleavage. Unsurprisingly, self-identified ideologues (on both the left and the right) are generally more polarized than non-ideological voters. This finding will help us understand the magnitude of the main estimates of interest: judicial attacks at different levels of ruling party personalism.

For these tests, we divide the sample into two equally sized categories (for low and high levels of ruling party personalism) and re-estimate the baseline model to assess the effect of judicial attacks in each subsample.[13] Figure 6.3 reports these results. The three estimates in the left plot show the finding for attacks on the state as well as left and right ideology among the group of countries *without* personalist ruling parties. The estimate for *Attacks on the state* is negative but not statistically different from zero. This suggests that attacks on the state have little effect on polarization when the ruling party has a low level of personalism. The estimates for ideology in the left plot are both positive and significant, indicating that, unsurprisingly, ideological voters are more polarized than centrist

---

[13] Ruling parties denoted as *personalist* are those with a ruling party personalism score greater than 0.45 on a 0–1 scale. All other ruling parties are denoted as non-personalist. Results in reproduction files show that using a cutpoint of 0.5 to place ruling parties into high and low categories of personalism yields a similar result.

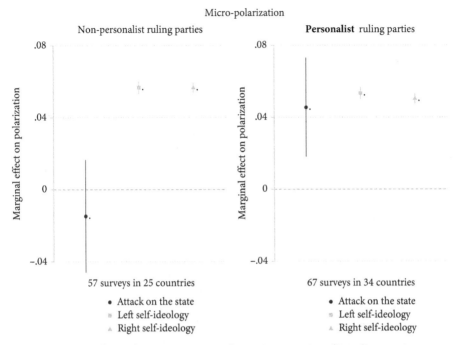

Figure 6.3 Attacks on the state increase polarization in personalist ruling parties

voters.[14] The three estimates in the right plot show the effects of attacks and ideology *when the ruling party is personalist*. Both left- and right-wing ideology voters are more polarized than non-ideological voters, as in the left plot. However, the estimate for incumbent attacks on the state is positive and significant in the right plot—and roughly the same size as the effect of ideology. This indicates that when personalist parties rule, attacks on the state yield increased polarization. And the size of this polarizing effect is roughly the same as that for ideology. The same is not true for attacks on the judiciary when ruling party personalism is at lower level.

The micro-data not only allow us to look at voters who back different parties within the same country, but they also enable us to compare personalist voters to those who support non-personalist parties. To look at differences among voters who support different parties in the same country, we must use the measure of party personalism from the Varieties of Party data set (Lührmann et al., 2020). These data code each major party in each election, including opposition parties. Whereas our original measure of ruling party personalism only captures the concept for the ruling party in each year, the party-level personalism data measure

---

[14] The standard errors, and hence the error bars, for attacks on the state are large, relative to the variance of the ideology estimates, because attacks on the state only vary by country year and not by individual respondent.

the concept for all parties in each election in each country. We code a voter as 'personalist' if the party they voted for 'mainly' or 'solely' focused on the will and priorities of the individual leader.[15] Roughly 16 per cent of voters in the data fall into this category.

We thus test whether the patterns in Figure 6.3 apply to personalist voters and non-personalist voters alike.[16] We find that while personalist voters are more polarized, on average, than non-personalist party voters, judicial attacks are associated with greater polarization among both groups of voters. This suggests that attacks on the state—at least when operationalized as government attacks on the judiciary—polarize all voters, not just those who support personalist parties. Further, this pattern is again stronger when the ruling party is more personalist, in line with our expectations about elite cues. When incumbent leaders attack the state, partisan elites and voters are forced to choose sides—either condemning the attack or condoning it. And choosing sides may reshape partisan identities in ways that exacerbate affective polarization (Van Bavel and Pereira, 2018; Törnberg, 2022).

Macro-Polarization. We next turn to a broader analysis of macro-polarization. Tests of our theory using the macro-data complement the micro-analysis in important ways. First, they enable us to assess how ruling party personalism shapes polarization in a broader sample, using global data from over a hundred countries across three decades from 1991 to 2020. This is valuable given that the CSES sample of countries overrepresents democracies in Europe, which tend to feature lower than average levels of party personalism, fewer incumbent attacks on the state, and lower levels of polarization.

Second, because the global data contain many cases where ruling personalist parties attack the state (e.g., Turkey) as well as cases where this does not occur (e.g., Malaysia), we can use causal mediation analysis to assess whether ruling party personalism increases polarization via incumbent attacks on the state. This type of analysis, discussed in detail below, helps establish whether attacks on the state are a causal mechanism linking ruling party personalism to polarization.

With the macro-level data, we want to answer two questions: (1) does ruling party personalism increase mass polarization? And (2) do leaders backed by a personalist party boost polarization by attacking the state? For this analysis, we use the V-Dem data on macro-polarization (described above) and our original measure of ruling party personalism (introduced in Chapter 2).

To test the first proposition, we conduct two types of test, a lagged outcome model and an initial outcome model. The lagged outcome model addresses temporal correlation in the macro-polarization data and assesses how ruling party personalism shapes year-on-year changes in the level of macro-polarization. We

---

[15] The variable v2paind is ordinal with five values; we use the highest two values to denote 'personalist voter'.

[16] These tests are reported in the online appendix.

test various specifications to ensure covariate selection is not biasing results: no covariates (save democracy age); baseline model (adjustment for democracy age, initial democracy level, and election year); a specification that adjusts for institutional rules (presidential and electoral system); and, finally, a dynamic panel specification with a lagged outcome variable as well as country fixed effects. In all specifications the estimate for ruling party personalism is positive and significant, ranging from 4.5 per cent to almost 7 per cent of one standard deviation in the outcome.[17] In unreported specifications we test the baseline and dynamic panel models with additional adjustments for variables related to parties: ruling party populism, party age (i.e., new parties), party economic ideology, and the initial level of party system institutionalization when the leader is elected into power. In each of these tests, we find consistently robust estimates for ruling party personalism.

Next we test the same specifications but with an initial outcome model. In these tests, the outcome is the *total* change in polarization from the initial level in the year each leader is elected into office. For example, for the US under President Trump, the outcome is the change in the level of polarization in the US from 2016 (election year) to 2020 (last year of the leader spell). All specifications adjust for the initial level of polarization in the leader election year to ensure that ruling party personalism is not simply picking up the level of polarization in the country when the leader is elected. For each specification, the estimate for ruling party personalism is again positive and significant. These estimates, however, are substantially larger (ranging from 0.19 to 0.30) than those in the lagged outcome models (ranging from 0.044 to 0.058) because the former capture the total effect of ruling party personalism over the course of each leader's tenure in power, whereas the estimates in the lagged outcome tests capture the yearly effect of ruling party personalism. The results therefore show that polarization is a product of incumbent behaviour: ruling party personalism increases subsequent polarization. This finding is consistent with the idea that parties shape public opinion (e.g., Zaller, 1992; Green et al., 2008; Slothuus and Bisgaard, 2021). Parties, according to this research, are 'opinion-forming agenc[ies]' (Campbell et al., 1980, 128). Indeed, leaders often increase polarization by activating pre-existing, latent attitudes towards particular groups. If personalist leaders manipulate public opinion to boost polarization—instead of simply leveraging existing polarization—to erode democracy, this turns extant research linking polarization and democratic backsliding on its head. Polarization may not be a cause of backsliding but rather a method—indeed perhaps one of many methods—by which personalist leaders shape citizens' attitudes to diminish vertical accountability on their way to accumulating power.

The Mediating Effect of Attacks on the State. Next we unpack how actions of leaders backed by personalist parties shape polarization using causal mediation

---

[17] These results are reported in Figure 6.A-1 in the Appendix to this chapter. The results remain robust when testing an interactive fixed effects estimator.

176   THE ORIGINS OF ELECTED STRONGMEN

analysis. We use the measure of attacks on the judiciary discussed in the previous section as the mediator for causal mediation analysis, which allows us to test whether party personalism boosts polarization via incumbent attacks on the state.

Causal mediation analysis allows us to examine whether a treatment, in our case ruling party personalism, influences an outcome (polarization) through a particular mechanism or mediator (judicial attacks). This type of analysis, however, rests on two key assumptions.[18] First, we have to assume that treatment assignment—that is, our measure of ruling party personalism—is independent of both the outcome (polarization) and the mediating factor (attacks on the judiciary). We mitigate the possibility that polarization causes selection into ruling party personalism by adjusting for the initial (or lagged) level of polarization.[19] Given that new and less consolidated democracies may be more at risk of incumbent attacks than more established democracies (Svolik, 2008) we also adjust for democracy age and the initial level of democracy when the leader is elected into power. The second key assumption is that incumbent attacks on the judiciary (the mediator) are independent of polarization (potential outcome); in this case we have to assume that polarization does *not* boost the likelihood of attacks on the judiciary, conditional on adjusting for the country's level of polarization when the leader is elected (initial outcome model) or the level of polarization in the prior year (lagged outcome model).

We conduct mediation analysis for the both the yearly effect of ruling party personalism (lagged outcome model) and the total effect for each leader spell (initial outcome model), consistent with the approaches reported in Figure 6.A-2. Figure 6.4 reports the results. The column on the left, for the yearly analysis, indicates that 20 per cent of the total effect of ruling party personalism on personalism occurs via judicial attacks. That is, party personalism boosts polarization directly (80 per cent) and via an indirect pathway by increasing judicial attacks, which, in turn, increase polarization. The right column reports a similar finding for the total average effect: just under a third of the personalism effect occurs by boosting judicial attacks. This analysis demonstrates that a non-trivial way in which party personalism shapes polarization is via incumbent attacks on a highly visible organ of the state with the potential to constrain leaders, namely the judiciary. When leaders are not bound by their own party, they are likely to attack these executive constraints, which in turn, contributes to rising polarization.

Thus far we have demonstrated that judicial attacks are associated with more polarization, an effect that is greatest when the attacks are carried out by incumbent parties that are highly personalist. Just as importantly, these attacks on the

---

[18] The assumptions of sequential ignorability are: (a) conditional on observed confounders, treatment assignment is independent of potential outcomes and mediators; and (b) conditional on observed confounders and treatment assignment, the mediator is independent of potential outcomes.

[19] Results reported in the appendix to Chapter 2 and also show that prior trends in macro-polarization are *not* correlated with selection into ruling party personalism.

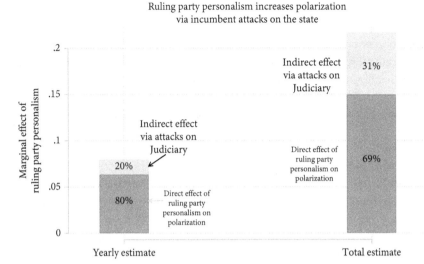

Figure 6.4 Party personalism boosts polarization via attacks on the state

state increase polarization among voters of both personalist and non-personalist parties. We provided evidence, as well, that ruling party personalism increases macro-polarization and that this occurs via incumbent attacks on the state.

We now turn to the second societal consequence of ruling party personalism: the shift in supporters' views of acceptable democratic behaviour that this brings.

6.5.2 Does Ruling Party Personalism Shift Norms?

Next, we empirically evaluate our argument that ruling party personalism leads to shifts in supporters' views of the types of behaviours that are acceptable in a healthy democracy. Assessing this relationship is challenging because of the difficulties involved in accurately capturing public attitudes about democratic transgressions (Ahmed, 2022). Not only do interpretations of the word 'democracy' vary substantially among survey respondents across different contexts but respondents' understanding of what constitutes 'democracy' may be endogenous to partisanship (Carlin et al., 2018; Carey et al., 2019; Bergan, 2021).[20]

Just as pernicious, however, is the fact that standard surveys about voters' support for democracy (e.g., World Values Survey and the CSES modules) do *not* ask

---

[20] Additionally, social desirability bias may inflate explicit expressions of support for a particular type of government (Shen and Truex, 2021).

questions that measure respondents' 'willingness to trade-off democratic principles for other valid but potentially conflicting considerations' (Svolik, 2020, 392). For example, a naive question about support for democracy does not ask whether voters care more about norms of democratic behaviour from their leader or other issues that distinguish the leader from their competitors, such as the performance of the economy, policy alignment, or affinity for the identity of the leader. To understand how norms about appropriate behaviour shape vertical accountability, surveys would need to tap into this trade-off between democratic values and other issues.

Thus, instead of directly testing our argument by examining surveys of popular support for the term 'democracy', we test one of the implications of our argument. We posit that ruling party personalism and the conduct that comes with it changes the sorts of behaviours supporters see as compatible with democracy; we would therefore expect supporters' own behaviours to change in response to personalist parties being in government. In particular, we would expect them to be more likely to support violations of democratic norms after the party has been in power.

To evaluate this, we look at an extreme indicator of breached norms: political violence at the time of an election. At its core, democracy implies *peaceful* as well as free and fair electoral contests to exert political will. The application of violence to secure one's political goals, therefore, runs counter to central democratic tenets. As Dahl (1966, xiii) notes, democracy entails 'organized political parties that compete peacefully in elections'. In this way, political violence—particularly at the time of elections—is a direct breach of democratic modes of conduct.

We examine whether ruling party personalism leads to a higher likelihood of election-related violence. That said, we would not expect all elections in which personalist incumbent parties run to lead to violence; only those in which they lose. For this reason, in this section we explore whether ruling party personalism is associated with greater political violence in elections that incumbents *lose*. Many incumbent personalist leaders win re-election—and often go on to dismantle the democracies they govern—and in these cases these parties and their supporters have little incentive to pursue violence. As long as their team wins an election, they should prefer peace to violence. However, in some instances, these leaders (or their parties) come out on the losing side, albeit often by slim margins, as discussed earlier in this chapter.

The tests in this section therefore enable us to evaluate whether ruling party personalism has lasting effects on democracy even where these parties are voted out of office. Should their departure be linked with a greater risk of electoral violence, then it suggests that democracy is still not safe from the deleterious effects of personalist party rule, even when they are no longer in leadership.

The aforementioned cases of the US under Trump and Brazil under Bolsonaro are certainly consistent with this expectation: in both instances, a leader backed by a personalist party lost an election, prompting non-state actors to resort to political violence, and ultimately calling into question the future health of the democracies they had governed. Here, we evaluate whether this link between ruling party personalism and election-related violence in the face of an incumbent loss, as observed in these instances, is systematic.

We first look at views on political violence among ordinary citizens. We expect that supporters of personalist ruling parties will be more likely than other voters to justify political violence, specifically when their party experiences an electoral loss. We then examine incidences of election-related violence committed by non-state actors. We expect that the risk of political violence will increase in elections that ruling personalist parties lose.

Voter Support for Political Violence. To begin, we explore when ordinary voters are likely to support political violence at the time of an election, using micro-level data. First, we look at whether voters whose party loses an election are more likely to justify the use of political violence than are those who voted for the winner. Next, we examine whether these dynamics change if the party the respondent voted for is personalist. To preview our findings, we first show that voters of losing parties are more likely to justify violence but that, on average, personalist party voters are *not* more likely than other voters to do so. This is important, because it means that supporters of political violence are not simply more likely to be aligned with parties that are personalist.

This analysis, however, does not pinpoint *ruling* party personalism. To evaluate our core empirical expectation, we want to know what happens when *ruling* personalist parties lose. We thus examine whether losing shapes attitudes about political violence when ruling party personalism is high. The evidence we provide is consistent with our argument: as levels of ruling party personalism increase, supporters of personalist parties become more likely to justify political violence in elections where their party loses.

To conduct these tests, we use survey data from the European Values Survey (wave 5, 2017–20). Elections in Europe tend to be the least violent of any region in the world (Daxecker and Jung, 2018, 57), so using data from this region means we are likely assessing how parties shape individual attitudes towards political violence in a least likely set of cases.

The outcome measure for this analysis is a question that asks respondents whether they 'justify political violence'. Respondents place themselves on a ten-point scale, where higher values correspond to more justification for using political violence. Roughly 78 per cent of respondents 'never' justify political violence, while 22 per cent do to some extent. However, less than 1 per cent of respondents 'always' justify violence. To easily interpret marginal effects we test a binary indicator where support for violence is coded as 1 when respondents mark 5 or higher on the scale.[21] With this measure, just over 6 per cent of respondents report justifying political violence.[22]

The main treatment variable is a binary indicator of whether the party for which the respondent voted lost the most recent election. This enables us to examine how party affiliation shapes whether citizens justify political violence when their party *loses* an election, given that it is a scenario in which we should be most likely to see latent support for violence to manifest.

Roughly 65 per cent of respondents in the survey voted for a losing party; conversely about 35 per cent of respondents voted for a winner. In a simple test of a difference of means, we find that support for political violence is slightly higher for losers (7 per cent) than for winners (5.9 per cent). This difference may appear relatively small but it is statistically significant in a large sample of respondents (over 28,000 in twenty-two countries). Further, a change of this size (roughly 1 per cent) in attitudes that are held by a small minority (6.5 per cent) of citizens is not trivial. In short, the descriptive pattern suggests that losing an election—relative to winning one—increases voters' propensity to support political violence.

Next we examine how voting for a personalist party shapes this pattern. We test econometric models with specifications that adjust for individual-level demographic characteristics, such as age, sex, employment, income, and education.[23] We use the measure of party personalism from the Varieties of Party project (discussed in earlier chapters) because it is coded for all major parties—and not just incumbent ruling parties. This allows us to compare voters for different parties—both the winning party and the losing parties—in the same country.

We begin by showing the impact of voting for a personalist party on support for political violence. We do so because it is important to assess whether supporters of political violence are simply more likely to align with personalist parties. Figure 6.A-3 in the Appendix to this chapter reports the estimates. Importantly, this test shows that personalist party voters are *not*, on average, more likely to justify political violence than are other voters. This means that voters who justify violence are *not* simply selecting into personalist parties.[24]

The estimate for *Election loser*, in this test, is about 1 per cent and significant. This result is consistent with the raw data patterns, which reveal a small boost in

---

[21] Reproduction materials show all results hold with ordinal variable analysis.

[22] We emphasize that survey questions and respondents' self-reported support for political violence (particularly in surveys such as the European Values Study) may inflate support for political violence simply due to respondents' inattention to the survey. Further, ambiguous question wording and lack of context in defining violence can substantially influence reported support for violence. This means that our findings using these data bear important caveats (Westwood et al., 2022; Hill and Roberts, 2023).

[23] We address country-level heterogeneity with random effects, testing mixed effects linear probability estimators.

[24] This null result for personalist party supporters contrasts with our findings for *populist* party supporters. In tests reported in the verification files, we find that the group of voters who support populist parties are more likely, on average, to justify violence than other voters. Thus, voters who are more likely to justify violence may be selecting into populist parties.

justifying political violence among election losers. Thus we find that while personalist voters are not, on average, more likely to support political violence, voters who back a losing party are more likely, on average, to justify violence.

Next we divide the data into two groups of voters—those who vote for a party that loses an election and those who vote for the winner—and re-estimate the model for each group. The results of these tests are also reported in Figure 6.A-3. Among election winners, we find that personalist voters are no more likely to support political violence than are other voters. Among election losers, however, the finding is substantially different: personalist voters who lose an election are more likely to justify violence than are voters for other parties that lose. The magnitude of this effect is 2.5 per cent, which is relatively large considering that the average support for violence in the sample is 6.5 per cent. This suggests that personalist voters are only more supportive of political violence than other voters when their party loses.

It is possible, however, that we see these findings simply because supporters of personalist parties are more likely to be sore losers, not because they are responding to the behaviour of the leader and party while in office (as we argue). To test the implications of our theory about ruling party personalism, we therefore need to examine whether *ruling* party personalism is what shapes supporters' views on political violence when their party loses. In the next set of tests we again restrict the sample to voters who support a losing party and examine whether personalist voters are more likely to justify violence than non-personalist voters. Thus, we are again testing the personalist voter effect. This time, however, we examine how the personalist voter effect varies across levels of ruling party personalism.

Importantly, a personalist party that loses an election may or may not have been the incumbent party because in some elections there may be more than one personalist party on the ballot. This means that if the behaviour of personalist ruling parties while in office is consequential, we would *not* expect to see a relationship between personalist party voters and justification of political violence at low levels of ruling party personalism. Instead, we would only expect to see a relationship between personalist voters and justification for violence at high levels of ruling party personalism. While this is not a perfect test, if we find that, among voters who back a losing party, personalist party voters are more likely to support political violence as levels of ruling party personalism increases, it would suggest that it is the behaviour of these parties while in office that is consequential for justifying political violence.

In this test, reported in the left plot in of Figure 6.5, we measure *ruling* party personalism using the variable we coded ourselves and introduced in the second chapter. We use this measure for two reasons. First, our measure of ruling party personalism is based on objective information about the ruling party and its leader that avoids conflating the measure with the leader's behaviour in office. Further, while we find consistent results whether we use our own measure of ruling party

182 THE ORIGINS OF ELECTED STRONGMEN

personalism or the Varieties of Party variable, the findings we report using our measure are more conservative. We have thus chosen to present more cautious estimates of the underlying patterns.

Recall that, across all ruling parties, the personalist voter effect is roughly 2.5 per cent: among losers, voters who back a personalist party are 2.5 per cent more likely than non-personalist party voters to justify violence. The tests reported in the left plot of Figure 6.5 demonstrate how this effect varies across levels of ruling party personalism.[25] We find that at low levels of ruling party personalism, the personalist voter effect is small. For high levels of ruling party personalism, however, the personalist voter effect is positive and significant—indeed more than 5 per cent when the ruling party is at the highest levels of personalism. This means that personalist voters are only more likely to support violence than non-personalist voters when a personalist ruling party loses an election.

The right plot of Figure 6.5 shows the data pattern in a slightly different way. Here the sample includes all voters—both those who support the eventual winner and those who vote for parties that lose the election. The main treatment effect we test is the *loser effect*: how does voting for a losing party—relative to voting for the winning party—influence support for political violence? The vertical axis in the right plot is thus the marginal effect of voting for a losing party. Recall from the result in Figure 6.A-3 that, on average, across all voters in all countries in the sample, this loser effect is roughly 1 per cent. In the tests in the right plot of Figure 6.5, we examine how this loser effect varies for different levels of ruling party personalism, as shown on the horizontal axis. As importantly, we conduct separate tests for personalist voters and non-personalist voters.

The solid line and associated confidence interval in the right plot of Figure 6.5 shows how the loser effect *among personalist voters* varies across levels of ruling party personalism. At low levels of ruling party personalism, the loser effect among personalist voters is close to zero. As ruling party personalism increases, however, the loser effect increases. At high levels of ruling party personalism, the loser effect among personalist voters is more than 5 per cent—a large substantive effect when the sample average is just over 6 per cent. This finding suggests that personalist voters are most likely to justify violence when a highly personalist ruling party loses an election—but not when that party wins.

The dashed line in the right plot of Figure 6.5 shows how the loser effect *among non-personalist voters* changes across levels of party personalism. Again, when ruling party personalism is low, the loser effect is close to zero. But as ruling party personalism increases, losing—relative to winning—tends to decrease support for violence among non-personalist voters. This means that, among non-personalist

---

[25] The plots in Figure 6.5 are from a kernel estimator with country fixed effects that allows for non-linear interaction effects.

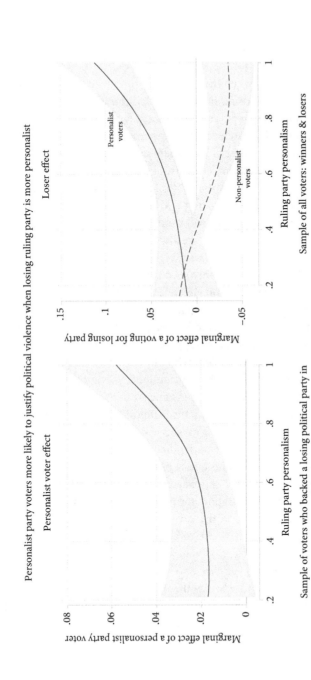

Figure 6.5 Ruling party personalism and support for political violence

voters, losing an election when the incumbent ruling party is personalist reduces support for violence.

Put another way, losing an election does not appear to move voters towards violence for any type of voter when the incumbent ruling party is not personalist. In contrast, the patterns for the loser effect are quite different for personalist and non-personalist voters when the incumbent ruling party is highly personalist: for a personalist voter, losing increases their support for violence, but for a non-personalist voter losing reduces their support for violence.

As Figure 6.5 shows, the results imply that personalism in the incumbent ruling party influences how the party's supporters respond to an election loss. At low levels of ruling party personalism, supporting a losing personalist party has no effect on whether a voter will justify political violence. At high levels of ruling party personalism, however, supporting a losing personalist party substantially increases the likelihood that a voter will support political violence. Interestingly, though the size of the effect is smaller, we also find that high ruling party personalism makes non-personalist voters *less* likely to support political violence when their party loses. Though we can only speculate why, it may be because ruling party personalism polarizes views on violence too (with supporters becoming apt to justify it and opponents less so), in light of our findings earlier in this chapter.

Taken together, the evidence offered here suggests that justifying political violence is largely the province of voters supporting personalist parties that lose the reins of government. This is consistent with our argument that ruling party personalism sets in motion dynamics that shift supporters' views of what constitutes acceptable democratic behaviour, in this instance resulting in greater tolerance for political violence when their party is on the losing side of an election.

It is important to note the following caveats about our results for violence. First, they stem from comparisons across individuals and countries in a single region of the world, albeit one that features a least likely set of cases. These comparisons do not constitute experimental evidence at the micro-level. Further, the European Values Study questions about support for political violence may be inflated due to respondents' inattentiveness to the survey or to question wording that lacks context. We leave it to future research to build on the findings here and further investigate how the electoral losses of incumbent parties that are personalist shape voter attitudes about political violence.

In what follows, we examine whether these micro-level patterns translate into a greater chance of political violence in elections that personalist ruling parties lose.

Incidences of Non-State Election Violence. Here, we transition from looking at voters' perspectives on political violence at the time of electoral losses to actual incidences of electoral violence when incumbents lose. We focus on *non-state* election violence because we are interested in the actions of ordinary citizens. We anticipate that ruling party personalism will increase the chance of non-state election violence in contests in which the party loses.

To measure non-state election violence, we use data from the Varieties of Democracy data set.[26] This measure captures violence before, during, and after election day committed by non-state actors (e.g., private citizens, political militias, and even party affiliated vigilantes or armed youth wings). It specifically excludes violence carried out by the government, the ruling party, or their agents. For our purposes, this makes it a better measure than standard measures of civil conflict and political violence, which typically record the total number of deaths due to political violence, irrespective of whether the government or non-state actors were the perpetrators. That said, the measure is not restricted to either government aligned groups or opposition groups but includes both. It is based on country-expert assessments for each election year.

Our analysis covers 589 executive elections from 1991 to 2020. Roughly half of these elections took place in Europe, while the fewest occurred in the Middle East and North Africa. Among these executive elections, incumbents lost just under half of the time (48 per cent).

To begin, we look at the trends in non-state violence in executive elections over the past three decades. As the left plot in Figure 6.6 illustrates, levels of violence have increased during this period, particularly since the global economic crisis around 2008. The right plot disaggregates these data based on whether the ruling party won or lost the election. It shows that for much of the period levels of non-state election violence were higher when ruling parties won elections than when they lost them. That said, this has been reversed in recent years, primarily because levels of violence have increased so much in elections that ruling parties lose. We propose that rising ruling party personalism has played a role in driving these changes.

To evaluate this, we conduct a series of tests (reported in the online appendix) looking at the relationship between ruling party personalism (using our original measure introduced in Chapter 2), incumbent electoral losses, and non-state election violence. We begin by estimating the independent effects of ruling party personalism and incumbent election losses on non-state election violence. We find that ruling party personalism is associated with more election violence, while incumbent election losses are not.

That said, election violence does not occur in a vacuum. It is often a reaction to the ruling party's attempts to use the state to intimidate opposition candidates and supporters, a tactic that is particularly likely in elections the incumbent party fears it could lose. For this reason, we conduct the same test, but include a control

---

[26] We use the variable v2elpeace, which measures violent force used to achieve political objectives by non-state actors. The definition excludes crime, including organized crime, but encompasses 'politically oriented militias and youth groups', including partisan groups. We flip the scale of this variable so that higher values indicate more violence.

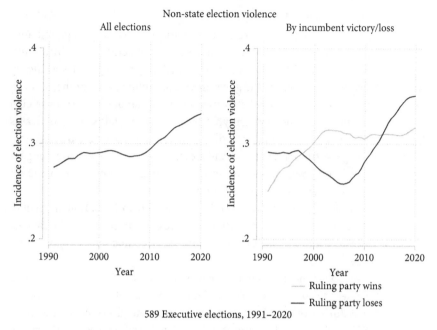

Figure 6.6 Trends in non-state election violence

for government intimidation.[27] Here, we find just the opposite: incumbent losses are associated with more violence but ruling party personalism is not.

Next, we test a specification that accounts for democratic consolidation (age of democracy and initial democracy score when the leader is elected into office), prior levels of state and civil violence, presidentialism, and a time trend. This specification captures the main cross-country differences in observed election violence, as well as the prior dynamic of political violence in the year preceding the election. Again we find that incumbent losses are associated with more election violence but ruling party personalism is not.

If our argument is correct, however, we should observe more election violence specifically when incumbent parties that are personalist lose elections. We therefore test an interaction model and report the results in Figure 6.7.[28] We find that when the ruling party is less personalist, we see a relatively peaceful election in the face of an incumbent's electoral loss. As ruling party personalism increases, however, the incumbent losing an election—relative to the incumbent winning an election—leads to more political violence.

---

[27] We use the variable v2elintim from Coppedge (2021).
[28] The test uses a kernel estimator that allows for non-linear interaction effects. We adjust for: democracy age; initial level of democracy; government intimidation; presidential system; prior year civil violence and prior year state-led violence, as well as a time trend.

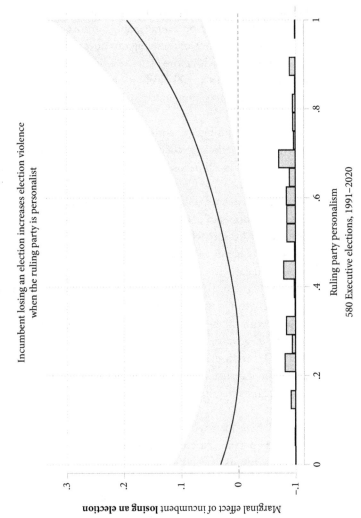

Figure 6.7 Election violence when personalist parties lose

188   THE ORIGINS OF ELECTED STRONGMEN

We conduct two additional tests to probe this pattern. First, we examined whether losing an election increases government intimidation or state-led violence—and whether ruling party personalism shapes this. We find that it does not. This suggests that election losses do not necessarily breed more pernicious state behaviour as ruling party personalism increases. The pattern we find, in other words, appears to be connected to non-state election violence, not state-led election violence. Second, we retested the interaction model and excluded African cases, where election violence is highest on average, and European cases, where election violence is lowest. Excluding each of these regions does not alter the main finding: election losses are associated with more violence when the (losing) ruling party is more personalist. This suggests a relatively robust global pattern where ruling party election losses breed more non-state violence when the incumbent party is personalist.

An important caveat to these findings remains, however. With these data we cannot untangle when the election violence occurs: ideally, we would like to evaluate whether it happens *after* an election loss, not necessarily before or during it. Further, the data here do not enable us to differentiate whether the increase in election-related political violence we observe with ruling party personalism is occurring at the hands of supporters of personalist parties or supporters of other parties. While we cannot know for sure *who* is committing this violence, we see it as most likely happening at the hands of personalist party supporters, in light of the survey evidence presented earlier.

Taken together, the overall evidence offered here suggests that personalist party supporters are no more likely to justify political violence than other voters are. That said, after experience with the party in power, this shifts. After personalist parties have held the reins of government, we are more likely to see their supporters justify political violence in elections that these parties lose. Moreover, given that levels of non-state violence are particularly high in contests that personalist parties lose, this suggests that it is the supporters of these parties who are perpetrating it.

The findings we present here have troubling implications for the long-term outlook of countries that see personalist parties win the leadership. In a healthy democracy, voters respect the results of elections and have confidence in the peaceful transfer of power that elections bring with them. In this way, acceptance of electoral losses is a hallmark of democratic rule. For peaceful electoral transitions to stabilize democracy, voters must ultimately not be too disheartened when their party loses; they must have trust in the system that oversaw the process. Instead, we see that when leaders backed by personalist parties come to power, their supporters' belief in one of the most important democratic norms of behaviour—the peaceful transfer of power via free and fair elections—deteriorates when their party comes out on the losing side of them.

6.6 Conclusion

Effective resistance to incumbent takeovers requires actions on the part of either state institutions or ordinary voters, or both. The last chapter showed how ruling party personalism lessens the chance of the former; this chapter explained how it lessens the chance of the latter.

In the last chapter, we demonstrated that personalist parties raise the risk of democratic decline because these parties provide a less robust constraint on leaders' efforts to expand executive power. We illustrated that personalist parties can spell trouble for democracy because the elites in these parties have less incentive and capacity to push back on a leader's consolidation of control relative to those in non-personalist political parties.

In this chapter, we showed that the behaviour of leaders backed by personalist parties once in office has consequences for the societies they govern. The actions leaders, supported by these parties, pursue to expand their powers polarize society and shift supporters' views of acceptable democratic behaviours, both of which lessen the chance that leaders will face accountability from ordinary voters. Moreover, even when such leaders lose office, the broadening of supporters' views of acceptable democratic behaviour raises the risk of violence around elections.

First, personalist leaders' attacks on state institutions are contentious, intensifying polarization and raising the stakes of holding office. This incentivizes supporters to continue to align with the leader even in the face of anti-democratic conduct. Second, ruling personalist parties shift supporters' views of acceptable democratic behaviours, increasing their tolerance for future anti-democratic actions. Together these factors reduce the chance that personalists who seek to undermine democracy will see defections or push-back from their supporters. This matters because, for democracy to survive, 'citizens have to be willing to act to preserve democratic institutions and punish incumbents for anti-democratic behaviour. In the absence of this ultimate check by ordinary citizens, democratic institutions can be hollowed out and bent to serve authoritarian purposes' (Fossati et al., 2021, 12).

Importantly, these relationships are reinforced by top-down messaging from personalist leaders and party elites that casts doubt on detractors and provides partisan cues that frame the leader's actions as 'normal' in a healthy democracy. As such, both polarization and the shift in citizen perspectives of acceptable democratic behaviours will be worse with ruling party personalism, thereby decreasing the chance that leaders will face vertical accountability.

As this chapter documented, how personalist parties conduct business alters the social fabric of their societies in ways that rally supporters and lessen the chance they will take issue with actions that subvert democracy, thereby diminishing checks on the executive from below.

190   THE ORIGINS OF ELECTED STRONGMEN

6.7 Appendix A: Regression Results

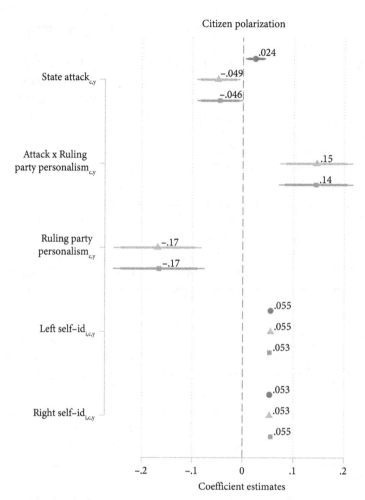

Figure 6.A-1 Judicial attacks increase polarization

SOCIETAL PATHWAYS 191

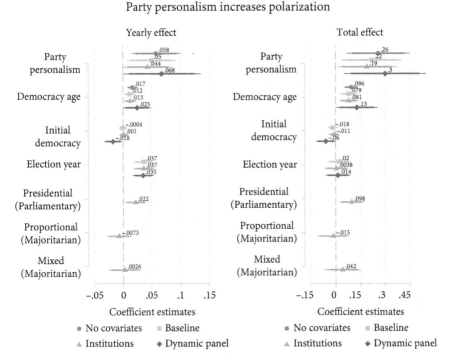

Figure 6.A-2 Ruling party personalism and polarization

192 THE ORIGINS OF ELECTED STRONGMEN

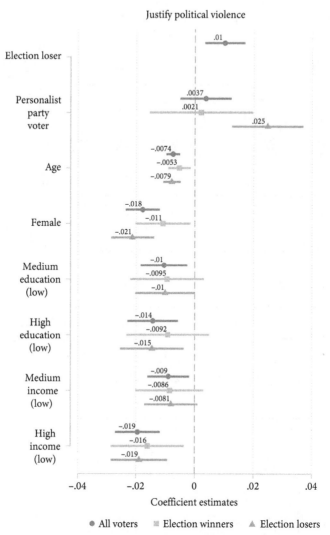

Figure 6.A-3 Election losers, personalist voters, and support for political violence

7

Personalist Politics, Democracy, and the Path Ahead

The social scientist William Graham Sumner wrote in 1914, 'I cannot trust a party; I can trust a man. I cannot hold a party responsible; I can hold a man responsible. I cannot get an expression of opinion which is single and simple from a party; I can get that only from a man' (Keller, 1914). Though written more than a century ago, this sentiment encapsulates the lure of personalist politics today.

Indeed, strongman leaders are on the rise. Long confined to the realm of autocracies, elected strongmen have now become a common feature of democracies too. Across a variety of domains—ranging from media reporting to political campaigns—politics has become increasingly centred around individuals, with elected leaders taking on outsized influence relative to their political parties or the institutions that surround them. The media too have taken note of this trend and declared the current era as one characterized by the 'return of the strongman' (Hamilton, 2017).

Observers point to a variety of reasons for the rise of elected strongmen and the personalization of politics more broadly. Today's media landscape, for one, prioritizes the individual over the organization, short-circuiting the need for party building to win office. Political parties are increasingly being built around individuals, and, lacking a robust policy platform, represent little more than the politicians who found them. Moreover, a well-documented wave of partisan dealignment has swept across many parts of the globe. As voters feel increasingly dissatisfied and detached from long-standing political parties, it has created openings for new leaders and their parties to fill.

Yet, despite the plethora of ideas about why more personalist parties are being elected to office, there is less understanding of their political consequences, particularly in terms of what they mean for democracy. This book has sought to fill this void. In it, we looked at the impact of personalist political parties—or parties that exist primarily to launch a leader into power and further his or her personal political career rather than to advance policy—on the quality of democracy. Using original global data measuring the extent of personalism within democratic political parties in the past three decades, we showed that ruling party personalism is indeed on the rise across the globe and is a key factor fuelling the

The Origins of Elected Strongmen. Erica Frantz, Andrea Kendall-Taylor, and Joseph Wright, Oxford University Press.
© Erica Frantz, Andrea Kendall-Taylor, and Joseph Wright (2024). DOI: 10.1093/oso/9780198888079.003.0007

democratic recession we see today. Where leaders come to power backed by personalist parties—what the pundits call elected strongmen—the risks of democratic backsliding rise.

Throughout this book, we carefully documented these effects and, critically, the pathways through which personalist parties corrode democracy—insights that help researchers and policy-makers to better target solutions. First, we demonstrated that personalist parties are fundamentally different from other parties: their leaders are more likely to create them, personally fund them, and control candidate nominations, resulting in an elite party cadre lacking political experience and whose careers are closely tied to the fate of the leader. These unique features of personalist parties, we argue, decrease the incentive and capacity of party officials to push back against a leader's efforts to consolidate power. When the party elite view their own career as tied to that of the leader, rather than the long-term reputation of the party, they will accept and even support illiberal actions to keep the personalist party in power.

As evidence, we showed that those leaders backed by personalist parties are more likely to be successful in their efforts to dismantle horizontal checks on their power, weakening institutional constraints on the executive. These attacks on state institutions not only directly undermine democracy, but also have far-reaching societal effects that facilitate democratic decline. In particular, elected strongmen and the personalist parties that back them intensify political polarization and weaken supporters' commitment to democratic norms of behaviour. Personalist party supporters' views of acceptable norms change to such an extent that—in those instances where these parties lose an election—they are more likely to resort to violence. In these ways, personalist parties weaken vertical accountability from ordinary citizens, facilitating a leader's efforts to undermine democracy.

These two pathways—the weakening of horizontal and vertical constraints on leaders backed by personalist parties—explain how personalist parties corrode democracy. This book, therefore, broadens our understanding of the political impact of the new strongman era. It also provides new insight into the dynamics underlying the well-documented contemporary challenges to democracies—challenges that now come predominately from elected leaders. Ruling party personalism, we show, is a key factor at the heart of the current wave of democratic decline.

In this concluding chapter, we summarize the central themes of the preceding chapters, the ideas proposed, and the major empirical findings. We then turn to a discussion of the policy recommendations that come out of this research. We offer a series of suggestions to help combat the effects of party personalism and safeguard democracy from the challenges that elected strongmen pose.

7.1 Summary of the Book

Chapter 1 began by describing the now widely observed upsurge in democratic backsliding that has occurred over the past three decades. We linked this development to the global rise of personalist political parties, a trend consistent with the growing personalization of politics observers have documented in democratic systems. We reviewed the manifestations and causes of the new personalist era, and then previewed our argument regarding its consequences for democracy. We started from the premise that it is all but impossible to gauge the intentions of political leaders before they enter office. We therefore assume that while many leaders look for opportunities to expand their power, those backed by personalist parties will be more likely to be successful in their efforts. Personalist parties lack both the incentive and the capacity to restrain a leader's effort to consolidate control, raising the risk of democratic backsliding from within. We situated our argument in the existing literature on democratic erosion and explained how we integrate and build on this work, before highlighting the book's central contributions.

In Chapter 2, we defined personalist parties as we conceptualize them, highlighting the importance of the leader's relationship with his or her political party. In personalist parties, the party tends to be little more than a vehicle to advance the leader's personal political career. This gives personalist leaders more control over the party than other senior party elites. We explained our approach to measuring personalism in the support party of democratic leaders and our original data collection effort. Our measure of party personalism, we note, incorporates information that predates the leader's assumption of power to ensure it is not endogenous to leaders' behaviours in office. Thus, we construct a measure of personalism that does not conflate the explanatory agent—personalist parties—with the outcome of interest, namely anti-democratic behaviour once in office. Next, we compared our concept to existing ones, paying close attention to how party personalism differs from populism, another oft-cited explanation for democratic backsliding in the literature and mainstream media. We then offered basic facts and features of personalist support parties. We showed that party personalism is not simply a feature of one or two regions of the world, but that it is on the rise worldwide. We also showed that personalist parties are not ideologically different from non-personalist parties, nor are they a reflection of electoral systems. These insights help make clear what personalist political parties are, as we describe them in the book.

Chapter 3 detailed our theory of how personalist parties undermine democracy. We contend that personalist parties are structured in ways that lessen the party's incentive and capacity to constrain the leader. In line with our theoretical assumptions, using both macro- and individual-level, micro-data, we showed that personalist parties are less likely to feature elites with party and governing experience. For this reason, elites in personalist parties are more likely to see their careers as being dependent on the fate of the leader rather than that of the party, making them more likely to accept and even support illiberal actions to keep the personalist party in power. In addition, we showed that leaders of personalist parties are more likely to control party resources and nominations, resulting in parties with weaker local organizations. Moreover, we provided evidence that cabinet appointee tenures are shorter when leaders' support parties are personalist, suggesting that partisan cabinet elites are likely to be reluctant to push back against a personalist leader's agenda. These patterns are consistent with our expectation that personalist parties are less likely or able to resist a leader's efforts to expand executive control. This chapter thus provided the backdrop for understanding how the personalization of political parties gives rise to electoral strongmen who will undermine democracy, which the remaining chapters document.

Chapter 4 provided direct evidence that party personalism increases the risk of democratic backsliding. We began by offering two detailed case studies from El Salvador and Hungary to illustrate the full arc of our argument. We then presented a battery of empirical tests that link ruling party personalism with democratic decline. We first showed that where personalism in the support party of the leader is high, we see the repression of freedoms of expression and association increase. Next, we examined how this impacts democratic backsliding more broadly. We found that party personalism increases the likelihood of democratic backsliding, regardless of whether it is measured incrementally, sharply, or by total democratic collapse. Importantly, we showed, as well, that party personalism exerts its greatest impact when ruling parties have legislative majorities. The message to emerge from this chapter is clear: greater personalism in the leaders' support party is harmful to democracy. The two chapters to follow provide empirical evidence demonstrating the pathways through which this occurs.

Chapter 5 documented the institutional pathways. It showed how personalist parties facilitate executive attacks on a country's institutions. First, we discussed the effective functioning of executive constraints in healthy democracies and how party personalism situates elected strongmen to erode them. Next, we showed that because personalist parties lack the incentive and capacity to push back against leaders' attempts to consolidate power, executive constraints decline following the election of these parties to power. In particular, we found that party personalism decreases constraints from the state's legislative, judicial, and bureaucratic institutions. Consistent with our expectations, we found that the erosion of executive constraints brought on by party personalism is even worse when the party has a legislative majority. This implies that personalist parties, unlike non-personalist parties, provide few roadblocks to a power-seeking leader's agenda. Moreover, we found that party personalism increases the likelihood that leaders will initiate additional attempts to expand their power, including by changing term limits. By weakening executive constraints, party personalism paves the way for subsequent actions that undermine democracy.

Chapter 6 documented societal pathways. It showed that personalist leaders' anti-democratic behaviour decreases the chance that citizens will act to check the leader from below. We first asked whether declining citizen views of democracy might be responsible for weakened vertical constraints on personalist leaders. We dispel this connection, drawing from our own findings in Chapter 2, as well as recent research. We suggest instead that citizens may value and support democracy and nonetheless back a leader and a party who subvert it. We highlighted two mutually reinforcing reasons why democratically supportive citizens tolerate anti-democratic actions. The first is political polarization. Existing research shows that polarization incentivizes voters to put up with actions that are harmful for democracy if those actions will prevent the party they oppose from gaining power. Using micro- and macro-evidence, we showed that leaders of personalist parties do not just instrumentalize existing polarization to help them come into power—as much of the existing literature suggests—but that these leaders actively amplify it, increasing their supporters' acceptance of anti-democratic behaviours. Second, personalist parties alter their supporters' view of what acceptable democratic behaviour looks like, ultimately weakening their own commitment to democratic norms. Because such shifts are challenging to observe in practice, we focus on a particularly egregious breach of norms: support for electoral violence. We showed that ruling party personalism increases the chance that supporters will justify the use of violence in elections incumbent parties lose.

Together, the analyses make clear that ruling party personalism poses great harm to democracy. Key actors in personalist political parties lack the incentive and capacity to restrain the leadership, such that their leaders succeed in loosening executive constraints. This in turn intensifies political polarization and reduces supporters' commitment to democratic norms of behaviour. Having weakened both horizontal and vertical pathways of accountability, the door is wide open for leaders backed by personalist parties to push their countries towards authoritarianism.

7.2 Countering the Perils of Personalism

The personalization of politics poses real dilemmas for defenders of democracy. What role can citizens play in defending democracy in their own countries if large swaths of voters accept or even endorse anti-democratic actions carried out by the leaders they support? How can democracy practitioners increase the resilience of democracy in other countries where illiberal leaders have been voted into office with the support of sizable segments of society? Indeed, the business of defending democracy has become more challenging as freely elected leaders gradually dismantle democracy from the top down, even in settings where citizens still strongly support democratic norms and standards.

Democracy practitioners have already begun to adapt to the new challenges posed by the modern wave of democratic decay. The research presented in this book can complement and reinforce current assessments about what actions will be required to safeguard democracy. Although many of the insights this research has highlighted are not new, they do underscore the importance of certain factors, helping practitioners to prioritize some actions over others, especially where resources for democracy assistance are limited. For example, the insight that political parties matter is not new, and democracy practitioners have long been focused on political party development. The research presented in this book underscores that such a focus is warranted, while also offering specific ways that parties could be made more resilient to the threats posed by elected strongmen.

In the remainder of this chapter, we discuss the recommendations that stem from the research we have presented.

First and foremost, this book has established that the election of leaders backed by personalist parties is an early warning sign that democracy is at an elevated risk of decline. Analysts and political observers alike have struggled to discern, in advance, which leaders pose problems for democracy. As we discussed earlier in this book, many political analysts and policy-makers praised Turkish President Erdoğan as a model of democracy. Likewise, it was not immediately apparent that Hungarian Prime Minister Orban would roll back democracy as he did, or that Poland's Law and Justice Party would dismantle executive constraints, particularly given that these were countries long assumed to have crossed the threshold of consolidated democracy. It is often the case that once the anti-democratic trajectory in a particular country becomes apparent, it is too late to reverse a leader's early gains, underscoring the need for early intervention. This is because once a leader successfully expands executive control and dismisses party officials who oppose such moves from the inner circle, it sends a clear signal to other elites that they must fall in line or risk being expelled from positions of power. Our research uses information that predates a leader's election to provide early warning that where leaders backed by personalist parties come to power, such risks grow. At a minimum, this insight provides practitioners with a clear and easily observable indicator of a heightened risk of democratic decay—an indicator that could guide the allocation of limited resources to those countries facing this heightened risk.

The second major message to emerge from this research is that better protecting democracies from erosion from within—the dominant way that contemporary democratic collapse is occurring—requires attention to political parties, as indicated above. This book reaffirms the critical role that political parties play in supporting healthy democracy. We leave it to scholars of party building to derive the best strategies for doing so, but suggest several types of measures that could increase the resilience of new parties to power-seeking leaders.

For example, strengthening parties' local capacity and connections to local communities can better position parties—both new and old—to counter the negative effects of elected strongmen. For one, strengthening established parties' connections to local communities can combat the partisan dealignment—or the process through which voters become less connected to their political party—that is, creating space for new, personalist parties to succeed at the polls. Equipping political parties and politicians to engage at the local level more effectively, including through increased grassroots mobilization and community events, can slow the spread of personalist parties.

Similarly, building the capacity of local party officials and party infrastructure can constrain opportunistic leaders. Experience from the US 2020 election illustrates this. At local levels, then-President Trump sought to overturn the presidential election results in his favour, alleging fraud despite having no evidence of foul play. Though many Republican Party elites at the national level did not push back against this power grab, particularly those with upcoming primary electoral campaigns, many local-level Republican officials spoke out in key states such as Michigan and Georgia. Two state-level Republican leaders in Michigan asserted the victory of his competitor even after a personal visit from Trump; and key Republican electoral officials in Georgia directly contradicted Trump's false claims about election malfeasance and refused to adjust the vote tallies to give Trump the win.

Interestingly, although local capacity is important, fundraising dynamics may operate by a different logic. There is evidence, for example, that candidates are less likely to run personalized campaigns when the local party organization gets a greater percentage of its total income from the central party (Cross et al., 2020). By contrast, funds raised on the ground lead to more personalized campaigns. While personalized campaigns are not synonymous with personalized parties, it is possible that attention to how party funding structures influence whether parties are personalist may be fruitful.

Outside the party, there is also an important role for civil society. While a country's formal institutions may struggle to constrain a leader, robust civil societies can play a role in increasing the headwinds that elected strongmen face. In particular, democracy watchdogs, the media, and other relevant civil society organizations should be more attuned to the rise of personalist parties and the ways in which they degrade democracy. Democracy practitioners and aid organizations can invest in equipping such watchdog and media groups to better understand the phenomenon and the early warning signs such that these organizations can shine a light on and raise alarm bells early. One way to better equip these groups is to facilitate the sharing of best practices between civil society groups in countries that have experienced the challenges posed by elected strongmen with groups in other countries where personalist parties have been elected to office for the first time. In addition to increasing understanding, such exchanges could also facilitate the sharing of best practices and strategies to push back on the actions of these leaders and their parties.

Our research underscored that more attention must be paid to early, small actions by elected strongmen to expand their personal influence. These early actions can take on outsized importance over time, and therefore warrant greater public scrutiny and outcry. For example, early, small changes to party constitutions and political party rules can facilitate a leader's anti-democratic actions further down the road. While party constitutions and political party rules are often dismissed as arcane, they do provide a critical check on a leader's power. In Hungary, for example, before Orban became prime minister he made changes to the Fidesz Party constitution to ensure he could determine that Fidesz candidates who were friendly to his ambitions were on the ballot at all levels. Democracy assistance organizations should train civil society organizations, democracy watchdogs, and local media to pay special attention to such actions that will enhance a leader's influence.

Civil society can also mobilize to push back against an elected strongman's problematic actions, even when sizable segments of the population support the leader. In Brazil, for example, scholars Benjamin Bradlow and Mohammad Ali Kadivar document the important role that civil society played in protecting the country's social programmes and democratic system during Bolsonaro's tenure (Bradlow and Kadivar, 2023). The authors show that these groups played a key role in helping the country weather the COVID-19 pandemic, even while Bolsonaro denied its existence. A coalition of health organizations, grassroots movements, and academics lobbied Congress to agree to an emergency social grant to support millions of Brazilians who could not work because of illness or lockdowns. Although Bolsonaro opposed this legislation, he agreed to sign it when it became clear that it had majority support in Congress. Likewise, urban housing movements and community groups continued to operate and, according to the authors, 'helped expose the president's raw incompetence ... [and] in doing so, they dragged down his approval rating'. Since the election violence in January 2023, civic groups have also joined pro-democracy protests and ultimately made clear that any further efforts to undermine the country's electoral institutions would face fierce resistance.

The world's democracies are indeed under stress. Revisionist authoritarian powers like Russia and China are working hard to undermine liberal democracy. These actors interfere in foreign elections, push disinformation, cultivate sympathetic elites, and pursue other influence operations to weaken democracy from the outside in. Meanwhile, democracies have been under increasing duress from actors within their own systems. Democratically elected leaders backed by parties they have created and dominated erode the constraints on their power. These elected strongmen have become one of the greatest threats to democracy today. This research has documented the threat and charted how these leaders work to dismantle democracy. Equipped with this understanding, policy-makers, elected leaders, civil society, and citizens alike will be placed in a better position to safeguard democracy. For the past decade, elected strongmen have gained the upper hand. It is time to turn the tide.

References

Abramowitz, Alan, and McCoy, Jennifer. 2019. United States: Racial Resentment, Negative Partisanship, and Polarization in Trump's America. *The ANNALS of the American Academy of Political and Social Science*, **681**(1), 137–56.

Acemoglu, Daron, and Robinson, James A. 2006. *Economic Origins of Dictatorship and Democracy*. New York: Cambridge University Press.

Adam, Silke, and Maier, Michaela. 2010. Personalization of Politics: A Critical Review and Agenda for Research. *Annals of the International Communication Association*, **34**(1), 213–57.

Ahmed, Amel. 2022. Is the American Public Really Turning Away from Democracy? Backsliding and the Conceptual Challenges of Understanding Public Attitudes. *Perspectives on Politics*, **21**(3), 967–78.

Al Jazeera. 2021a. El Salvador Elections: President Bukele Set to Gain More Control', 27 February. Available at: https://www.aljazeera.com/news/2021/2/27/el-salvador-elections-president-bukele-set-to-gain-more-control (accessed 16 November 2021).

Al Jazeera. 2021b. Crisis Brewing as El Salvador's Congress Votes Out Top Judges, 2 May. Available at: https://www.aljazeera.com/news/2021/5/2/crisis-brewing-as-el-salvador-congress-votes-out-top-judges.

Albertus, Michael, and Grossman, Guy. 2021. The Americas: When Do Voters Support Power Grabs? *Journal of Democracy*, **32**(2), 116–31.

Aldrich, John H. 1995. *Why Parties? The Origin and Transformation of Political Parties in America*. Chicago: University of Chicago Press.

Alvarado, Jimmy, Labrador, Gabriel, and Arauz, Sergio. 2020. The Bukele Clan That Rules with Nayib. *El Faro*, 17 June.

Álvares, Débora, and de Sousa, Marcelo Silva. 2021. Bolsonaro Urges Brazil Senate to Impeach High Court Justice. Associated Press, 20 August.

Alyanek, Oguz, and Kurt, Umit. 2021. The Sultan and His Sycophants: Erdogan Is Leading Turkey towards a Bleak Future. opendemocracy.net, 16 February. Available at: https://www.opendemocracy.net/en/north-africa-west-asia/the-sultan-and-his-sycophants-erdoğan-is-leading-turkey-towards-a-bleak-future/.

Amnesty International. 2017. Poland: On the Streets to Defend Human Rights. *Amnesty International*, 37/7147/2017.

Anderson, Christopher J., Bol, Damien, and Ananda, Aurelia. 2021. Humanity's Attitudes about Democracy and Political Leaders: Patterns and Trends. *Public Opinion Quarterly*, **85**(4), 957–86.

Applebaum, Anne. 2018 (October). *A Warning From Europe: The Worst Is Yet to Come*. The Atlantic.

Applebaum, Anne. 2020. *Twilight of Democracy: The Seductive Lure of Authoritarianism*. New York: Doubleay.

Araya, Ignacio Arana. 2023. Dominant Personality and Politically Inexperienced Presidents Challenge Term Limits. *Journal of Politics*, forthcoming, 1–35.

Associated Press. 2019. El Salvador: Anti-Corruption Candidate Naybi Bukele Wins Presidential Election. *The Guardian*, 3 February.

REFERENCES 203

Aydin-Duzgit, Senem. 2019. The Islamist-Secularist Divide and Turkey's Descent into Severe Polarization. *Democracies Divided: The Global Challenge of Political Polarization.* Washington, DC: Brookings Institution Press.

Aydintasbas, Asli. 2015. Erdogan Is Pushing His Luck. *Politico,* 6 September. Available at: https://www.politico.eu/article/erdogan-turkish-palace-ankara/.

Balmas, Meital, Rahat, Gideon, Sheafer, Tamir, and Shenhav, Shaul R. 2014. Two Routes to Personalized Politics: Centralized and Decentralized Personalization. *Party Politics,* **20**(1), 37–51.

Bankuti, Miklos, Halmai, Gabor, and Scheppele, Kim Lane. 2012. Hungary's Illiberal Turn: Disabling the Constitution. *Journal of Democracy,* **23**(3), 138–46.

Barker, Rodney. 2001. *Legitimating Identities: The Self-Presentations of Rulers and Subjects.* New York: Cambridge University Press.

Barr, Robert R. 2009. Populists, Outsiders and Anti-Establishment Politics. *Party Politics,* **15**(1), 29–48.

Barrera, Carlos. 2021. Let the President Control Everything. *El Faro,* 25 February.

Baturo, Alexander. 2014. *Democracy, Dictatorship, and Term Limits.* Ann Arbor, MI: University of Michigan Press.

BBC News. 2022. SA Minister Calls on Ramaphosa to Resign over Scandal. *BBC News,* 7 December.

Beauchamp, Zack. 2018. *It Happened There: How Democracy Died in Hungary.* Vox, 13 September.

Bell, Curtis. 2016. The Rulers, Elections, and Irregular Governance Dataset (REIGN). Broomfield, CO: OEF Research.

Bergan, Daniel E. 2021. Introduction: Democratic Norms, Group Perceptions, and the 2020 Election. *Journal of Political Marketing,* **20**(3–4), 251–4.

Berglund, Frode, Holmberg, Soren, Schmitt, Hermann, and Thomassen, Jacques. 2005. Party Identification and Party Choice. *The European Voter: A Comparative Study of Modern Democracies.* Oxford: Oxford University Press, 106–24.

Berman, Sheri. 2021. The Causes of Populism in the West. *Annual Review of Political Science,* **24**, 71–88.

Berman, Sheri, and Snegovaya, Maria. 2019. Populism and the Decline of Social Democracy. *Journal of Democracy,* **30**(3), 5–19.

Bermeo, Nancy. 2016. On Democratic Backsliding. *Journal of Democracy,* **27**(1), 5–19.

Bernhard, Michael. 2021. Democratic Backsliding in Poland and Hungary. *Slavic Review,* **80**(3), 585–607.

Bernhard, Michael, Hicken, Allen, Reenock, Christopher, and Lindberg, Staffan I. 2020. Parties, Civil Society, and the Deterrence of Democratic Defection. *Studies in Comparative International Development,* **55**, 1–26.

Bisgaard, Martin, and Slothuus, Rune. 2018. Partisan Elites as Culprits? How Party Cues Shape Partisan Perceptual Gaps. *American Journal of Political Science,* **62**(2), 456–9.

Bizzarro, Fernando, Hicken, Allen, and Self, Darin. 2017. The V-Dem Party Institutionalization Index: A New Global Indicator (1900–2015). *V-Dem Working Paper Series,* **48**, 1–26.

Blondel, Jean, and Thiébault, Jean-Louis. 2010. *Political Leadership, Parties and Citizens: The Personalisation of Leadership.* New York: Routledge.

Bohmelt, Tobias, Ezrow, Lawrence, and Lehrer, Roni. Forthcoming. Populism and Intra-Party Democracy. *European Journal of Political Research.*

Bouka, Yolande. 2015. *A House Divided in Burundi: Rifts at the Heart of the Ruling Party.* Pretoria: Institute for Security Studies.

Bradlow, Benjamin H., and Kadivar, Mohammad Ali. 2023. *How Brazil Can Prevent an Authoritarian Resurgence. Foreign Affairs*, 12 January.

Brookes, James. 1990. Fujimori Elected Peru's President over Vargas Llosa. New York Times, 11 June.

Buckley, Neil, and Byrne, Andrew. 2018. The Rise and Rise of Viktor Orban. *Financial Times*, 25 January.

Bucur, Cristina. 2017. A Mould-Breaking Cabinet? Changes and Continuities in the Formation of the 2017 French Government. *French Politics*, **15**(3), 340–59.

Bueno de Mesquita, Bruce, and Siverson, Randolph M. 1995. War and the Survival of Political Leaders: A Comparative Study of Regime Types and Political Accountability. *American Political Science Review*, **89**(4), 841–55.

Bugaric, Bojan. 2019. Could Populism Be Good for Constitutional Democracy? *Annual Review of Law and Social Science*, **15**, 41–58.

Bump, Philip. 2021. Party Polarization Hit a High under Trump: Can Biden Reel It Back? *Washington Post*, 20 January.

Bustikova, Lenka, and Guasti, Petra. 2019. The State as a Firm: Understanding the Autocratic Roots of Technocratic Populism. *East European Politics and Societies*, **33**(2), 302–30.

Calise, Mauro. 2015. The Personal Party: An Analytical Framework. *Italian Political Science Review*, **45**, 301–15.

Campbell, Angus, Converse, Philip E., Miller, Warren E., and Stokes, Donald E. 1980. *The American Voter*. Chicago: University of Chicago Press.

Capati, Andrea. 2019. The Personalisation of Politics in the Age of Social Media: What Risks for European Democracy? *IAI Commentaries*.Istituto Affari Internazionali: Rome.

Carey, John, Clayton, Katherine, Helmke, Gretchen, Nyhan, Brendan, Sanders, Mitchell, and Stokes, Susan. 2022. Who Will Defend Democracy? Evaluating Tradeoffs in Candidate Support among Partisan Donors and Voters. *Journal of Elections, Public Opinion and Parties*, **32**(1), 230–45.

Carey, John M., and Shugart, Matthew Soberg. 1995. Incentives to Cultivate a Personal Vote: A Rank Ordering of Electoral Formulas. *Electoral studies*, **14**(4), 417–39.

Carey, John M., Helmke, Gretchen, Nyhan, Brendan, Sanders, Mitchell, and Stokes, Susan. 2019. Searching for Bright LInes in the Trump Presidency. *Perspectives on Politics*, **17**(3), 699–718.

Carlin, Ryan E, Hartlyn, Jonathan, Hellwig, Timothy, Love, Gregory J, Martínez-Gallardo, Cecilia, and Singer, Matthew M. 2018. Public Support for Latin American Presidents: The Cyclical Model in Comparative Perspective. *Research & Politics*, **5**(3), 1–8. Available at: https://doi.org/10.1177/2053168018787690.

Carreras, Miguel. 2014. Outsider Presidents, Institutional Performance, and Governability in Latin America. PhD dissertation, University of Pittsburgh.

Carreras, Miguel. 2017. Institutions, Governmental Performance and the Rise of Political Newcomers. *European Journal of Political Research*, **56**(2), 364–80.

Carreras, Miguel, Morgenstern, Scott, and Su, Yen-Pin. 2015. Refining the Theory of Partisan Alignments: Evidence from Latin America. *Party Politics*, **21**(5), 671–85.

Carter, David, and Signorino, Curtis. 2010. Back to the Future: Modeling Time Dependence in Binary Data. *Political Analysis*, **18**(3), 271–92.

Cheibub, José Antonio. 2007. *Presidentialism, Parliamentarism, and Democracy*. New York: Cambridge University Press.

Chhibber, Pradeep. 2013. Dynastic Parties: Organization, Finance and Impact. *Party Politics*, **19**(2), 277–95.

REFERENCES   205

Chiopris, Caterina, Nalepa, Monika, and Vanbert, Georg. 2021a. Authoritarian Backsliding. Working Paper, University of Chicago and Duke University.

Chiopris, Caterina, Nalepa, Monika, and Vanberg, Georg. 2021b. A Wolf in Sheep's Clothing: Citizen Uncertainty and Democratic Backsliding. Working Paper, University of Chicago, Tech. Rpt.

Cilliza, Chris. 2019. Donald Trump Just Keeps 'Joking' about Serving More Than 2 Terms as President. *CNN*, 18 June.

Claassen, Christopher. 2020. Does Public Support Help Democracy Survive? *American Journal of Political Science*, **64**(1), 118–34.

Claassen, Ryan L., and Ensley, Michael J. 2016. Motivated Reasoning and Yard-Sign-Stealing Partisans: Mine Is a Likable Rogue, Yours Is a Degenerate Criminal. *Political Behavior*, **38**(2), 317–35.

Clayton, Katherine, Davis, Nicholas T., Nyhan, Brendan, Porter, Ethan, Ryan, Timothy J., and Wood, Thomas J. 2021. Elite Rhetoric Can Undermine Democratic Norms. *Proceedings of the National Academy of Sciences*, **118**(23), 1–6.

Cleary, Matthew R., and Ozturk, Aykut. 2022. When Does Backsliding Lead to Breakdown? Uncertainty and Opposition Strategies in Democracies at Risk. *Perspectives on Politics*, **20**(1), 205–21. doi:10.1017/S153759272000366.

Collier, David, and Adcock, Robert. 1999. Democracy and Dichotomies: A Pragmatic Approach to Choices about Concepts. *Annual Review of Political Science*, **2**(1), 537–65.

Coppedge, Michael et al. 2021. V-Dem Codebook v11.1. Varieties of Democracy (V-Dem) Project.

Corrales, Javier. 2016. Can Anyone Stop the President? Power Asymmetries and Term Limits in Latin America, 1984–2016. *Latin American Politics and Society*, **58**(2), 3–25.

Corrales, Javier. 2022. *Autocracy Rising: How Venezuela Transitioned to Authoritarianism.* Washington, DC: Brookings Institution Press.

Crisp, Brian. 2009. Álvaro Uribe, President of Colombia. *Encyclopedia Britannica*. Available at: https://www.britannica.com/biography/Alvaro-Uribe-Velez (accessed 7 June 2019).

Cross, William P., Katz, Richard S., and Pruysers, Scott (eds.) 2018. *The Personalization of Democratic Politics and the Challenge for Political Parties.* London: ECPR Press.

Cross, William P., Currie-Wood, Rob, and Pruysers, Scott. 2020. Money Talks: Decentralized Personalism and the Sources of Campaign Funding. *Political Geography*, **82**, 1–11.

Dada, Carlos. 2020. Central America Dismantles Democracy. *Dissent*, **67**(4), 95–106.

Dagi, Ishan. 2008. Turkey's AKP in Power. *Journal of Democracy*, **19**(3), 25–30.

Dahl, Robert A. 1966. *Political Oppositions in Western Democracies.* New Haven, CT: Yale University Press.

Dahl, Robert A. 1971. *Polyarchy: Participation and Opposition.* New Haven, CT: Yale University Press.

Dal Bó, Ernesto, Dal Bó, Pedro, and Snyder, Jason. 2009. Political Dynasties. *The Review of Economic Studies*, **76**(1), 115–42.

Dalton, Russell J., and Wattenberg, Martin P. 2002. *Parties without Partisans: Political Change in Advanced Industrial Democracies.* New York: Oxford University Press.

Davenport, Christian. 2007. *State Repression and the Domestic Democratic Peace.* Cambridge: Cambridge University Press.

Davenport, Christian, and Inman, Molly. 2012. The State of State Repression Research since the 1990s. *Terrorism and Political Violence*, **24**(4), 619–34.

Daxecker, Ursula, and Jung, Alexander. 2018. Mixing Votes with Violence: Election Violence around the World. *SAIS Review of International Affairs*, **38**(1), 53–64.

206 REFERENCES

de Bellaigue, Chistopher. 2016. Welcome to Demokrasi: How Erdogan Got More Popular Than Ever. *The Guardian*, 30 August.

Deegan-Krause, Kevin, and Haughton, Tim. 2021. When Voters Chase Novelty. *Foreign Policy*, 12 November.

Deutsche Welle. 2018. French Interior Minister Gerard Collomb Resigns. Deutsche Welle, 3 October.

Devermont, Judd. 2021. Guinea: The Causes and Consequences of West Africa's Latest Coup. Available at: https://www.csis.org/analysis/guinea-causes-and-consequences-west-africas-latest-coup.

Diamond, Larry. 2021. Democratic Regression in Comparative Perspective: Scope, Methods, and Causes. *Democratization*, **28**(1), 22–42.

Diamond, Larry J. 1994. Toward Democratic Consolidation. *Journal of Democracy*, **5**(3), 4–17.

Ding, Iza, and Slater, Dan. 2021. Democratic Decoupling. *Democratization*, **28**(1), 63–80.

Dione, Babacar, and Larson, Krista. 2021. Senegal Opposition Leader Released as New Clashes Erupt. *Associated Press*, 8 March.

Döring, Holger, and Regel, Sven. 2019. Party Facts: A Database of Political Parties Worldwide. *Party Politics*, **25**(2), 97–109.

Druckman, James N. 2003. The Power of Television Images: The Tirst Kennedy-Nixon Debate Revisited. *The Journal of Politics*, **65**(2), 559–71.

Druckman, James N., and Levendusky, Matthew S. 2019. What Do We Measure When We Measure Affective Polarization? *Public Opinion Quarterly*, **83**(1), 114–22.

Dugas, John C. 2003. The Emergence of Neopopulism in Colombia? The Case of Álvaro Uribe. *Third World Quarterly*, **24**(6), 1117–36.

Dulani, Boniface. 2021. Long-Serving African Presidents Say the People Want Them to Stay on: Is That True? *The Washington Post*, 5 November.

Dulani, Boniface, and van Donge, Jan Kees. 2005. African Parliaments between Governance and Government. *A Decade of Legislature–Executive Squabble in Malawi, 1994–2004*. New York: Palgrave Macmillan, 201–25.

Economist, The. 2004. The Importance of Backing Erdogan, 29 January.

Economist, The. 2017. Turkey's Slide into Dictatorship, 15 April.

Economist, The. 2018. El Salvador's Rising Political Star, 10 March.

Economist, The. 2020a. Nayib Bukele's Power Grab in El Salvador, 7 May.

Economist, The. 2020b. Senegal, West Africa's Most Stable Democracy, Teeters, 2 February.

Elgie, Robert. 2018. The Election of Emmanuel Macron and the New French Party System: A Return to the Éternel Marais? *Modern & Contemporary France*, **26**(1), 15–29.

Erdoğan, Emre, and Öney, Sezin. 2014. And the Winner of Turkey's Presidential Election Is ... Populism'. *Washington Post*, 8 August.

Everett, Burgess, Bade, Rachael, and Cheney, Kyle. 2017. Republicans Give Trump a Pass on Judge Attacks. *Associated Press*, 6 February.

Ferreira da Silva, Frederico, Garzia, Diego, and De Angelis, Andrea. 2021. From Party to Leader Mobilization? The Personalization of Voter Turnout. *Party Politics*, **27**(2), 220–33.

Fjelde, Hanne. 2020. Political Party Strength and Electoral Violence. *Journal of Peace Research*, **57**(1), 140–55.

Foa, Roberto Stefan, and Mounk, Yascha. 2017. The Signs of Deconsolidation. *Journal of Democracy*, **28**(1), 5–15.

Forero, Juan. 2001. A Hawk's Candidacy Gains in Besieged Colombia. *New York Times.* Available at: https://www.nytimes.com/2001/03/30/world/a-hawk-s-candidacy-gains-in-besieged-colombia.html (accessed 7 June 2019).

Fossati, Diego, Muhtadi, Burhanuddin, and Warburton, Eve. 2021. Why Democrats Abandon Democracy: Evidence from Four Survey Experiments. *Party Politics,* **28**(3), 554–66.

Frantz, Erica. 2018. *Authoritarianism: What Everyone Needs to Know.* New York: Oxford University Press.

Frantz, Erica, Kendall-Taylor, Andrea, Nietsche, Carisa, and Wright, Joseph. 2021. How Personalist Politics Is Changing Democracies. *Journal of Democracy,* **29**(5), 918–38.

Frantz, Erica, Kendall-Taylor, Andrea, Li, Jia, and Wright, Joseph. 2022. Personalist ruling parties in democracies. *Democratization,* 1–21.

Freedom House. 2017a. Freedom in the World 2017: Ecuador. Available at: https://freedomhouse.org/country/ecuador/freedom-world/2017.

Freedom House. 2017b. Freedom in the World 2017: Hungary. Available at: https://freedomhouse.org/country/hungary/freedom-world/2017.

Freedom House. 2019. Freedom in the World 2019: Hungary. Available at: https://freedomhouse.org/country/hungary/freedom-world/2019.

Freedom House. 2020. Freedom in the World 2020: Senegal. Available at: https://freedomhouse.org/country/senegal/freedom-world/2020.

Freedom House. 2021a. Freedom in the World 2020: El Salvador. Available at: https://freedomhouse.org/country/el-salvador/freedom-world/2020.

Freedom House. 2021b. Freedom in the World 2021: Ecuador. Available at: https://freedomhouse.org/country/ecuador/freedom-world/2021.

Freedom House. 2021c. Freedom in the World 2021: El Salvador. Available at: https://freedomhouse.org/country/el-salvador/freedom-world/2021.

Freedom House. 2021d. Freedom in the World 2021: Turkey. Available at: https://freedomhouse.org/country/turkey/freedom-world/2021.

Galston, William A. 2018. The Populist Challenge to Liberal Democracy. *Journal of Democracy,* **29**(2), 5–19.

Garzia, Diego. 2011. The Personalization of Politics in Western Democracies: Causes and Consequences of Leader-Follower Relationships. *The Leadership Quarterly,* **22**(4), 697–709.

Garzia, Diego. 2013. Changing Parties, Changing Partisans: The Personalization of Partisan Attachments in Western Europe. *Political Psychology,* **34**(1), 67–89.

Garzia, Diego. 2014. *Personalization of Politics and Electoral Change.* Basingstoke: Palgrave Macmillan.

Garzia, Diego. 2017. Personalization of Politics between Television and the Internet: Leader Effects in the 2013 Italian Parliamentary Election. *Journal of Information Technology and Politics,* **14**(4), 403–16.

Garzia, Diego, and Ferreira da Silva, Frederico. 2019. Personalization of Politics. In: Maisel, Louis Sandy (ed.), *Oxford Bibliographies of Political Science.* New York: Oxford University Press.

Garzia, Diego, Ferreira da Silva, Frederico, and De Angelis, Andrea. 2021. *Leaders without Partisans: Dealignment, Media Change, and the Personalization of Politics.* London: Roman and Littlefield Publishers/ECPR Press.

Garzia, Diego, Ferreira da Silva, Frederico, and De Angelis, Andrea. 2022. Partisan Dealignment and the Personalisation of Politics in West European Parliamentary Democracies. *West European Politics,* **45**(2), 311–34.

REFERENCES

Geddes, Barbara, Wright, Joseph, and Frantz, Erica. 2014. Autocratic Breakdown and Regime Transitions: A New Data Set. *Perspectives on Politics*, **12**(2), 313–31.

Geddes, Barbara, Wright, Joseph, and Frantz, Erica. 2018. *How Dictatorships Work*. New York: Cambridge University Press.

Gerring, John, Oncel, Erzen, Morrison, Kevin, and Pemstein, Daniel. 2019. Who Rules the World? A Portrait of the Global Leadership Class. *Perspectives on Politics*, **17**(4), 1079–97.

Gerschewski, Johannes. 2021a. Erosion or Decay? Conceptualizing Causes and Mechanisms of Democratic Regression. *Democratization*, **28**(1), 43–62.

Gerschewski, Johannes. 2021b. Explanations of Institutional Change: Reflecting on a 'Missing Diagonal'. *American Political Science Review*, **115**(1), 218–33.

Gidron, Noam, Adams, James, and Horne, Will. 2020. *American Affective Polarization in Comparative Perspective*. Cambridge: Cambridge University Press.

Giglioli, M.F.N. 2020. Plutocratic Leadership in the Electoral Arena: Three Mitteleuropean Cases of Personal Wealth in Politics. *Comparative European Politics*, **18**, 309–29.

Ginsburg, Tom. 2003. *Judicial Review in New Democracies: Constitutional Courts in Asian Cases*. New York: Cambridge University Press.

Goat, Elliott, and Banuta, Zsofia. 2019. Fresh Evidence of Hungary Vote-Rigging Raises Concerns of Fraud in European Elections. *Open Democracy*, 17 May.

Goodman, Peter S. 2018. The West Hoped for Democracy in Turkey: Erdogan Had Other Ideas. *New York Times*, 18 August.

Gorokhovskaia, Yana, Shahbaz, Adrian, and Slipowitz, Amy. 2023. Freedom in the World 2023: Marking 50 Years in the Struggle for Democracy. Freedom House. Available at https://freedomhouse.org/report/freedom-world/2023/marking-50-years.

Gortazar, Naiara Galarraga. 2023. Brazil: A Laboratory for the Global Fight against Disinformation. *El Pais*, 8 March.

Graham, Matthew H., and Svolik, Milan W. 2020. Democracy in America? Partisanship, Polarization, and the Robustness of Support for Democracy in the United States. *American Political Science Review*, **114**(2), 392–409.

Green, Donald, Palmquist, Bradley, and Schickler, Eric. 2008. *Partisan Hearts and Minds*. New Haven, CT: Yale University Press.

Grillo, Edoardo, and Prato, Carlo. 2023. Reference Points and Democratic Backsliding. *American Journal of Political Science*, **67**(1), 71–88. Available at: https://doi.org/10.1111/ajps.12672.

Grossman, Guy, Kronick, Dorothy, Levendusky, Matthew, and Meredith, Marc. 2022. The Majoritarian Threat to Liberal Democracy. *Journal of Experimental Political Science*, **9**(1), 36–45.

Grzymala-Busse, Anna, Kuo, Didi, Fukumaya, Francis, and McFaul, Michael. 2020. *Global Populisms and Their Challenges*. Stanford: Stanford University Freeman Spogli Institute for International Studies.

Guasti, Petra. 2020. Populism in Power and Democracy: Democratic Decay and Resilience in the Czech Republic (2013–2020). *Politics and Governance*, **8**(4S3), 473–84.

Guess, Andrew, and Coppock, Alexander. 2020. Does Counter-Attitudinal Information Cause Backlash? Results from Three Large Survey Experiments. *British Journal of Political Science*, **50**(4), 1497–515.

Gunther, Richard, and Diamond, Larry. 2003. Species of Political Parties: A New Typology. *Party Politics*, **9**(2), 167–99.

Haggard, Stephan, and Kaufman, Robert. 2021. *Backsliding: Democratic Regress in the Contemporary World*. New York: Cambridge University Press.

Hamilton, Graeme. 2017. Return of the Strongman: 'It's a Perfect Storm against Democracy Right Now'. *National Post*, 11 August.

Hansen, Suzy. 2017. Inside Turkey's Purge. New York Times Magazine, 17 April. Available at: https://www.nytimes.com/2017/04/13/magazine/inside-turkeys-purge.html (accessed 7 June 2019).

Haughton, Timothy, and Deegan-Krause, Kevin. 2021. *The New Party Challenge: Changing Cycles of Party Birth and Death in Central Europe and Beyond*. Oxford: Oxford University Press.

Hawkins, Kirk A. 2009. Is Chávez Populist? Measuring Populist Discourse in Comparative Perspective. *Comparative Political Studies*, **42**(8), 1040–67.

Heil, Andy. 2022. Six Takeaways from Fidesz and Orban's Big Hungarian Election Win. *Radio Free Europe Radio Liberty*, 4 April.

Hermans, Liesbeth, and Vergeer, Maurice. 2009. Personalization in E-Campaigning: A CrossNational Comparison of Personalization Strategies Used on Candidate Websites of 17 Countries in EP Elections 2009. *New Media and Society*, **15**(1), 72–92.

Hicken, Allen, and Martínez Kuhonta, Erik. 2011. Shadows from the Past: Party System Institutionalization in Asia. *Comparative Political Studies*, **44**(5), 572–97.

Hill, Seth J., and Roberts, Margaret E. 2023. Acquiescence Bias Inflates Estimates of Conspiratorial Beliefs and Political Misperceptions. *Political Analysis*, **31**(4), 575–90.

Hlousek, Vit. 2015. Two Types of Presidentialization in the Party Politics of Central Eastern Europe. *Italian Political Science Review*, **45**(3), 277–99.

Holtz-Bacha, Christina, Langer, Ana Ines, and Merkle, Susanne. 2014. The Personalization of Politics in Comparative Perspective: Campaign Coverage in Germany and the United Kingdom. *European Journal of Communication*, **29**(2), 153–70.

Horowitz, Michael C., Sta, Allan C., and Ellis, Cali M. 2015. *Why Leaders Fight*. Cambridge: Cambridge University Press.

Horz, Carlo M. 2021. Electoral Manipulation in Polarized Societies. *The Journal of Politics*, **83**(2), 483–97.

Hunter, Wendy, and Power, Timothy J. 2019. Bolsonaro and Brazil's Illiberal Backlash. *Journal of Democracy*, **30**(1), 68–82.

Ignazi, Piero. 1996. The Crisis of Parties and the Rise of New Political Parties. *Party Politics*, **2**(4), 549–66.

International Crisis Group. 2022. *Brazil's True Believers: Bolsonaro and the Risks of an Election Year*. Brussels, Belgium. 16, June. Available at: https://www.crisisgroup.org/latin-america-caribbean/brazil/brazils-true-believers-bolsonaro-and-risks-election-year (accessed 29 November 2023).

Iverson, Torben, and Soskice, David. 2006. Electoral Institutions and the Politics of Coalitions. *American Political Science Review*, **100**(2), 165–81.

Iyengar, Shanto, Sood, Gaurav, and Lelkes, Yphtach. 2012. Affect, Not Ideology: A Social Identity Perspective on Polarization. *Public Opinion Quarterly*, **76**(3), 405–31.

Janda, Kenneth. 1980. *Political Parties: A Cross-National Survey*. New York and London: Free Press and Collier Macmillan.

Johnson, Joel W., and Wallack, Jessica S. 2012. Electoral Systems and the Personal Vote. *Harvard Dataverse*, **1**. https://doi.org/10.7910/DVN/AMRXJA.

Kagan, Robert. 2021. Our Constitutional Crisis Is already Here. The Washington Post, 23 September.

Kaltwasser, Cristóbal Rovira, Taggart, Paul, Espejo, Paulina Ochoa, and Ostiguy, Pierre. 2017. *The Oxford Handbook of Populism*. Oxford: Oxford University Press.

REFERENCES

Karvonen, Lauri. 2010. *The Personalisation of Politics: A Study of Parliamentary Democracies*. Colchester: ECPR Press.

Katz, Richard S., and Crotty, William J. 2006. *Handbook of Party Politics*. London: Sage.

Kefford, Glenn, and McDonnell, Duncan. 2018. Inside the Personal Party: Leader-Owners, Light Organizations and Limited Lifespans. *The British Journal of Politics and International Relations*, **20**(2), 379–94.

Keller, Albert Galloway (ed.) 1914. *The Challenge of Facts and other Essays*. New Haven, CT: Yale University Press.

Kendall-Taylor, Andrea, and Frantz, Erica. 2016. How Democracies Fall Apart. *Foreign Affairs*, 5 December.

Kendall-Taylor, Andrea, Frantz, Erica, and Wright, Joseph. 2017. The Global Rise of Personalized Politics: It's Not Just Dictators Anymore. *The Washington Quarterly*, **40**(1), 7–19.

Kendall-Taylor, Andrea, Lindstaedt, Natasha, and Frantz, Erica. 2019. *Democracies and Authoritarian Regimes*. New York: Oxford University Press.

Keyman, E. Fuat. 2014. The AK Party: Dominant Party, New Turkey and Polarization. *Insight Turkey*, **16**(2), 19–31.

Kingzette, Jon, Druckman, James N, Klar, Samara, Krupnikov, Yanna, Levendusky, Matthew, and Ryan, John Barry. 2021. Affective Polarization and Democratic Norms. *Public Opinion Quarterly*, **85**(2), 663–7.

Kiratas. 2021. Polarization Settles in El Salvador de Bukele. Kiratas. Available at: https://www.kiratas.com/polarization-settles-in-el-salvador-de-bukele/.

Kirsch, Helen, and Welzel, Christian. 2019. Democracy Misunderstood: Authoritarian Notions of Democracy around the Globe. *Social Forces*, **98**(1), 59–92.

Korosenyi, Andras. 2013. Political Polarization and Its Consequences on Democratic Accountability. *Corvinus Journal of Sociology and Social Policy*, **4**(2), 3–30.

Korosenyi, Andras, Illes, Gabor, and Gyulai, Attila. 2020. *The Orban Regime: Plebiscitary Leader Democracy in the Making*. United Kingdom: Routledge.

Kostadinova, Tatiana, and Levitt, Barry. 2014. Toward a Theory of Personalist Parties: Concept Formation and Theory Building. *Politics & Policy*, **42**(4), 490–512.

Kouba, Karol. 2016. Party Institutionalization and the Removal of Presidential Term Limits in Latin America. *Revista de Ciencia Politica*, **36**(2), 433–57.

Kräämer, Karl-Heinz. 2003. Nepal in 2002: Emergency and Resurrection of Royal Power. *Asian Survey*, **43**(1), 208–14.

Krcmaric, Daniel, Nelson, Stephen C., and Roberts, Andrew. 2020. Studying Leaders and Elites: The Personal Biography Approach. *Annual Review of Political Science*, **23**(1), 133–51.

Kriesi, Hanspeter. 2012. Personalization of National Election Campaigns. *Party Politics*, 825–44.

Kroeger, Alex M. 2020. Dominant Party Rule, Elections, and Cabinet Instability in African Autocracies. *British Journal of Political Science*, **50**(1), 79–101.

Kruikemeier, Sanne, van Noort, Guda, Vliegenthart, Rens, and Vreese, Claes H. De. 2013. Getting Closer: The Effects of Personalized and Interactive Online Political Communication. *European Journal of Communication*, **28**(1), 53–66.

Kruse, Stefan, Ravlik, Maria, and Welzel, Christian. 2019. Democracy Confused: When People Mistake the Absence of Democracy for Its Presence. *Journal of Cross-Cultural Psychology*, **50**(3), 315–35.

REFERENCES 211

Kuenzi, Michelle, and Lambright, Gina. 2001. Party System Institutionalization in 30 African Countries. *Party Politics*, **7**(4), 437–68.

Kumar, Anita, and Orr, Gabby. 2020. Inside Trump's Pressure Campaign to Overturn the Election. *Politico*, 21 December.

Labrador, Gabriel, Quintanilla, Jaime, Arauz, Sergio, and Alvarado, Jimmy. 2019. Amigos, socios, y parientes en el nuevo gobierno. *El Faro*, 2 June.

Laczo, Ferenc. 2020. Ten Years of Viktor Orban: The Rise of 'Soft Authoritarianism'. Studio Europa Maastricht, Maastricht University, 25 November.

Laebens, Melis G, and Lührmann, Anna. 2021. What halts democratic erosion? The changing role of accountability. *Democratization*, **28**(5), 908–28.

Landau, David. 2020. Personalism and the Trajectories of Populist Constitutions. *Annual Review of Law and Social Science*, **16**(1), 293–309.

Latinobarometer. 2022. Latinobarometer. Available at: https://www.latinobarometro.org/lat.jsp.

Laver, Michael. 1981. *The Politics of Private Desires*. London: Penguin Books.

Laver, Michael, and Schofield, Norman. 1998. *Multiparty Government: The Politics of Coalition in Europe*. University of Michigan Press.

Lendvai, Paul. 2018. The Most Dangerous Man in the European Union. *The Atlantic*, 7 April 2018.

Lenz, Gabriel S., and Lawson, Chappell. 2011. Looking the Part: Television Leads Less Informed Citizens to Vote Based on Candidates' Appearance. *American Journal of Political Science*, **55**(3), 574–89.

Levi, Margaret. 1989. *Of Rule and Revenue*. Berkeley: University of California Press.

Levitsky, Steven. 1999. Fujimori and Post-Party Politics in Peru. *Journal of Democracy*, **10**(3), 78–92.

Levitsky, Steven, and Cameron, Maxwell A. 2003. Democracy without Parties? Political Parties and Regime Change in Fujimori's Peru. *Latin American Politics and Society*, **45**(3), 1–33.

Levitsky, Steven, and Way, Lucan A. 2010. *Competitive Authoritarianism: Hybrid Regimes after the Cold War*. Cambridge: Cambridge University Press.

Levitsky, Steven, and Ziblatt, Daniel. 2018. *How Democracies Die*. New York: Crown Publishing.

Levitsky, Steven, Loxton, James, and Van Dyck, Brandon. 2016. *Challenges of Party-Building in Latin America*. Cambridge: Cambridge University Press. Chap. Introduction: Challenges of Party-Building in Latin America.

Lewis, Paul H. 1972. The Spanish Ministerial Elite, 1938–1969. *Comparative Politics*, **5**(1), 83–106.

Lijphart, Arend. 1991. Constitutional Choices for New Democracies. *Journal of Democracy*, **2**(1), 72–84.

Lindberg, Staffan I. 2007. Institutionalization of Party Systems? Stability and Fluidity among Legislative Parties in Africa's Democracies. *Government and Opposition*, **42**(2), 215–41.

Linden, Jon. 1997. Philippine High Court Dashes Ramos's Second-Term Chances. *The Wall Street Journal*, 11 June.

Linz, Juan J. 1990. The Perils of Presidentialism. *Journal of Democracy*, **1**(1), 51–69.

Lipset, Seymour Martin. 1959. Some Social Requisites of Democracy: Economic Development and Political Legitimacy. *American Political Science Review*, **53**(1), 69–105.

Londregan, John B., and Poole, Keith T. 1990. Poverty, the Coup Trap, and the Seizure of Executive Power. *World Politics*, **42**(2), 151–83.

212 REFERENCES

Lu, Christina. 2021. What's Going on in Senegal? *Foreign Policy*, 12 March.

Lucas, Edward. 2008. Whataboutism. *The Economist*, 31 January.

Lührmann, Anna. 2020. *Codebook Varieties of Party Identity and Organization (V-Party)*. Varieties of Democracy (V-Dem) Project.

Lührmann, Anna. 2021. Disrupting the Autocratization Sequence: Towards Democratic Resilience. *Democratization*, **28**(5), 1017–39.

Lührmann, Anna, and Lindberg, Staffan I. 2019. A Third Wave of Autocratization Is Here: What Is New About It? *Democratization*, **26**(7), 1095–113.

Lührmann, Anna, Dupont, Nils, Higashijima, Masaaki, Kavasoglu, Yaman Berker, Marquardt, Kyle L., Bernhard, Michael, Doring, Holger, Hicken, Allen, Laebens, Melis, Lindberg, Staffan I., Neundorf, Anja, Ruth, Saskia, Weghorst, Keith R., Wiesehomeier, Nina, Wright, Joseph, Reuter, Ora John, Alizada, Nazifa, Bederke, Paul, Gastaldi, Lisa, Grahn, Sandra, Hindle, Garry, Ilchenko, Nina, von Romer, Johannes, Wilson, Steven, Pemstein, Daniel, and Seim, Brigitte. 2020. *Varieties of Party Identity and Organization (V-Party) Dataset V1*. Varieties of Democracy (V-Dem) Project.

Lupu, Noam. 2016. *Party Brands in Crisis: Partisanship, Brand Dilution, and the Breakdown of Political Parties in Latin America*. New York: Cambridge University Press.

Madison, James. 1788. Federalist No. 51: The Structure of the Government Must Furnish the Proper Checks and Balances Between the Different Departments. Washington, D.C.: Library of Congress. Available at: https://guides.loc.gov/federalist-papers/text-51-60 (accessed 30 November 2023).

Mainwaring, Scott. 1998. Party Systems in the Third Wave. *Journal of Democracy*, **9**(3), 67–81.

Mainwaring, Scott, and Perez-Linan, Anibal. 2014. *Democracies and Dictatorships in Latin America: Emergence, Survival, and Fall*. Cambridge: Cambridge University Press.

Mainwaring, Scott, and Scully, Timothy. 1995. *Building Democratic Institutions: Party Systems in Latin America*. Stanford, CA: Stanford University Press.

Mainwaring, Scott, and Torcal, Mariano. 2006. Party System Institutionalization and Party System Theory after the Third Wave of Democratization. *Handbook of Party Politics*, **11**(6), 204–27.

Mainwaring, Scott, and Zoco, Edurne. 2007. Political Sequences and the Stabilization of Interparty Competition: Electoral Volatility in Old and New Democracies. *Party Politics*, **13**(2), 155–78.

Mair, Peter. 1984. Party Politics in Contemporary Europe: A Challenge to Party? *West European Politics*, **7**(4), 170–84.

Mansbridge, Jane, and Macedo, Stephen. 2019. Populism and Democratic Theory. *Annual Review of Law and Social Science*, **15**, 59–77.

Marino, Bruno, Diodati, Nicola Martocchia, and Verzichelli, Luca. 2021. The Personalization of Party Politics in Western Europe (1985–2016): Evidence from an Expert Survey. *Acta Politica*. Available at: https://doi.org/10.1057/s41269-021-00210-x.

Martinez-Gallardo, Cecilia. 2012. Out of the Cabinet: What Drives Defections from the Government in Presidential Systems? *Comparative Political Studies*, **45**(1), 62–90.

McAllister, Ian. 2007. The Personalization of Politics. In: Russell J. Dalton and Hans-Dieter Klingemann (eds.), *The Oxford Handbook of Political Behavior*. Oxford: Oxford University Press.

McCoy, Jennifer, and Somer, Murat. 2019. Toward a Theory of Pernicious Polarization and How It Harms Democracies: Comparative Evidence and Possible Remedies. *The Annals of the American Academy of Political and Social Science*, **681**(1), 234–71.

McCoy, Jennifer, and Somer, Murat. 2021. Overcoming Polarization. *Journal of Democracy*, **32**(1), 6–21.

McCoy, Jennifer, Rahman, Tahmina, and Somer, Murat. 2018. Polarization and the Global Crisis of Democracy: Common Patterns, Dynamics, and Pernicious Consequences for Democratic Polities. *American Behavioral Scientist*, **62**(1), 16–42.

McKernan, Bethan. 2019. From Reformer to 'New Sultan': Erdogan's Populist Evolution. *The Guardian*, 11 March.

McKie, Kristin. 2017. Comparative Continuismo: Presidential Term Limit Contravention across Developing Democracies. Notre Dame: Kellogg Institute for International Studies, University of Notre Dame, 425.

McKie, Kristin. 2019. Presidential Term Limit Contravention: Abolish, Extend, Fail, or Respect? *Comparative Political Studies*, **52**(10), 1500–34.

Meijers, Maurits J., and Zaslove, Andrej. 2020. Measuring Populism in Political Parties: Appraisal of a New Approach. *Comparative Political Studies*, **54**(2), 372–407.

Melendez-Sanchez, Manuel. 2021. Latin America Erupts: Millennial Authoritarianism in El Salvador. *Journal of Democracy*, **32**(3), 19–32.

Meng, Anne. 2020. *Constraining Dictatorship: From Personalized Rule to Institutionalized Regimes*. Cambridge: Cambridge University Press.

Meredith, Sam. 2018. Who is the 'Trump of the Tropics?' Brazil's Divisive New President, Jair Bolsonaro—in his own words. *CNBC*, 29 October.

Mettler, Suzanne, and Lieberman, Robert C. 2020. *Four Threats: The Recurring Crises of American Democracy*. New York: St. Martin's Press.

Metz, Rudolf, and Varnagy, Reka. 2021. 'Mass', 'Movement', 'Personal', or 'Cartel' Party? Fidesz's Hybrid Organisational Strategy. *Politics and Governance*, **9**(4), 317–28.

Metz, Manon, Kruikemeier, Sanne, and Lecheler, Sophie. 2020. Personalization of Politics on Facebook: Examining the Content and Effects of Professional, Emotional and Private Self-Personalization. *Information, Communication & Society*, **23**(10), 1481–98.

Meyer-Sahling, Jan-Hinrik, and Toth, Fanni. 2020. Governing Illiberal Democracies: Democratic Backsliding and the Political Appointment of Top Officials in Hungary. *NISPAcee Journal of Public Administration and Policy*, **13**(2), 93–113.

Middlebrook, Kevin J. 2000. *Conservative Parties, the Right, and Democracy in Latin America*. Baltimore, MD: Johns Hopkins University Press.

Miller, Michael K. 2021. A Republic, If You Can Keep It: Breakdown and Erosion in Modern Democracies. *The Journal of Politics*, **83**(1), 198–213.

Molotsky, Irvin. 1987. Reagan Wants End of Two-Term Limit. *New York Times*, 29 November.

Mounk, Yascha. 2018a. Hungary's Election Was a Milestone in the Decline of Democracy. *Slate*, 9 April.

Mounk, Yascha. 2018b. *The People vs. Democracy: Why Our Freedom Is in Danger and How to Save It*. Cambridge, MA: Harvard University Press.

Mudde, Cas. 2007. *Populist Radical Right Parties in Europe*. Cambridge: Cambridge University Press.

Mudde, Cas. 2014. The 2014 Hungarian Parliamentary Elections, or How to Craft a Constitutional Majority. *Washington Post*, 14 August.

Mudde, Cas, and Kaltwasser, Cristóbal Rovira. 2012. *Populism in Europe and the Americas: Threat or Corrective for Democracy?* Cambridge: Cambridge University Press.

Mudde, Cas, and Kaltwasser, Cristóbal Rovira. 2017. *Populism: A Very Short Introduction*. Oxford: Oxford University Press.

Mudde, Cas, and Kaltwasser, Cristóbal Rovira. 2018. Studying Populism in Comparative Perspective: Reflections on the Contemporary and Future Research Agenda. *Comparative Political Studies*, **51**(13), 1667–93.

Mughan, Anthony. 1993. Party Leaders and Presidentialism in the 1992 Election: A Post-War Perspective. *British Elections and Parties Yearbook*, **3**(1), 193–204.

Mughan, Anthony. 2000. *Media and the Presidentialization of Parliamentary Elections*. New York: Springer.

Muller, Jan-Werner. 2016. *What Is Populism?* Philadelphia: University of Pennsylvania Press.

Muller, Thomas C., Isacoff, Juditch F., and Lansford, Tom. 2012. *Political Handbook of the World 2012*. Washington, DC: CQ Press.

Munck, Gerardo L, and Verkuilen, Jay. 2002. Conceptualizing and Measuring Democracy: Evaluating Alternative Indices. *Comparative Political Studies*, **35**(1), 5–34.

Musella, Fortunato. 2015. Personal Leaders and Party Change: Italy in Comparative Perspective. *Italian Political Science Review*, **45**(3), 227–47.

Nalepa, Monika, and Cinar, Ipek. 2021. *Mass or Elite Polarization as the Driver of Authoritarian Backsliding? Evidence from 8 Polish Surveys*. University of Chicago.

Nash, Nathaniel. 1994. A New Breed of Strongman in the South. *New York Times*, 16 January.

Navia, Patricio, and Perello, Lucas. 2021. It's Not Just El Salvador. Democracies Are Weakening Across Central America. *America's Quarterly*, 1 March.

Nelson, Stephen C. 2020. Playing Favorites: How Shared Beliefs Shape the IMF's Lending Decisions. *International Organization*, **68**(2), 297–328.

Neuman, Scott. 2020. Troops Occupy El Salvador's Legislature to Back President's Crime Package. *National Public Radio*, 10 February.

News Wires. 2021. Thousands Protest in El Salvador against 'Dictator' President Bukele. *News Wires*, 18 October. Available at: https://www.france24.com/en/americas/20211018-thousands-protest-in-el-salvador-against-dictator-president-bukele.

Nicas, Jack, and Spigariol, Andre. 2023. Bolsonaro Faces Investigation for Inspiring Brazil's Capital Riot. *New York Times*, 13 January.

Nicas, Jack, Milhorance, Flavia, and Ionova, Ana. 2022. How Bolsonaro Built the Myth of Stolen Elections in Brazil. *New York Times*, 25 October.

Niesse, Mark. 2021. Georgia Elections Chief Counters False Claims in Letter to Congress. *Atlanta Journal Constitution*, 7 January.

North, Douglass C., and Weingast, Barry R. 1989. Constitutions and Commitment: The Evolution of Institutions Governing Public Choice in Seventeenth-Century England. *The Journal of Economic History*, **49**(4), 803–32.

Nowack, Daniel. 2021. Process Tracing the Term Limit Struggle in Malawi: The Role of International Democracy Promotion in Muluzi's Bid for a Third Term. *Africa Spectrum*, **55**(3), 291–320.

NPR. 2022. Embattled UK Prime Minister Boris Johnson Resigns. *National Public Radio*, 7 July.

Nyrup, Jacob, and Bramwell, Stuart. 2020. Who Governs? A New Global Dataset on Members of Cabinets. *American Political Science Review*, **114**(4), 1366–74.

Ologou, Expédit B. 2021. Democracy Capture in Benin. *Democracy Capture in Africa*. Accra: Ghana Center for Democratic Development, 33–57.

Orhan, Yunus Emre. 2021. The Relationship between Affective Polarization and Democratic Backsliding: Comparative Evidence. *Democratization*, **29**(4), 714–35.

REFERENCES 215

OSCE. 2018. Hungary: Parliamentary Elections. *Organization for Security and Cooperation in Europe*, 27 June.

Passarelli, Gianluca. 2015. *The Presidentialization of Political Parties: Organizations, Institutions and Leaders*. Basingstoke: Palgrave Macmillan.

Pech, Laurent, and Bard, Petra. 2022. The Commission's Rule of Law Report and the EU Monitoring and Enforcement of Article 2 TEU Values. *European Parliament*, **PE 727.551**(PE 727.551).

Pedersen, Helene Helboe, and Rahat, Gideon. 2021. Political Personalization and Personalized Politics within and beyond the Behavioural Arena. *Party Politics*, **27**(2), 211–19.

Pepinsky, Thomas. 2014. The Institutional Turn in Comparative Authoritarianism. *British Journal of Political Science*, **44**(3), 631–53.

Perez-Linan, Anibal, Schmidt, Nicolas, and Vairo, Daniela. 2019. Presidential Hegemony and Democratic Backsliding in Latin America, 1925–2016. *Democratization*, **26**(4), 606–25.

Plattner, Marc F. 2019. Illiberal Democracy and the Struggle on the Right. *Journal of Democracy*, **30**(1), 5–19.

Poguntke, Thomas, and Webb, Paul. 2007. *The Presidentialization of Politics: A Comparative Study of Modern Democracies*. Oxford: Oxford University Press.

Point, Le. 2018. The Dictator: How Far Will Erdogan Go? 25 May.

Pommiers, Eléa. 2017. Les ministres de la société civile sont-ils vraiment étrangers à la politique? *Le Monde*, 19 May.

Posner, Eric A. 2017. Can It Happen Here? Donald Trump and the Paradox of Populist Government. University of Chicago Public Law and Legal Theory Paper Series, **605**.

Postman, Neil. 2006. *Amusing Ourselves to Death: Public Discourse in the Age of Show Business*. London: Penguin.

Powell, Eleanor Neff, and Tucker, Joshua A. 2014. Revisiting Electoral Volatility in Post-Communist Countries: New Data, New Results and New Approaches. *British Journal of Political Science*, **44**(1), 123–47.

Przeworski, Adam, and Limongi, Fernando. 1997. Modernization: Theories and Facts. *World Politics*, **49**(2), 155–83.

Puddington, Arch, and Roylance, Tyler. 2017. Populists and Autocrats: The Dual Threat to Global Democracy. *Freedom House*.

Querubin, Pablo. 2016. Family and Politics: Dynastic Persistence in the Philippines. *Quarterly Journal of Political Science*, **11**(2), 151–81.

Quinlan, Stephen, and McAllister, Ian. 2022. Leader or Party? Quantifying and Exploring Behavioral Personalization 1996–2019. *Party Politics*, **28**(1), 24–37.

Rahat, Gideon. 2022. Party Types in the Age of Personalized Politics. *Perspectives on Politics*, 1–16.

Rahat, Gideon, and Kenig, Ofer. 2018. *From Party Politics to Personalized Politics? Party Change and Political Personalization in Democracies*. Oxford: Oxford University Press.

Rahat, Gideon, and Sheafer, Tamir. 2007. The Personalization(s) of Politics: Israel, 1949–2003. *Political Communication*, **24**(1), 65–80.

Randall, Vicky, and Svåsand, Lars. 2002. Party Institutionalization in New Democracies. *Party Politics*, **8**(1), 5–29.

Reiljan, Andres. 2020. 'Fear and Loathing across Party Lines' (also) in Europe: Affective Polarisation in European Party Systems. *European Journal of Political Research*, **59**(2), 376–96.

Renwick, Alan, and Pilet, Jean-Benoit. 2016. *Face on the Ballot: The Personalization of Electoral Systems*. Oxford: Oxford University Press.

216 REFERENCES

Resnick, Danielle. 2014. *Urban Poverty and Party Populism in African Democracies*. Cambridge: Cambridge University Press.

Resnick, Danielle. 2017. Populism in Africa. *The Oxford Handbook of Populism*. Oxford: Oxford University Press, 101–20.

Reuters Staff. 2017. Support for Hungary's Ruling Fidesz Highest in Six Years in October: Pollster. *Reuters*, 2 November.

Rhodes-Purdy, Matthew, and Madrid, Raúl L. 2020. The Perils of Personalism. *Democratization*, **27**(2), 321–39.

Riker, William H. 1962. *The Theory of Political Coalitions*. Vol. 173. New Haven, CT: Yale University Press.

Ríos-figueroa, Julio. 2007. Fragmentation of Power and the Emergence of an Effective Judiciary in Mexico, 1994–2002. *Latin American Politics and Society*, **49**(1), 31–57.

Robinson, Eugene. 1990. Dark Horse Confuses Peru's Election. *Washington Post*, 7 April. Available at: https://www.washingtonpost.com/archive/politics/1990/04/07/dark-horse-confuses-perus-election/81675346-e38a-4cb5-9387-4631fe6473c7/.

Rooduijn, Matthijs, and Pauwels, Teun. 2011. Measuring Populism: Comparing Two Methods of Content Analysis. *West European Politics*, **34**(6), 1272–83.

Roth, Kenneth. 2018. The Pushback against the Populist Challenge. *Human Rights Watch*. New York, NY. https://www.hrw.org/sites/default/files/201801world_report_keynote.pdf

Ruediger, Marco Aurélio. 2022. Online disinformation and questioning of election results: fifteen months of posts about electronic voting machine fraud and auditable printed votes on Facebook. Rio de Janeiro, Brazil. FGV DAPP. Available at: https://democraciadigital.dapp.fgv.br/wp-content/uploads/2022/02/ENEstudo-7_Fraude-nas-urnas_FichaISBN.pdf (accessed 29 November 2023).

Sadurski, Wojciech. 2019. *Poland's Constitutional Breakdown*. Oxford: Oxford University Press.

Samuels, David J, and Shugart, Matthew Soberg. 2003. Presidentialism, Elections and Representation. *Journal of Theoretical Politics*, **15**(1), 33–60.

Samuels, David J, and Shugart, Matthew S. 2010. *Presidents, Parties, and Prime Ministers: How the Separation of Powers Affects Party Organization and Behavior*. New York: Cambridge University Press.

Santora, Marc, and Bienvenu, Helene. 2018. Hungary Election Was Free but Not Entirely Fair, Observers Say. *New York Times*, 9 April.

Sartori, Giovanni. 1989. Video-Power. *Government and Opposition*, **24**(1), 39–53.

Schedler, Andreas. 1998. What Is Democratic Consolidation? *Journal of Democracy*, **9**(2), 91–107.

Scheppele, Kim Lane. 2011. Hungary's Constitutional Revolution. *New York Times*, 19 December.

Schumacher, Gijs, and Giger, Nathalie. 2017. Who Leads the Party? On Membership Size, Selectorates and Party Oligarchy. *Political Studies*, **65**(1), 162–81.

Segura, Edwin. 2020. Bukele cierra su primer año de trabajo con alta aprobación. *La Prensa Gráfica*, 24 May.

Segura, Edwin. 2021. Bukele llega a la mitad de su gestión con alta aprobación. *La Prensa Gráfica*, 15 November.

Segura, Edwin. 2022. Bukele cierra su tercer año y medio de festión con 88% de aprobación. *La Prensa Gráfica*, 12 December.

Sharon-Krespin, Rachel. 2009. Fethullah Gülen's Grand Ambition. *Middle East Quarterly*, Winter, 55–66.

Shen, Xiaoxiao, and Rory Truex. 2021. In Search of Self-Censorship. *British Journal of Political Science*, **51**(4), 1672–84.

Singer, Matthew M. 2018. The Meaning, Origin, and Consequences of Populist Politics. *Oxford Research Encyclopedia Online*. Available at: https://doi.org/10.1093/acrefore/9780190228637.013.623 (accessed 18 December 2019).

Singer, Matthew M. 2023. Fiddling while Democracy Burns: Partisan Reactions to Weak Democracy in Latin America. *Perspectives on Politics*, **21**(1), 9–26.

Slothuus, Rune, and Bisgaard, Martin. 2021. How Political Parties Shape Public Opinion in the Real World. *American Journal of Political Science*, **65**(4), 896–911.

Smith, Daniel M, and Martin, Shane. 2017. Political Dynasties and the Selection of Cabinet Ministers. *Legislative Studies Quarterly*, **42**(1), 131–65.

Smith, Daniel Markham. 2012. Succeeding in Politics: Dynasties in Democracies. PhD dissertation, University of California, San Diego, CA.

Somer, Murat. 2019. Turkey: The Slippery Slope from Reformist to Revolutionary Polarization and Democratic Breakdown. *The ANNALS of the American Academy of Political and Social Science*, **681**(1), 42–61.

Stanyer, James. 2012. *Intimate Politics: Publicity, Privacy and the Personal Lives of Politicians in Media Saturated Democracies*. Cambridge: Cambridge University Press.

Stasavage, David. 2020. *The Decline and Rise of Democracy: A Global History from Antiquity to Today*. Princeton, NJ: Princeton University Press.

Stiftung, Bertelsmann. 2018. BTI 2018 Country Report—Benin. Available at: https://bti-project.org/fileadmin/api/content/en/downloads/reports/country_report_2018_BEN.pdf.

Strom, Kaare. 1990. A Behavioral Theory of Competitive Political Parties. *American Journal of Political Science*, **34**(2), 565–98.

Svolik, Milan. 2008. Authoritarian Reversals and Democratic Consolidation. *American Political Science Review*, **102**(2), 153–68.

Svolik, Milan W. 2019. Polarization versus Democracy. *Journal of Democracy*, **30**(3), 20–32.

Svolik, Milan W. 2020. When Polarization Trumps Civic Virtue: Partisan Conflict and the Subversion of Democracy by Incumbents. *Quarterly Journal of Political Science*, **15**(1), 3–31.

Szajkowski, Bogdan. 2005. *Political Parties of the World*. London: John Harper Publishing

Szakacs, Gergely, and Than, Krisztina. 2015. Hungary's Right-Wing Alliance Loses Two-Thirds Majority. *Reuters*, 23 February.

Taber, Charles S, and Lodge, Milton. 2006. Motivated Skepticism in the Evaluation of Political Beliefs. *American Journal of Political Science*, **50**(3), 755–69.

Tai, Yuehong 'Cassandra', Hu, Yue, and Solt, Frederick. 2022. Democracy, Public Support, and Measurement Uncertainty. *American Political Science Review*, 1–7. doi:10.1017/S0003055422000429.

Tavits, Margit. 2005. The Development of Stable Party Support: Electoral Dynamics in PostCommunist Europe. *American Journal of Political Science*, **49**(2), 283–98.

Temin, Jon. 2020. When Leaders Override Term Limits, Democracy Grinds to a Halt. *Lawfare*, 29 October.

Törnberg, Petter. 2022. How Digital Media Drive Affective Polarization through Partisan Sorting. *Proceedings of the National Academy of Sciences*, **119**(42), e2207159119.

Tworzecki, Hubert. 2019. Poland: A Case of Top-Down Polarization. *The Annals of the American Academy of Political and Social Science*, **681**(1), 97–119.

Vaccaro, Andrea. 2021. Comparing Measures of Democracy: Statistical Properties, Convergence, and Interchangeability. *European Political Science*, **20**(4), 666–84.

Van Aelst, Peter, Sheafer, Tamier, and Stanyer, James. 2012. The Personalizations of Mediated Political Communication: A Review of Concepts, Operationalizations and Key Findings. *Journalism*, **13**(2), 203–20.

Van Bavel, Jay J., and Pereira, Andrea. 2018. The Partisan Brain: An Identity-Based Model of Political Belief. *Trends in Cognitive Aciences*, **22**(3), 213–24.

Vida, Melissa. 2019. While El Salvador's Security Improves, It Loses Ground in Freedom of Press. *Global Voices Advox*, 1 October.

Vidra, Zsuzsanna. 2019. Did the Hungarian Local Elections Break Polarization and Extremism? *Open Democracy*, 27 October.

VonDoepp, Peter. 2019. *The Politics of Presidential Term Limits*. The Politics of Presidential Term Limits in Malawi. Oxford: Oxford University Press, 291–310.

De Vries, Catherine E., and Hobolt, Sara B. 2020. *Political Entrepreneurs: The Rise of Challenger Parties in Europe*. Princeton, NJ: Princeton University Press.

Waldner, David, and Lust, Ellen. 2018. Unwelcome Change: Coming to Terms with Democratic Backsliding. *Annual Review of Political Science*, **21**(1), 93–113.

Washington Post. 2013. Prime Minister Erdogan's Strongman Response to Turkey's Protests. *Washington Post*, 3 June.

Webb, Paul, Poguntke, Thomas, and Kolodny, Robin. 2012. The Presidentialization of Party Leadership? Evaluating Party Leadership and Party Government in the Democratic World. *Comparative Political Leadership*. London: Palgrave Macmillan.

Werlich, David P. 1991. Fujimori and the 'Disaster' in Peru. *Current History*, **90**(553), 61.

Westwood, SJ, Grimmer, J, Tyler, M, and Nall, C. 2022. Current Research Overstates American Support for Political Violence. *Proceedings of the National Academy of Sciences*, **119**(2), e2116870119.

Weyland, Kurt. 2001. Clarifying a Contested Concept: Populism in the Study of Latin American Politics. *Comparative Politics*, **34**(1), 1–22.

Weyland, Kurt. 2020. Populism's Threat to Democracy: Comparative Lessons for the United States. *Perspectives on Politics*, **18**(2), 389–406.

Weyland, Kurt, and Madrid, Raul L. 2019. *When Democracy Trumps Populism: European and Latin American Lessons for the United States*. New York: Cambridge University Press.

Whitehead, Laurence. 2001. *The International Dimensions of Democratization: Europe and the Americas*. Oxford: Oxford University Press.

Wike, Richard, Simmons, Katie, Stokes, Bruce, and Fetterolf, Janell. 2017. Globally, Broad Support for Representative and Direct Democracy. Pew Research Center, 16 October.

Wilson, Matthew C, Medzihorsky, Juraj, Maerz, Seraphine F, Lindenfors, Patrik, Edgell, Amanda B, Boese, Vanessa A, and Lindberg, Staffan I. 2022. Episodes of Liberalization in Autocracies: A New Approach to Quantitatively Studying Democratization. *Political Science Research and Methods*, 1–20. doi:10.1017/psrm.2022.11.

Wines, Michael, and Bazelon, Emily. 2020. Census Officials Say They Can't Meet Trump's Deadline for Population Count. *New York Times*, 19 November.

World Bank. 2012. World Development Indicators 2012. Available at https://openknowledge.worldbank.org/handle/10986/6014 (accessed 14 February 2017).

Wuttke, Alexander, Schimpf, Christian, and Schoen, Harald. 2020. When the Whole Is Greater than the Sum of Its Parts: On the Conceptualization and Measurement of Populist Attitudes and Other Multidimensional Constructs. *American Political Science Review*, **114**(2), 356–74.

Zakaria, Fareed. 1997. The Rise of Illiberal Democracy. *Foreign Affairs*, **76**, 22.

Zakharov, Alexei V. 2016. The Loyalty-Competence Trade-Off in Dictatorships and Outside Options for Subordinates. *The Journal of Politics*, **78**(2), 457–66.

Zaller, John R. 1992. *The Nature and Origins of Mass Opinion*. Cambridge: Cambridge University Press.

Zengerle, Patricia. 2016. Trump Says He Will Accept Election Result—If He Wins. *Reuters*, 19 October. Available at: https://www.reuters.com/article/us-usa-election/trump-says-he-will-accept-election-result-if-he-wins-idUSKCN12J0ZM.

Ziblatt, Daniel. 2017. *Conservative Political Parties and the Birth of Modern Democracy in Europe* New York: Cambridge University Press.

Zrt, Ipsos Hungary. 2017. Public Opinion in Hungary: November 30 – December 20, 2017. Center for Insights in Survey Research.

Index

For the benefit of digital users, indexed terms that span two pages (e.g., 52–53) may, on occasion, appear on only one of those pages.

Introductory Note

Tables and figures are indicated by an italic *t* and *f* following the page/paragraph number.

accountability
  horizontal 11, 125, 134–135, 149–150
  vertical 3–4, 125, 151, 153–154, 189
Africa 42–44, 113, 148, 154–155, 188
Agrofert 63, 72
Ahmed, Shahabuddin 26
Americas 43–44, 113, 148, 154–155
Amnesty International 109–110
Andres Perez, Carlos 59, 87
Anliker, Federico 68
anti-pluralism 34
appointments 8, 30, 70–71, 74–75, 87–92, 90*f*, 91*f*, 96*f*, *see also* nominations
Arinc, Bulent 69
Arroyo, Gloria Macapagal 112
Asia 42–43, 113, 148
authoritarianism
  drift to 2
  in El Salvador 102
  in Hungary 105, 107–108
  and party institutionalization 39
  and party personalism 18, 28, 118–119
  and reforms 11
  in Turkey 123, 162, 163
  and voters 155
autocracies 1, 5n.6, 36n.14, 39, 111
Autocratic Regimes Data Set 10–11
autogolpes 11–12, 22

Babacan, Ali 69
Babis, Andrej 40, 63, 70–72
Bachelet, Michelle 59
Bangladesh 26, 117–118
Barros, Felipe 164
Belarus 1
Benin 2, 146, 167*f*, 167–168
  Progressive Union 167–168
Biden, Joe 154
Bolivia 13, 122–123
Bolsonaro, Jair 31, 154, 156, 161, 163–165, 200
Bradlow, Benjamin 200

Brazil 158, 161, 163–165, 200
  Congress 200
  Social Liberal Party (PSL) 164
  Superior Electoral Court (TSE) 164–165
  Supreme Court 165
Bukele, Nayib 59, 68, 99–104, 128, 151, 170
Bukele, Xavier Zablah 68
bureaucracies 135, 137–139, 145–146
Burundi, National Council for the Defense of Democracy-Forces for the Defense of Democracy (CNDD-FDD) 71–72
Bush, George H.W. 32–33
Bush, George W. 31–33

cabinet appointments 74–75, 87–92, 90*f*, 91*f*, 96*f*
Caldera, Rafael 40, 59, 87
campaign finance 53–54, 62, 72 *see also* funding
capacity 64, 71–74, 93
Cardoso, Fernando Henrique 164
case studies 99–108, 161–165
Castiglioni, Luis 133
Chapel Hill Expert Survey (CHES) 47–48n.21
Chavez, Hugo
  and democratic backsliding 1–2, 10, 113
  and judicial attacks 171
  and party personalism 2, 8, 31, 40, 59, 87
  and polarization 168
  and populism 33
China 200
citizens 21, 153, 154–161, 197
civil liberties 1, 96*f*, 98, 108–111, 131*f*
civil societies 199–200
coalitions 75, 126, 200
Colombia
  Colombia First Movement (Movimento Primero Colombia) 26–27n.6
  Conservative Party 26–27, 26–27n.6, 70
  Liberal Party 26–27n.6
Comparative Candidate Survey (CCS) 79–84, 81*f*, 83*f*, 86

INDEX   221

Comparative Study of Election Systems (CSES) 168–171, 174, 190*f*
Condé, Alpha 13
Correa, Rafael 13–14, 59, 112, 117–118, 121
countering party personalism 197–200
coups
    and democratic collapse 11–13, 12*f*, 13, 120–123, 124*f*
    military 11–13, 124*f*, 98, 113, 117–118
    in Turkey 162–163
COVID-19 pandemic 102, 200
crime, violent 99–100
Czech Republic, Action by Dissatisfied Citizens (ANO) 40, 63, 70–72

Database of Political Institutions (DPI) 26–27
democracy
    age of 40–42, 100, 113
    attitudes to 154–155, 177–178
    concept of 10–11
    declining support for 53
    defence of 197–199
    empirical patterns 74–92
    executive constraints on 71–74, 134–140
    harmed by party personalism 7–9, 21, 197
    illiberal 108–109, 111
    undermined by party personalism 64–67, 98
democracy scores 43, 117–118, 122*t*, 122
democratic backsliding
    and attitudes to democracy 154–155
    concept of 10
    and democratic collapse 13, 112–113, 122*t*, 120–125
    and democratic decay 111–112
    and democratic erosion 112
    descriptive patterns 113–117, 114*f*, 116*f*
    econometric tests 117–120
    and executive constraints 133–134
    existing explanations of 14–16
    and legislature control 125–130, 129*t*, 127*f*
    measurement of 10–11
    and party personalism 3–4, 4*f*, 20, 63–64, 92–93, 118*t*, 98–99, 108, 111–120, 130–131, 193–196
    and polarization 155–156, 159
    and populism 42–43, 47, 50
    research 18
    and societal pathways 153
    in Turkey 35–38, 37*f*
democratic collapse 1–2, 12*f*, 10–14, 42–43, 112–113, 114*f*, 118*t*, 118–119, 119*f*, 120–125, 122*t*, 124*f*
democratic decay *see* democratic backsliding

democratic decline 1–4, 4*f*, 17–19, 41*f*, 40–42, 114*f*, 104, 112, 198
democratic survival 100
Der Spiegel 66
descriptive patterns
    of democratic backsliding 113–117
    of democratic collapse 123–125
dictatorships 18, 75, 147
Duarte, Nicolanor 133
Duda, Andrjez 112, 117–118, 141, 144
Duterte, Rodrigo 31

Eastern Europe 43
economic ideology 45, 46*f*
economic issues 99–100
Economist, The 35–36, 66, 97, 101, 102
Ecuador 13–14, 50, 112–113, 117–118
elections 52–54, 154, 162–163
election violence 153, 178–188, 183*f*, 186*f*, 187*f*, 197, 200
electoral reforms 106
electoral rules 50–52, 55
electoral systems 10–11, 61*f*, 42–43, 50–52, 59–60, 109
elites *see* partisan elites
El Salvador 1, 98, 99–104, 170–171
    ARENA (Alianza Republicana Nacionalista) 101, 103–104
    Constitutional Court 103
    FMLN (Frente Farabundo Martípara la Liberacíon Nacional) 101, 103–104
    GANA (Grand Alliance for National Unity) 101
    New Ideas (Nuevas Ideas) 68, 101–103, 128
    Supreme Court 170
Erdoğan, Recep Tayyip
    and democratic backsliding 2, 33
    and failed coup attempt 123
    and judicial attacks 171
    and lack of executive constraints 69, 138n.5
    as model of democracy 35–36, 66, 198
    and polarization 161–163
    political career 63, 66
    and populism 35–37, 47
Europe 43–44, 113, 148, 188
European Values Survey 179, 184
Executive Approval Project 128
executive constraints
    in democracies 134–140
    empirical tests 140–149
    erosion of 196–197
    and incumbent support parties constraints 132–133

222 INDEX

executive constraints (*Continued*)
  and the legislature 135–137
  and party personalism 20–21, 132–134, 143*f*,
    138–139, 142–144, 149–150

Facebook 101
Federalist Papers 132, 135
Finland 171
France, La République En Marche! Party
    (LREM) 24, 64, 73
Freedom House 1, 97–98
  'Populists and Autocrats: The Dual Threat to
    Global Democracy' 33
freedom of association 10–11, 98, 108–109
freedom of expression 10–11, 98, 108–110
Fujimori, Alberto 11–12, 16, 22, 59, 63
funding 72–73, 85*f*, 86–87, 95*f*, 199

Garcia, Alan 22
geographical distribution 42–44, 44*t*
Georgia 50
  Georgian Dream 128
Georgia, US 199
Global Leadership Project (GLP) 75–77, 78*f*
Global Populisms project 47–48n.21
government experience 80–84
Guerini, Stanislas 24
Guinea 13
Gül, Abdullah 36, 63, 69

Haiti 26
horizontal accountability 11, 125, 134–135,
    149–150
horizontal constraints 151, 194
Human Rights Watch 33
Hungary 98–100, 104–109, 111, 159
  Constitutional Court 105–106
  Election Commission 106
  Fidesz 33, 48, 63, 65–66, 72, 104–108, 200
  Media Council 106
  Socialist Party 105

ideology 44–45, 46*f*, 172–173, 173*f*
illiberal democracy 108–109, 111
incentive 64, 67–71, 74, 92, 135
incumbent approval 128–130, 129*t*
incumbent support parties 67–74, 132–133,
    136–137
incumbent takeovers 11–14, 12*f*, 17, 122, 123,
    124*f*,
Indonesia 158
institutional arrangements 50–52, 55
institutional constraints
  attacks on 3–4, 11, 196–197

and party personalism 9, 20–21, 132–134,
    143*f*, 149–150
  in practice 139–140
  removal of 103, 105–106
institutions
  attacks on state *see also* executive constraints
    in Brazil 164–165
    and democratic backsliding 3–4
    and elections 154
    and polarization 153, 156–158, 169–170,
      172–177, 173*f*, 177*f*, 189, 190*f*, 194
    in Turkey 162
    and vertical accountability 151
  and executive constraints 135
Internet 6
Israel 170
  Likud Party 48–49

Japan 171
Javid, Sajid 70
Johnson, Boris 70
judiciaries
  control of 103–106
  and executive constraints 135, 137–139,
    144–145
  incumbent attacks on 170–172, 175–177,
    190*f*

Kaczyński, Jaroslaw 68, 166
Kaczyński, Lech 68, 141
Kadivar, Mohammad Ali 200
Kagan, Robert 152
Kicis, Bia 164

Latin America 15–16, 43–44, 156
Lebanon 43–44
legislature
  control of the 102–104, 127*f*, 125–130, 129*t*
  erosion of 196–197
  and executive constraints 135–138, 141–145,
    142*t*,
  and term limit extension attempts 149
Le Point 66
local party strength 8–9, 95*f*, 71–72, 74, 86–87,
    85*f*, 92–93, 199
loser parties 180–184, 183*f*, 192*f*
Lula da Silva, Luiz Inacio 154, 163–164

macro-level polarization 166–169, 169*f*,
    174–175
Macron, Emmanuel 24, 31, 64, 73
Madison, James 108–109, 132, 135
majoritarian electoral system 51–52, 61*f*, 60,
    96*f*, 109, 191*f*

INDEX 223

Malawi 132–133, 144
Marcos, Ferdinand 11–12
mass communication 6
media reporting 5–6, 54, 106–107
mediation analysis 175–177
Michigan, US 199
micro-level polarization 168–174, 169f, 173f
Middle East 43–44
migration 107
military coups 11–13, 124f, 98, 113, 117–118
mixed electoral system 50–52, 60, 61f, 96f, 191f
Modi, Narendra 121
Morales, Evo 13, 31, 122–123
Moreno, Lenín 13–14
Muluzi, Bakili 132–133, 139, 144
Mutharika, Bingu wa 31

Nepal 13n.13
Netanyahu, Benjamin 48–49, 121
New York Times 22, 164–165
Nicaragua 2
Nkurunziza, Pierre 71–72
nominations 70–71, 74, 84–86, 85f, 92–93, 95f, 105–106 *see also* appointments
non-personalist parties 8–9, 69–70, 72–73, 183f, 182–184
norms of behaviour
  and partisan elites 151–153, 158–161
  and party personalism 153, 160–161, 177–188, 194
  and weakening of vertical constraints 155, 159–161

Obama, Barak 65
opposition parties 43, 98, 125–126, 136, 156–157
Orban, Viktor 32–33, 63, 65–66, 70, 72, 99–100, 104–109, 111, 121, 151, 198, 200
Ortega, Daniel 2, 121

Pakistan 170
Paraguay 133
  Colorado 133
parliamentary systems 38–39, 50–52, 74, 75, 91
partisan dealignment 6, 54, 193, 199
partisan elites
  and cabinet appointees 74–75, 87–92, 90f, 91f, 96f
  candidate surveys 79–84, 81f, 83f
  and cues 158, 160–161, 164–165
  and executive constraints 132
  and the legislature 137
  and norms of behaviour 151–153, 158–161

and party personalism 8–9, 19–20, 158–159, 195–196
political experience 25–26, 67–71, 73–84, 78f, 79t, 81f, 83f,
party age 115–116, 116f
party creation 59–60, 64, 66–67, 114f, 113–117, 116f, 123, 141–142, 142t
party dominance 125–130, 136
PartyFacts ID codes 26–27
party institutionalization 39, 55, 59, 115–116, 116f
party members 8, 63–71, 132–133
party personalism
  and anti-system candidates 40
  and appointments 8, 30, 70–71, 88–89
  and bureaucratic constraint 146
  and cabinet appointees 74–75, 87–92, 90f, 91f, 96f
  and campaign finance 53–54, 62, 72
  and capacity 64, 71–74, 93
  and citizens 21
  concept of 19, 23–24, 34–35, 38–40, 195
  countering 197–200
  and defence of democracy 197–198
  definition 24–25, 54, 195
  and democracy scores 117–118
  and democratic backsliding 3–4, 4f, 15–16, 20, 63–64, 92–93, 118t, 98–99, 108, 111–120, 130–131, 193–196
  and democratic collapse 119f, 124f
  and democratic decline 17–19, 41f, 40–42, 198
  and dictatorships 18
  and economic ideology 45, 46f
  and election violence 184–188, 186f, 187f, 197
  and electoral rules 50–52
  and electoral systems 50–52, 59–60, 61f
  empirical patterns 74–92
  and executive constraints 20–21, 67–74, 132–134, 143f, 140–141, 149–150
  facts and features of 19, 40–52, 54–55, 194
  and funding 72–73, 86–87, 85f, 95f
  geographical distribution of 42–44, 44t
  harming democracy 7–9, 21, 197
  and ideology 44–45, 46f
  and incentive 64, 67–71, 74, 92
  and incumbent attacks on the judiciary 171–174, 173f
  indicators of 29–31, 30t
  and institutional arrangements 50–52, 55
  and institutional constraints 20–21, 132–134, 149–150
  and judicial constraints 138–139, 144–145

224 INDEX

party personalism (*Continued*)
  and legislature control 125–130, 127*f*, 129*t*,
    136–137, 142–144
  levels of 2–4, 22–23
  and local party strength 8–9, 71–72, 74, 85*f*,
    86–87, 92, 93, 95*f*
  measurement of 17–19, 25–33, 54, 56–62,
    58*t*, 57*f*, 60*f*, 61*f*, 62*f*, 93, 195
  and media reporting 54
  and nominations 70–71, 74, 84–86, 85*f*,
    92–93, 95*f*
  and norms of behaviour 160–161, 177–188,
    194
  and parliamentary systems 51–52
  and partisan dealignment 54
  and partisan elites 8–9, 19–20, 67–74,
    195–196
  and party creation 64
  and party dominance 125–130
  and party institutionalization 39, 55, 59
  and polarization 21, 156–159, 166–177, 169*f*,
    177*f*, 191*f*, 197
  and political experience 73, 75–84, 78*f*, 79*t*,
    81*f*, 83*f*
  and political outsiders 40
  and political violence 21, 153, 178–188, 183*f*,
    192*f*
  and populism 33–38, 47–50, 49*f*
  and presidential systems 38–39, 50–52,
    59–60, 150*f*, 61*f*
  and reasons for winning elections 52–54
  and repression of civil liberties 98, 108–111,
    131*f*
  rise of 5–7, 4*f*, 193
  and societal pathways 151–153, 189–190, 197
  and term limit extension attempts 148–149,
    150*f*
  trends 40–42
  undermining democracy 64–67, 98
  and weakening of horizontal constraints 194
  and weakening of vertical constraints 194
  weakness 71
  and welfare state ideology 45, 46*f*
party rules 200
Pascal-Trouillot, Ertha 26
personalism *see* party personalism
personalist political parties *see* party
    personalism
Peru 11–12, 16, 22
  Cambio 90 22, 63, 128
  Peruvian Aprista Party (APRA) 22
Philippines 11–12, 147
Poland 109–110, 117–118, 141, 166,
    170–171

Law and Justice Party (PiS) 68, 117–118, 141,
    145, 166, 171, 198
polarization
  in Benin 167*f*, 167–168
  in Brazil 164
  and democratic backsliding 14–15, 120,
    155–156, 159
  in El Salvador 104
  in Hungary 107
  and incumbent attacks on the
    judiciary 171–174, 190*f*
  and party personalism 9, 21, 151–153,
    156–159, 169*f*, 166–177, 177*f*, 191*f*, 197
  in Poland 166
  in Turkey 162–163
  in United States 167*f*, 167–168
  use of term 3–4n.4
  in Venezuela 167*f*, 167–168
  and weakening of vertical
    constraints 155–159
political experience
  of partisan elites 25–26, 67–71, 73–84, 78*f*,
    79*t*, 81*f*, 83*f*
  and party personalism 73, 75–84, 78*f*, 79*t*,
    81*f*, 83*f*
  and populism 77–79, 79*t*, 82
political outsiders 16, 40, 63
political violence 21, 153, 178–188, 183*f*, 192*f*
popularity 128–130, 129*t*
populism
  concept of 33–35
  and democratic backsliding 14–15, 37*f*,
    42–43, 47, 50
  and nominations 86
  and party creation 115, 116*f*
  and party personalism 33–38, 47–50, 49*f*
  and political experience 77–79, 79*t*, 82
presidential systems
  and cabinet appointees 74–75
  and democratic collapse 120–121
  and executive constraints 141
  and party personalism 38–39, 50–52, 59–60,
    61*f*
  and term limit extension attempts 15, 148,
    150*f*
presidents 42–43, 61*f*, 50–51, 88
prime ministers 26, 42–43, 50–51, 61*f*, 88
proportional electoral system
    51–52
protests 104, 162

Ramaphosa, Cyril 70
Ramos, Fidel 147
Reagan, Ronald 148

rebellion 122
ruling party personalism *see* party personalism
Russia 200

Sall, Macky 34–35, 63, 97–98, 125, 126, 151
Sanguinetti, Julio María 59
Senegal 34–35, 97–98, 125
  Alliance for the Republic (APR) 34–35, 63, 97, 126
  Senegalese Democratic Party (PDS) 63, 97
  Socialist Party 97
  United for Hope (Benno Bokk Yaakaar (BBY)) coalition 126
Serbia 1
Shinawata, Thaksin 113, 117–118, 121
Simicska, Lajos 72
Sirleaf, Ellen Johnson 121
social media 6, 101, 103–104, 164–165
societal constraints 3–4
societal pathways 151–153, 189–190, 197
Sonko, Ousmane 34–35, 97–98
South Africa 113
  African National Congress (ANC) 70
state institutions
  attacks on *see also* executive constraints
    in Brazil 164–165
    and democratic backsliding 3–4
    and elections 154
    and polarization 153, 156–158, 169–170, 172–177, 173f, 177f, 189, 190f, 194
    in Turkey 162
    and vertical accountability 151
strongmen
  elected 3, 17, 22, 53, 193, 200
  era of 2–3
  and party personalism 22–23
Summer, William Graham 193

Talon, Patrice 2, 146, 167–168
television 6
term limit extension attempts 147–149, 150f
Thailand 113, 117–118
Time Magazine 2, 66
traditional parties 16, 101
Trump, Donald
  attitude to democracy 65
  and bureaucratic constraints 137
  and democratic backsliding 10, 121
  and institutional constraints 139
  and lack of executive constraints 69
  and local party constraints 72, 133, 199
  and loss of re-election 154
  and party personalism 31–33, 152–153
  and polarization 168, 175
  as political outsider 31

and populism 48–49
and term limits 148
use of social media 171
Turkey 2, 35–38, 37f, 43–44, 123, 161–163
  Justice and Development Party (AKP) 33, 35–37, 37f, 63, 66, 69, 128, 161–163
Twitter 101, 103–104, 170, 171

United States 10, 113, 117–118, 133, 137, 158, 167, 167f, 168, 171, 175, 199
  Census Bureau 137
  Democrats 152
  Republican Party 48–49, 69, 72, 137, 152–153, 168, 199
Uribe, Alvaro 26, 26–27n.6

Varga, Judit 157
Varieties of Democracy data set 10–11, 59, 97–98, 110, 111–112, 141, 144–145, 185
Varieties of Party data set 26–27, 34–36, 38, 45, 47–49, 59, 77–80, 82, 84, 86, 126, 173–174, 180, 181–182
Velazquez, Ramon Jose 87
Venezuela 1–2, 8, 10–12, 112, 113, 167f, 167–168, 171
  COPEI 40
  Democratic Action (AD) 59
  Fifth Republic Movement (MVR) 1–2, 8, 33, 40, 59, 128
  National Convergence 40, 59
  Revolutionary Bolivarian Movement (MBR-2000) 2
vertical accountability 3–4, 125, 151, 153–154, 189
vertical constraints
  case studies 161–165
  empirics 166–188
  and party personalism 151
  weakening of 153–161, 194
violence *see* election violence; political violence
violent crime 99–100
voters 153–155, 183f, 179–184
voting behaviour 5–6

Wade, Abdoulaye 97
Washington Post 66
Wazed, Hasina 117–118
welfare state ideology 45, 46f
'whataboutism' 157
WhoGov project 88

Yayi, Boni 167–168

Zembelli, Carla 164
Zuma, Jacob 113

The manufacturer's authorised representative in the EU for product safety is
Oxford University Press España S.A. of el Parque Empresarial San Fernando de
Henares, Avenida de Castilla, 2 – 28830 Madrid (www.oup.es/en or product.
safety@oup.com). OUP España S.A. also acts as importer into Spain of products
made by the manufacturer.

www.ingramcontent.com/pod-product-compliance
Lightning Source LLC
Chambersburg PA
CBHW051629090425
24848CB00004B/77